STO

THE BRITISH ECONOMY:
TOWARD A DECENT SOCIETY

GRID SERIES IN ECONOMICS

Baer, *The Brazilian Economy*
Martin, *Principles of Economics: Macro*
Martin, *Principles of Economics: Micro*
Neale, *The British Economy: Toward a Decent Society*
Winger, *Cases in Managerial Economics*

THE BRITISH ECONOMY
TOWARD A DECENT SOCIETY

Walter C. Neale
University of Tennessee

Grid Publishing, Inc., Columbus, Ohio

1 2 3 4 5 6 5 4 3 2 1 0

Library of Congress Cataloging in Publication Data

Neale, Walter C
    The British economy.

    (Grid series in economics)
    Includes index.
    1. Great Britain—Economic policy—1945-   2. Great
Britain—Social policy.   3. Great Britain—Politics and
government—1964-   I. Title.
HC256.6.N4   330.9'41'0857   79-16553
ISBN O-88244-194-9 pbk.

CONTENTS

LIST OF TABLES

NOTE TO THE HARRIED READER

For the reader more interested in some than in other
aspects of the British economy, not all the book need be
read. Chapter 2 is integral to the whole argument, as
perhaps is Chapter 13. The origins and problems of the
welfare state are discussed in Chapters 2, 5, 11, and 12.
To extend the coverage to socialism as well, add Section II
of Chapter 4 and Chapter 10. Those aspects of policy which
are not peculiarly a part of the welfare state or socialism
are covered in Sections I and III of Chapter 4 and in
Chapter 9. The basic statistical data are in Chapters 7
and 8. The structural characteristics of the economy are
described in Chapters 4 through 8 and 11. Chapter 3 explains the system of government under which the economy
functions and the attitudes (and principles) of the
political parties.

ACKNOWLEDGMENTS

As is usually the case with a book, numbers of people
have given me help, all of which has been from useful to
essential. For insisting that I write the book and for an
encouraging reading of the draft, I am indebted to
J. S. Neale. J. Adams, K. Brown, and A. M. Sievers kindly
read the whole draft and politely pointed out where I could
do better. N. Alper, M. Chanock, J. F. Holly, F. M. Murtaugh,
and R. H. Peacock provided helpful criticisms on various
chapters. To all, my thanks.

Three graduate research assistants have done yeoman
and patient work, organizing and computing statistics, of
which only "the tip of the iceberg" appear in these pages:
E. Lin, D. Wilson Renner, and D. Stallings (who also helped
me make sense of Britain's relationships with the EEC).

R. Nesbitt, C. Shires and R. Wollwine typed draft
after draft, with care and imagination, and almost always
with courtesy. Without them, I know not what I would have
done.

I should also like to thank Davis-Poynter Limited for
permission to quote from Barbara Wootton, *Incomes Policy:
An Inquest and a Proposal* (London: 1974, pp. 80-81);
Oxford University Press for permission to quote from Andrew
Shonfield, *Modern Capitalism* (London/Oxford/N.Y.; 1969, pp.
128-29 & 134); and St. Martin's Press, Inc., to quote from
Robert Bacon and Walter Eltis, *Britain's Economic Problem:
Too Few Producers* (N.Y.: 1976, pp. 31 & 100).

My thanks also to Professor Harold Williamson of
Northwestern, for suggesting, just as I was beginning to
work on this book, that I was going to write an economic
ethnography of Britain--anyway, I've tried.

Finally and mostly, my deep gratitude to A. Mayhew,
whose role in the writing of this book lies somewhere
between continuous copy editor and co-author.

1

THEMES

Britain is going down the drain. The ship of state is sinking. Overburdened by a Robin Hood government which has made the merry men as weak as the deer they poached and as poor as the serfs they hoped to help, the British stand a lesson to us all, of how not to do, lest the Lord God of Hosts desert us too.

Not so. The British are a sensible people striving to create the decent society: not the richest society; not the most powerful society; certainly not the economically most efficient society--but a nice society to live in and to grow old in. Often they don't know quite what to do, or quite how to do it--but then, do the people of any country?

While its economy has traits in common with many other economies, the whole complex of traits creates a distinctively *British* economy. Yet the goals, policies, and problems of this British economy are, in varying degrees, those of all industrialized democracies, so that an account of the British economy must be simultaneously a description and an explanation of how Britain's distinctively British economy works and a discussion of the Welfare State.

The themes of this book are a description of the traits of the British economy--how they originated, and how they fit together to give the British economy its present institutions, processes, and problems--and an explanation of why the British, all together as British or separately as different groups, have been doing and proposing what they have been proposing.

[While most of the statistics presented in this book are for the United Kingdom as a whole, which includes Ulster (Northern Ireland), I do not discuss Ulster's history, structure, and problems because they are quite different from those of the rest of the United Kingdom.]

2

A CLASSFUL
SOCIETY

British society is a class society, markedly so in
England. One can, of course, point out that all societies
have social classes. Certainly there are no lines in British society as hard and as consequential as the line between
white and black in the USA. The point, especially in comparing Britain with the U.S., is that all other class lines
in Britain are clearer than in the U.S. and the consequences
of the class structure are more important. In many respects
the importance of class lines has been decreasing, and barriers to mobility between classes have become lower, but
identification with a class remains important and may have
become even more important in its effects on current economic policies.

A class society is difficult to describe in a logical
and objective way. It tends to share with sex and gefilte
fish the trait that you have to try them to know what they
are like. The clue to understanding a class system is to
realize that it is self-defined: it is the participants
themselves who feel and think, often more feel than think,
in terms of classes and who act in terms of their feelings
and expectations about class. There is a subjectivity
about class, as there is about race, such that, although
the outsider can learn to recognize the signs of class and
learn the rules of class behavior, he never feels as does
the native born.

THE FORMATIVE YEARS

Modern British class structure began to take shape in
the latter part of the 18th century. At that time, at the
beginning of the Industrial Revolution in Britain, the Kingdom was still largely rural. In comparison with continental

3

countries, to say nothing of the new United States, it was a center of commerce, finance, and industry. But it was small compared to later centers; most industry (woollens, iron) was dispersed through the countryside or in small towns. Three quarters of the population lived in rural parishes.

There were three social classes in the countryside; the landowning gentry (who wore red coats on fox hunts), the tenant farmers (who wore tweed coats at hunts), and the laboring poor (who did not ride to hounds at all). Small-holders farming their own land and various kinds of "copy-holders" and "cottagers" and others with varying rights to land and to the use of common, waste and woodland were not, strictly speaking, landless, but they tended to merge with the landless laborers. Many were better off than the pure laborer, but most were not any better off than such skilled laborers as the stockmen who cared for the animals on the large farms. Although there were mergings at the margins, most people were clearly in one class or another.

The gentry--later commonly called "county"--ran the countryside. A gentleman owned many acres, in the hundreds and upwards, sometimes all the land in a parish. Many had a "living", the right to appoint the minister of the Church of England parish church. The gentry supplied the Justices of the Peace who sat in judgment (pretty summary judgment) of petty cases and misdeameanors and were the administrators of law and policy in the countryside. When occasionally the JPs of a county met together they constituted an informal county council. It was the gentry who elected members to Parliament from rural constituencies.

There was a noble class--people with the feudal titles of Baron, Earl, Viscount, Duke--and membership in this class was more prestigious than merely being a gentleman. Since membership in this class also put one in the House of Lords, being a noble gave one a good deal of political power. Because nobles were frequently large landowners they were often in a position to decide who would be elected to the House of Commons.

At the end of the 18th century land was the most im-portant kind of wealth. Viewed from the perspective of 1700, Britain in 1800 was a land of immense commercial and manufacturing wealth. The stock of capital--in ships, in inventories of raw materials and semi-processed goods for manufacture (still largely making by hand, with some water power, in the workers' homes or in small establishments), in inventories of finished goods (especially for inter-

national trade), and in the iron industry (still largely in
small-scale smelters and foundries where men's arms were the
mechanical power)--had never been so large. But what was
large by comparison with the past was still small in comparison to the value of land. Ownership of land was mostly
inherited. Very few smallholders ever managed to expand
their farms and rise to anything like wealth. Some of the
wealth amassed by merchants was used to buy estates (as some
of the income of the landed gentry was lent to finance commerce), but most of the gentry inherited their estates and
position. Wealth and income were concentrated. National
income data does not exist for the period, but it has been
estimated (i.e., thoughtfully guessed) that less than five
percent of the population owned most of the land and capital
and received perhaps fifty percent of the income. Although
actively employed talent in trade and commerce had
already contributed a good deal to Britain's wealth
and income, and modern industry was beginning to contribute, it was nevertheless true that wealth was "ascribed"
(inherited), not "achieved" (earned).

What Disraeli was, half a century later, to call "the
two nations"--the privileged wealthy and the propertyless,
disfranchised laborers--already existed in rural England.
Class lines in the towns followed the pattern of class
lines in the countryside.

Present day classes are products of the economic and
political evolution of that late 18th century class structure as Britain became an urban, industrial nation. There
were major changes: the population became ninety-five
percent urban; the rural laborer became the urban wage
earner; the power of the aristocracy all but disappeared;
the landed gentry became a small minority of the upper
classes; bankers and businessmen, industrialists and all
sorts of professional people, along with the middle and
upper echelons of the civil service, came to constitute the
upper classes. The "working class" became the name of the
wage earning and blue-collar class. The "other" groups--
"middle class," "upper middle class," "upper class"--have
no single name, nor have they ever enjoyed that homogeneity
of self-identification which so clearly marks the "working
class." However, for a century "the middle class" has been
a pride and joy of Britain's middle classes: they and those
above them know that they are not "working class." The
lower middle classes fear to be confused with the working
class while the working class knows that the lower middle
classes are not "working class." The professions, civil
service, and the military absorbed the children of the

landed gentry. Families of the rising commercial and industrial classes "married into" the landed gentry and bought
estates and became "county." Probably most of the 18th
century ancestors of today's upper and middle classes were
not landed gentlemen or merchants engaged in the great
trading ventures of the 18th century. If the ones who were
landed or rich are remembered with pride, so also very often
are those ancestors who rose from "humble origins." The
great public schools (which is to say, the great private
boarding schools such as Eton, Rugby, Winchester) became the
training grounds which turned the sons of the rising capitalists into gentlemen.

The transformation began in the late 18th century, in
what has become known as the Industrial Revolution. The
necessary and mutually reinforcing technologies were developed during the 18th century. By the middle of the century
the principle for turning coal into coke by burning it with
too little oxygen opened the possibility of producing iron
in quantity. However, mines in Britain quickly filled with
water so that large scale exploitation of this discovery
had to wait upon James Watt and his steam engine, which
could pump water economically. Watt and his partner Boulton
had to wait upon Wilkinson to develop a technique of boring
which produced sufficiently small tolerances to make the
steam engine economic. Then one had the foundation of the
Industrial Revolution: coal to make coke; coke to make
iron; iron to make engines; engines to pump water from the
mines; coal to power the engines and to make coke . . . .
During the same years a series of inventions from the spinning jenny, which made it possible for a woman to turn out
much more thread, through the water frame to the mule had
reached the point where thread could be spun by machine if
there were water power to move the heavy wood-and-iron mules.
Just at this time Eli Whitney in the U.S. produced the cotton gin which made it possible to clean short and medium
staple cotton in huge quantities. Hook up the steam engine
to the spinning frame, then to the loom, and to the gin,
and there is the cotton textile industry and that great
growth of textile mills which was for so long regarded as
the Industrial Revolution (almost certainly mistakenly, for
it was the harnessing of inanimate energy with coke and iron
and engine which transformed the progress in textile technology into a revolution). Then came the beginning of a
modern chemical industry with the by-products of coking.
The engine was put on wheels, the wheels on rails, and thus
began the railway age and modern transportation. (Steel, it
should be remembered, was not part of this revolution.
Large scale production of steel had to wait upon the Besse-

mer and open hearth processes of the third quarter of the
19th century.)

Coke produced lots of iron. Lots of iron produced
many engines. Many engines burning much coal provided
energy in concentrations such as had never been seen before.
Enormous weights could be shifted and the heavy parts of
machines made to move. Coal in quantity provided intense
concentrations of heat which made possible the production
of new chemicals and the production of huge quantities of
old chemicals. Furnaces and engines concentrated energy.
Those who worked with the concentrated energy had to con-
centrate around the furnaces and engines and the machines
the engines ran. Thus modern industrial towns and cities
grew up, inevitable, unavoidable by-products of the concentrated energy which the new technologies released from coal.

By 1850 over half the population lived in towns and
cities. The cotton textile industry had grown up around
Manchester (in Lancashire, on the west coast north of Wales),
drawing women and children into the mills in vast numbers.
In Wales and along the Welsh border (the "Black Country")
coal mining had absorbed many men and not a few children.
Smelting and iron manufacturers became common in the region.
Iron manufactures, cutlery, pottery, and engineering
(engine-, machine-, and vehicle-building) developed in the
Midlands. To the northeast in Yorkshire the woollen and
worsted trades expanded greatly. The Glasgow region became
a center for cotton textiles and then for iron and for shipbuilding.

Most of the rural laboring class was absorbed into the
factory system and into the unskilled, semiskilled, and
skilled trades of urban society during the first three
quarters of the 19th century. With them came people who
had had some rights in the land but lost them during the
enclosures of the 1790s and subsequent years, when the open
fields and many of the common lands of England were divided
into properties in fee simple. Some lost their small rights
because they were simply cheated by unscrupulous rich and
powerful, more lost their small properties because they were
uneconomic as independent holdings. To these people were
added Scots driven out of the Highlands as farming gave way
to pasturage and pasturage gave way to estates for deer
hunting. The potato famine in Ireland brought thousands of
destitute to Liverpool and Glasgow. The development of
sheep pasturage in rural Wales combined with the opening of
coal mines added to the number who moved into modern industries. The picture of a countryside depopulated by mass

migration to the towns is not an accurate one. In much of
England the natural rate of growth of population was sufficient to populate the towns without depopulating the
countryside. In the southwest there was a marked fall in
population, but likely as much due to the decline of the
home weaving industry there as to changes in farming. Elsewhere in England rural populations did not decline, or did
not decline noticeably. In the Scottish Highlands the drop
in rural population was great, and has continued down to the
present. In Wales the people did not move far: what had
been arable valleys became mining villages and small mining
and foundry towns. Of course, the fact that it was an increase in the number of second and third sons and daughters
who survived childhood to go to the new towns and factories
did not in the least make them think any the less that they
were driven out of the country.

Then in the 1870s railroads opened up the interior of
North America, Argentina, and Russia. The flow of cheap
grain and cheap meat from these lands caused agricultural
depression throughout western Europe. On the continent
tariffs protected the farmers but in Britain the cheap food
was welcomed--in Britain landlords and farmers were a minority interest whereas on the continent they were not. This
agricultural depression induced many landholders to convert
arable to pasture (with their moderate, damp climate and
good soils the British isles are a wonderful place for converting grass into wool and meat and milk).

The urban working class went through a number of losing
battles. First there were the enclosures and the indigni-
ties of receiving relief from parish overseers of the poor,
experiences which colored the views of the first generation
of urban workers, who passed on their views to succeeding
generations. Acts passed by Parliament forbidding any
forms of worker organization embittered those who came to
the towns. The anti-combination and conspiracy acts were a
panicked response to the excesses (for that they certainly
were) of the mobs during the French Revolution and not
thought-out pieces of anti-labor legislation; but for the
wage-earner who wanted representation before his employer,
or an organization to present his hopes and fears in public,
nervous stomachs among his rulers did not justify them in
sending him off to Australia (which had replaced Georgia as
Britain's penal colony).

In the 1820s labor organizations became legal and the
1830s saw rise of the Grand National Trade Union and the
Chartist Movement. The Grand National Trade Union was open

to all, designed to represent every kind of worker and
even any person who wished to join.   Interests so diverse
and people working for so many different employers could
not possibly be effectively represented by so large a union
and it shortly collapsed.   The Chartists demanded political
reform: universal manhood suffrage with a secret ballot.
The landed and the newly enfranchised middle class had no
intention of giving the vote to the propertyless and the
working class was not prepared to rebel.   Economic depression in the 1840s and the failure of the revolutions of
1848 on the continent ended this Movement--leaving the
feeling and creating the tradition that the upper classes
would never do justice by the lower classes.

Whether the British working classes suffered unduly or
only duly during the Industrial Revolution; whether their
living standards rose or fell; whether the urban worker had
fewer or more dignities, whether he had less or more security than his father in the rural parish--whatever really
true answers to these questions will be revealed on Judgment Day--by 1850 the British wage earner had come to feel
that he was "working class" with interests inherently antag-
onistic to the interests of the upper and middle classes,
and that *he could never expect decent treatment from them*.
An urban working class had been created: objectively defined as wage earning, propertyless, and voteless, but
subjectively self-defined as victims of callous, greedy,
privileged, and rich-without-reason upper classes.

I do not know enough to make comparisons with events
and attitudes on the continent.   However, the contrast with
the United States is marked.   By the time the United States
became industrialized and urbanized every man had the vote.
If "the bosses" did not seem to come by their wealth all
that honestly or deservedly, at least they did not inherit
it.   For American wage earners the people who had deprived
them of their security were English landlords in England,
Scotland, and Ireland; German Junkers in Poland; the landed
aristocracy in Italy; princes and Prussians in Germany.
Objectively defined as wage-earning and propertyless,
American workers defined themselves subjectively as better
off with more opportunities than they might otherwise have
been.

There is a vast and disputatious literature about the
Industrial Revolution in Britain.   *The* issue--often explicit,
sometimes denied--is whether or not the Industrial Revolution was "a good thing:"   not whether later generations are
the better off for it, but whether those who lived through

it suffered greatly and whether their sufferings were somehow necessary, or an avoidable consequence of callousness,
greed, and bad public policy. On the one side socialists,
reformers, many historians, and a good many economic historians have insisted that the period from the 1790s to the
1840s was distinguished by that immiserization of the working class which Marx found so characteristic of capitalism.
On the other side many economists and a goodly number of
economic historians have argued that conditions were not
nearly so bad as they have often been portrayed, certainly
no worse than they were before that period, and that the
capitalists were not to blame.

The evidence and argument that has provided the language with the phrase, "the worst evils of the Industrial
Revolution," were the low level of wages, the employment of
women and especially of young children as young as six or
seven in the textile mills and in the mines, the almost complete absence of schooling and time for play for children,
the rising prices of staple foodstuffs, families living in
one or two rooms without running water or any arrangements
for sanitation, widespread drunkenness, and the repressive
actions of the authorities.

The response to this position has been to marshal
evidence that wages were not so low as claimed, that in fact
real wages rose during the period, except for those years
between 1795 and 1815 when rising prices should more properly be blamed on the long wars with Napoleon than upon the
system or upon the capitalists themselves; that children
had always worked before and had not gone to school; that
the testimony before Parliamentary committees was biased and
exaggerated by the dominant landholding class which wanted
to smear the rising manufacturers; that the "worst evils"
were exceptional; and that it was not the new class of manufacturers who created the slums but working class "jerry-
builders" (many from Ireland, a point which English authors
seem to find meaningful). Finally, the absence of urban
amenities is attributed to the fact that no country had
ever before faced the problem of housing the majority of its
population in cities: that it is unreasonable to expect the
first generation to deal with a totally new problem to arrive at a satisfactory solution.

It may not seem unreasonable to ask, "Well, who is
right?" but that question cannot be answered for a variety
of reasons. To begin with, we do not have enough precise
information to answer the quantitative questions with assurance. Records of some prices from here at one time, some

prices from there at another time, and a similar smattering
of wage rates indicate but do not prove that the real wages
of those employed in the new industries did rise over the
period. They do not tell us about the standard of living of
those out of employment, nor do we have accurate data on
how many were unemployed, let alone for how long. One of
the miseries of the Industrial Revolution was the declining
real incomes of skilled workers in the declining industries,
especially the handloom weavers, and the decline in their
earnings is not in doubt. How does one weigh an increase in
the wages of one group against a decline in the wages of
another group? And how does one evaluate the effects of
changing status? How does one judge the "evil" or the
"goodness" of paying young women more and husbands and
fathers less?

Then there is the "before and after" problem: children
who worked "before" worked in the countryside and children
who worked "after" worked in factories. The same "before
and after" problem applies to the position and welfare of
women. It is also true that British society "before" was
pretty callous and that "after" it was much more humane.
It was during this period that modern ideas of kindliness to
children began to spread (Dickens' *A Christmas Carol* and
Oliver Twist; Charles Kingsley's *The Water Babies*). Are
mine and mill owners, MPs and justices of the peace to be
blamed or to be excused for not being among the first to
adopt the emerging humane morality? Whatever the "objective"
measures of welfare "before" in the countryside and "after"
in the city, the nastier aspects of life were more obvious
in the city--at least, they were more obvious if one went to
look. To critics of the Industrial Revolution this is a
damning criticism; to those who take the other side it is
evidence that "looking" accounts for the increasingly
humane attitudes of the upper and middle classes.

Urban life requires policemen and firemen, sanitary
engineers and refuse collectors, water pipes and paved
streets--none of which are necessary in rural areas. The
countryside provides "out-of-doors" by its very nature;
cities must build parks. By the 1840s this was realized
and the authorities were beginning to do something about
these problems. Did it take an unconscionably long time
for the realization to dawn? Or did the ruling classes
learn as quickly as one might reasonably ask? Was the
evidence to the eyes clear in, say, 1810? Or were the
problems of urban life only obvious from, say, 1825?

Critics of the Industrial Revolution point out that it

was the ruling classes which made the rules and which enjoyed the benefits of the rules they made. The working
classes had no vote. But where were there mass democracies
in the world at that time? Manhood suffrage for whites in
the United States was not universal until the 1830s.

The debate, however, is not only about evidence and its
interpretation. Most importantly, the issue has been ideo-
logical--*ideo*logical, not logical. Somehow the view has
come to be accepted that if the Industrial Revolution in
Britain was a period of inexcusable "worst evils," then
capitalism and capitalists today are bad and should be
abolished. But if the period were not so bad and if the
capitalists and rulers of Britain in the first half of the
19th century were not inhumane and evil people, then capitalism is a good system for Britain today. One is struck
by the lack of logic. The system and the rulers a century
and a half ago could have been absolute stinkers without in
the least requiring that modern capitalism and present day
industrialists and Conservative leaders be bad too. Conversely, the rulers and the system of 1790-1840 could be
judged quite reasonably good for the time without in the
least invalidating arguments that there are much better
ways to run Britain today than the way it is being run or
the way in which the Conservatives might like to run it.
But we are here dealing with sets of emotions and beliefs
which define and support views of the self and one's role
in the world and the actual world in which one has a self
and a role. Such emotions and beliefs do not require logic
nor are they subject to logic (as we have known since Freud).
The "worst evils of the Industrial Revolution" are symbols
of working class protest as well as justifications for the
protest. The opposing (Conservative) arguments are not
merely efforts to bring reason to the debate or to destroy
the symbols of the socialists. They too have their positive
symbolic side: the fundamental virtues of the middle
classes, British success in the 19th century as proof that
private property is good, the view that British leadership
has spared Britain the revolutions and civil wars which
shook the continent and the United States.

THE YEARS OF REINFORCEMENT

Whatever the whole truth about what happened from the
beginning of the 19th century through the 1840s, there is
agreement that life improved after 1850. There was slow
growth in real incomes from the mid-century on, often in-
terrupted but trending upward. The suffrage was extended.

In 1867 all urban male householders were admitted to the
vote. The rural constituencies, where laborers did not get
the vote, were still much over-represented, but in 1884 the
Third Reform Act extended the vote to rural male householders and reduced the disparities in the sizes of constituencies. (In 1917 women over thirty were admitted to the
rolls of electors and all property qualifications for the
vote were removed. The voting age for women was reduced to
twenty-one in 1928.) From the 1850s to the 1890s there was
fairly steady growth of trade unions among skilled workers,
but not among the unskilled.

If the century which elapsed from the end of the "hungry forties" until the Labour Party took full charge of the
government in 1945 was one of intermittent rise in living
standards and increasing democratization of politics, it
was hardly without events which reinforced the attitudes
which the working class had already developed. In 1889 the
London dockers conducted a long strike, finally winning the
first effective union representation of unskilled or semi-
skilled workers. This was the start of industrial, as opposed to craft, unionism. It was followed by organization
among the unskilled in railroads, by more effective unionization among the miners, and in other industries. However,
unlike the period of the New Deal in the United States, it
was not the first step in a steady upward march, for severe
setbacks to unionization followed. In 1900 some of the
property of the Taff Vale railway line in South Wales was
damaged during a strike. The company sued both the union
and the individual strikers for damages and won. With such
a financial threat hanging over unions and their members
strikes were much reduced. In 1906, under the pressure of
a rising labor vote both for the Liberal Party and for the
newly founded Labour Party, the unions regained the total
immunity from such suits which they had enjoyed from 1871 to
the Taff Vale decision. But in 1908 one Osborne, a member
of the Amalgamated Society of Railway Servants, sued his
union for contributing to the Labour Party on the grounds
that under the Trade Union Act of 1876 a union could bargain
collectively but did not have any other rights. When Osborne
won his case Labour lost its only sizable source of finance.
In 1913 an act empowered unions to set up political funds
if approved by a ballot of the membership, but allowing
members who did not wish to contribute to opt out. The
result of the Taff Vale and Osborne decisions was to sharpen
the working class's distrust of courts, of the law, and of
lawyers—a distrust which continues to mark working class
attitudes to this day.

The years between the World Wars were marked by continuous unemployment. While unemployment was often much worse elsewhere during the 1930s, the British entered the Great Depression after a decade of depressed economic activity. Alone among the European countries, all of whom experienced inflation during the Great War, the British decided to go back on the gold standard at the prewar parity (£1 = $4.86). To achieve this aim required that British prices decline, so while other countries enjoyed fairly prosperous times in the decade after 1919-20, there was constant delationary pressure in Britain. Wages actually declined during the 1920s. In March, 1926, the coal miners went on strike and the Trades Union Congress called a general strike of all member unions in support of the miners. Outside of the unions the call was regarded as a threat of revolution; the middle classes volunteered to take all sorts of working class jobs to keep the country going, and after ten days the general strike was called off. The miners continued their strike but finally gave in. The failure of the general strike and defeat of the miners became symbols of what workers should be able to do and of what the capitalist system could do to the just demands of workers. In 1936 a number of unemployed workers marched from Jarrow in the northeast to London to protest the chronically high level of unemployment in the northeast which was one of the worst hit parts of Britain. The Jarrow March too has gone into the history of the left as an occasion of heroic failure-- of the determination of the working class and of the callousness of the capitalist system. If middle-aged people of the center and right in British politics today insist with justice that they were not even born at the time of the general strike and barely weaned when the Jarrow March occurred and so can hardly be blamed for the 1920s and 1930s, nevertheless they remain tarred by the memories of other people's grandparents.

THE WORKING CLASS INTO POLITICS

These years also saw the founding of the Labour Party and its rise to the status of His Majesty's loyal opposition as the second largest party. In the 1880s trade unionists who went into politics joined the Liberal Party. A number of them, supported by the TUC (Trades Union Congress), became MPs and formed a trade unionist wing of that Party. They were loyal Liberals. When Keir Hardie and a number of socialists and cooperative societies formed the Independent Labour Party in 1893 the TUC refused to support it. Keir Hardie has since become the patron saint of Labour, but he

was not a favorite then. A former errand boy who had become a "trapper" (ventillator operator) in the mines at age
10, he became a lay preacher and then a politician. Elected
to Parliament as an independent in 1892 he shocked the Commons. When every MP wore a top hat and a frock coat Hardie
wore tweeds and a miner's cloth cap. When the House proposed to pass a motion of sympathy with the French after
their president was assassinated he suggested a similar
motion for the bereaved families of a Welsh mine disaster.
When the House passed a motion of congratulation to Queen
Victoria on the occasion of the birth of a great grandson,
he opposed the motion to "protest against the Leader of the
House declining to take official cognizance of the terrible
colliery accident." This sort of behavior would not be
popular today; eighty years ago it was anathema. But Davids
who defy the establishment are the stuff of great traditions.

Then in 1900 the TUC set up a Labour Representation
Committee which became the Labour Party in 1906. With trade
union support withdrawn from the Liberal Party and with increasing organization among the unskilled and semiskilled,
the Labour Party began to replace the Liberals as the major
opposition to the Conservatives. At first the rise of
Labour was slow: 30 seats in a Parliament of 670 in 1906;
40 seats won in January, 1910, and 42 in December, 1910.
After the Great War came the "hang the Kaiser, make the
Germans pay" campaign which re-elected the wartime coalition
government of Conservatives and Liberals. Almost as a by-
product, the overwhelming victory of the Coalition left
Labour as the largest opposition party. It also became
overtly socialist, adopting a platform largely written by
Beatrice and Sidney Webb and reflecting the position of the
Fabian Society.

The Fabian Society began as a small group of left in-
tellectuals of all sorts. In 1888 George Bernard Shaw,
Sidney Webb, and others published *Fabian Essays in Socialism*, a book which became the authoritative view of British
socialism. Others joined the writers of *Fabian Essays* and
the Fabian Society grew until it became the philosophical
and research arm of British socialism and the Labour Party.
The Fabians were devoted to persuading the elite of British
society to become socialist and to openly (not secretly)
infiltrating the influential and ruling groups in Britain.
The Society took its name from Fabius Maximus, the Roman
general who outlasted Hannibal for a generation and wore
the Carthaginians down to their ultimate defeat. Gradualism,
and preparation for power, were the core of Fabian method.
Gradual it was, and it worked.

In the election of 1922 Labour won 142 seats out of 615, leaving the Liberals as the third party with 116 seats. The Conservatives lost the election of 1923, called on the issue of the Conservative proposals for higher tariffs, but it was not clear who had won. There were 191 Labour Members of the Parliament and 159 Liberal Members. The Liberals supported a Labour government for a year, but as a minority government dependent upon the support of the Liberals the Labour Party could administer but could not reform. In 1924 the Conservatives came back to power, but while Labour lost 40 seats the Liberals lost 119. In 1929, for the first time Labour became the largest party in Parliament: 288 seats to 260 Conservative seats, 59 Liberal seats, and 8 others. Again Labour formed a government, again to administer rather than to reform, for it still lacked an absolute majority. The depression brought on a National Government of all parties, but its creation split the Labour Party. Labour won only 52 seats in the election of 1931 (to 521 Conservative but only 37 Liberal seats). 1935 saw a rise to 154 Labour seats and a continued Liberal fall, to 20 seats, the Conservatives still holding 432 seats. The fall of France and the Battle of Britain put all thought of a wartime election aside, so it was not until 1945 that the Labour Party formed a government with an absolute majority and thus with the power to reform, to make its own program the law.

The precipitous decline of the Liberal Party after 1918 was an immediate consequence of the decision of Lloyd-George, the Liberal leader and head of the wartime coalition government, to continue the coalition after the war, thus splitting his own party; and of his subsequent inability to reunite the party or to "get out of the way" (he was the sort of hero who could not be pushed out of the way). However, underlying the decline of the Liberal Party was the fact that the working class now had a party of its own. The whole working class, let alone the working class as represented by the trade unions, would not have constituted a majority of the electorate (nor does it today), but it pre-empted the largest single bloc of potential votes for the Liberals so that potential Liberal voters increasingly felt that, in order not to "waste" their votes, they had to choose between becoming Conservatives or supporting Labour (and often calling themselves "Lib-Lab").

Modern British politics has thus grown out of the class structure as it took form during the 19th century. Many issues of policy today take their form because problems are seen in terms of the lessons and symbols of that century, reinforced by the experiences-become-symbols of the two decades before the Great War and of the interwar years.

EDUCATION AND EQUALITY

Perhaps class is nowhere so well illustrated as in the educational system—its structure, the changes that have occurred therein, and attitudes toward the schools. Before the Second World War the educational system tended to reinforce class lines and to give the upper classes much greater access to positions of wealth, power, and prestige than it gave the working class. The public schools (the private, fee-charging boarding schools) were the main route to careers in the professions and the higher levels of the civil service. They enjoyed that loyalty and enthusiasm which in the United States is sometimes given to one's college (although they often earned the lifelong hatred of some of their graduates, a hatred of the sort usually reserved for jails in the United States). Some provided an excellent education, and the poorest were probably a good deal better than the average American high school.

The universities drew most of their students from the graduates of the public schools, as did the medical schools. Law and accounting firms recruited their "articled clerks" from the same group (apprenticeship rather than professional schooling was the normal training for these professions). The armed forces recruited officers from the public schools. In addition to intellectual training these schools instilled attitudes and taught manners and a way of speech which marked their graduates as gentlemen. It was the ties of these schools that bound together the old-school-tie network. A story will illustrate: a former RAF officer, of middle class parentage, told me that after enlisting in the RAF he was interviewed to find out if he was qualified for assignment to flight school and a commission. Upon presenting himself to the panel, he was asked one question: "Where did you go to school?" It was a public school. He was sent to flight school.

There were "grammar schools," the state's day (not boarding) version of the public school. Some of the grammar schools were excellent, as good in the intellectual substance of what they taught as the best of the public schools, and most grammar schools were very good educational institutions. However, although they often did try, they did not as a rule manage to turn out gentlemen whose accents and tastes and attitudes fitted perfectly with those of the upper classes. The best of their products were accepted into the upper classes—one public secret of British social stability has been the ability and willingness of the upper classes to recruit into their ranks many of the brightest

and most ambitious of the children of the lower middle and
working classes. Grammar schools faced two almost insur-
mountable barriers to success in competing with the public
schools: (1) they simply were not public schools, by definition; and (2) day students tended to retain too many of the
traits of their parents and neighborhoods. While the mid-
dling and even lower level of public school graduate found
many attractive careers open to him, only the best of grammar school graduates were likely to find such spots.

The wartime Coalition government, as part of its planning for change and reform in postwar society, decided to
alter this state of affairs by providing more and better
education, free, to all classes. The result was the Education Act of 1944 which set up a system of three kinds of
schools: grammar schools (more of them), technical schools,
and "secondary modern" schools. After turning eleven a
child would take an examination called the "eleven plus."
Those who scored highest were admitted to a grammar school;
those who scored somewhat below this group could go to a
technical school; and the rest (the majority) went to a
secondary modern school. The idea was that the brightest
would be trained to rise to the top, no matter what their
class origins, and the next best given special opportunity
to develop skills. Failure to qualify for a grammar school
was not necessarily relegation to the class of hewers of
wood and drawers of water: students in the secondary moderns could study for "O" (for ordinary) level examinations
at age 15 or 16 and, if they passed, had further opportunity
to study for "A" (for advanced) level examinations and a
pass in two or three fields at the A level would admit one
to a university. However, more of the better teachers of
English and History and Chemistry and so on were to be found
in the grammar schools, which also had more of the other resources (books, laboratories) to train the students. Nevertheless, sufficient numbers from the secondary moderns did
make it through A levels to cast increasing doubt upon the
validity of the eleven plus examination as a sorter of men
and women (which eleven year olds were not, yet).

It was the expectation of Labour that the enlargement
of opportunity to go to grammar school, the identification
of bright youngsters, and a policy of actively pressing
opportunity upon the brighter children of the working class
would have three good results. It would assure that more
people of working class background rose to positions of influence and power in Britain. By mixing the classes together as children the new system would tend to break down
class barriers. And thirdly, it would be fairer. After a

decade disillusionment began to set in. While the new system did recruit many more of the working class into professional careers and budding positions of leadership, the
recruits tended to take on the traits of the upper classes
with whom they went to universities and who continued to
dominate the professions and the higher civil service.
There was even a fear that perhaps the system was draining
the working class of its talented members. Then, despite
the earlier good intentions to develop the grammar schools,
economic stringency in the postwar period prevented the
building and equipping of many more schools. Where there
had been a number of schools and the area richer (the counties of the south and southeast) upwards of a fifth of
eleven year olds were placed in grammar schools, but elsewhere (especially in the northeast of England) the ratio
fell below ten percent. This seemed unfair, doubly so to
Labour for it meant that where the working class was thick-
est, the opportunities were thinnest.

From the middle 1950s on the idea of comprehensive
schools has become more and more popular. These schools
combine the grammar, the technical, and the secondary modern
under one roof. While there is still "streaming"--academic,
technical, and general--the lines between the streams do not
exclude youngsters in one stream from taking courses in or
shifting into another stream. This system--it is hoped and
believed, and there is evidence that it is true--does mix
the social classes together more effectively and is tending
to break down class barriers (although it is doubtful that
the change is due to Labour's favorite piece of reasoning:
to wit, that working class boys will bash the noses of middle and upper class boys and thereby prove to all that
social equality is right and beautiful). By the middle 70s
the abolition of separate schools had become national policy,
and the education authorities in each county were being required to reorganize, build, and transfer so that all youngsters were being taught in comprehensive schools. There has
been resistance. In a number of localities, of conservative
as well as Conservative bent, it was felt that amalgamation
of the schools would weaken the teaching and the prestige of
the grammar stream. Where this feeling was strong the resistance largely took the form of foot-dragging, delay in
the hope that a more conservative Conservative government
would come into power and reverse the policy. Only in a
district near Manchester (Tameside, in Greater Manchester)
did the conflict reach the point of a dispute between education authority and the minister carried to the courts.

The struggle over "grammar vs. comprehensive schools,"

now almost certainly decided in favor of the comprehensives, has been revealing of British attitudes. The argument of those favoring the grammar schools has always been in terms of the merits of the education in them and the fear that their strengths will not survive amalgamation into comprehensives, and no one with experience of many American high schools can call the fear unrealistic. On the other hand, it is among members of the Conservative Party that one finds support for the separate grammar schools, and especially in those areas where the population is middle and upper class, so that one cannot help but suspect that the feeling is at least in part a fear that the distinctive and distinguishing social coloration given to the graduates of grammar schools will be lost. (I have not seen the matter discussed, but I have wondered if the parents who oppose comprehensive schools are not a bit afraid that their children may succeed in opting out of the rigorous traditional education of the grammar scheme--in a grammar school the student would have no other courses to take. Parents who have struggled to get their children to take Latin instead of Spanish and Spanish instead of "drivers' ed" will sympathize.)

The arguments of those favoring comprehensive schools are more revealing of the class issue involved. Beyond the revealing suggestion, always made with a certain relish, that a working class kid will bloody the nose of a middle class kid (I have not yet heard it cheerfully suggested that a budding Mohammed Ali of Jamaican parentage might knock out a Yorkshire miner's boy), the emphasis has always been on the elimination of privileged position and the socially desirable consequences of common experience. That this is a very important element, if not actually the most important element, in the case for the comprehensive school is strongly indicated by the left wing's continuing opposition to the still-existing public schools. There are repeated suggestions that they be abolished, or at least that their property be made taxable. Immediately after the Second World War a few special scholarship places were established in the public schools so that working class boys could enjoy the advantages of a public school education, but they were so few as to make no real difference to the social structure of the schools, and any working class boy who would take such a scholarship was likely to be a deserter from his class origins anyway. So opening these schools to the masses is no longer a popular idea, but making life impossible for these schools still has adherents. There is both reason and symbolic resentment in the position. Public schools still give their graduates advantages, both because they do provide an excellent education and because their reputations and the loyalties they inspire (the old school tie) do open doors to their graduates quite aside from the individual's merits. But the importance of the old school tie has declined greatly--it may have become worth very little indeed by 1979--and there are many other routes through grammar school streams and the much expanded system of higher education to careers of power and prestige. Thus one suspects that the continued efforts to abolish the public school, directly or by slow strangulation, reflect less a desire to reform society than a desire "to get the privileged bastards."

Another and for the future important aspect of the struggle is its close correlation with age. Supporters of the separate grammar school appear to be mostly of middle age or older (admittedly this is when people are parents). Younger adults do not seem to care much about the issues of grammar and public schools. Whereas in its youth a younger generation is apt to be more radical than its parents, in this case there appears to be a permanent divide. Not only are class and the overt signs of class not nearly so important to the rising generation; they never will be.

CLASS SINCE 1965

The lines of class cannot be measured. They are felt by participants in a class system. They are evident to observers in the ways people's behavior changes when they interact across class lines. They are also evident when talking to members of different classes, or in the lack of substantive communication about the nature of the world when one listens to people of different classes talking to each other. But characterizations of class illustrated "in the small" can never prove or disprove "the large," and hence disagreement can be, and is, continuous. What follows here is therefore impressionistic--I think it is correct, but I cannot prove it.

too much too risk

In the early 1960s all the young working class people rising into the professional classes worked hard to adopt the accents and style of the upper classes. One had to listen with great care to guess at a person's origins (Scotsmen and Irishmen) excepted). By the early 1970s young men and women who had been through a university were speaking in the accents and phrasings of their class and region of origin, and no penalties seemed to be attached. In the early 1960s people of different classes living in close proximity would frequent different pubs, or the upper class

people would go into the saloon bar and the working class
into the public bar--or where the classes "mixed" in the
public bar there was deference in the tones of the lower
orders and jolliness in the tones of the higher orders.
Not nearly so true today. In 1960 one could tell the class
of a person in a pub by his dress; by 1975 it was a doubtful
clue (egalitarians owe some debt to America's jeans).

Among younger people one senses an indifference to
class, a not caring. This is different from "not believing
in" class or disapproving of class. One can have principles,
and hopes for the future, one can work for the abolition of
class lines yet still feel them, still be conscious of the
differences, still think or fear they make a difference.
[For many American whites this has been an aspect of racial
integration--I have been on the side of the angels all my
life, but I certainly know whether I have blacks in a class
and have sorted out how well or badly they are doing long
before I have sorted out the same for white students.] The
"not caring"--one can know a person's parentage is Manchester
working class just as one can know a person's parentage is
Connecticut farmer without caring--may be well on the way to
making social class of little importance in British politics.

But this hardly means that class has disappeared as a
most important element in British society. The American
slogan of the 1960s--"Never trust anyone over 30"--might be
the proper slogan for those under thirty in Britain in 1979.
Class is real, is felt, is important to anyone born before
Attlee's first postwar government; and it is not totally un-
important to many born since. It will be some years, ten
anyway, maybe twenty, before one can begin to speak of
British society and policy without speaking about class; and
so deep are the perceptions of the world and the symbols of
discourse rooted in class that it may be more years than
that before one can analyze British problems without con-
sidering class.

In some ways the decreasing importance of class may be
making class more important. In an hierarchical class system the lower orders show and are apt to feel a deference
for the higher orders. A feeling of deference is by no
means inconsistent with resentment of the higher orders and
a dislike and resentment of one's own feelings of deference:
the combination can make relationships very nasty indeed.
Besides deference there is also *fear*. Fear is both a cause
and a consequence of deference, as well as of differences
in power and in the degree of vulnerability to the consequences of one's acts. There is likely to be abuse of

deference and of fear by those ranking higher in the class
system, often unconscious but nevertheless real. When
values are changing and many are ceasing to care about
class, evidence of deference, and particularly evidence of
the expectation or abuse of deference or fear, is going to
be especially offensive to those who both disapprove of
class and "do not care" to what class a person belongs.
They are apt to react strongly, to be more than willing to
carry the fight to great lengths to destroy the remaining
elements of class. The consequence may be that as class in
fact declines in total importance it becomes more important
in setting off militant responses on the part of working
class people and people who do not care, and last ditch confused defences by those who sincerely believe they have co-
operatively given up all the privileges which they had been
asked to give up.

GOVERNMENT AND POLITICS[1]

I. THE SYSTEM OF GOVERNMENT

Britain--more properly, the United Kingdom of Great
Britain and Northern Ireland--is a parliamentary democracy.
It is also a unitary state. Both facts distinguish the
processes of policy making and the administration of
government from their counterparts in our presidential
system.

The supreme authority in Britain is *Parliament*. According to the principle of "parliamentary supremacy" no
person nor any agency--including Parliament itself--can limit the powers of Parliament. This doctrine of "parliamentary supremacy" is, however, severely limited by Britain's
"unwritten constitution"--that agglomeration of laws, traditions, beliefs, and practices that have grown up since
Magna Carta. Parliament is almost (not quite, but almost)
as limited in its exercise of power as are the organs of
American government under our written constitution. The
guardians of this unwritten constitution are varied, in-
definite, and rather peculiar: the courts, but Parliament
can overrule the courts; the opposition in Parliament, but
it can always be out-voted by the majority; the electorate
at the next election, but Parliament can always postpone
the next election (as it did when World War II broke out);
and the self-restraint of those temporarily in positions of
power, reinforced by a vague but universal knowledge of and
devotion to "the rights of Englishmen."

Parliament consists of two Houses: The House of Commons and the House of Lords. The "Lords" is short for the
House of Lords, although in the House of Commons it is always referred to as "the other place." Those elected to

the House of Commons are called Members of Parliament or, more frequently, MPs (Lords are always Lords, never MPs).

All real power resides in the House of Commons. The leader of the party with a majority in the Commons becomes the prime minister. Winston Churchill once remarked that the British prime minister is "the most powerful dictator in the world—so long as he retains the support of the House of Commons:" a quip that expresses the powers of the House and summarizes the position of the prime minister as representative of that House and its powers.

The prime minister appoints the other ministers, all of whom together constitute "the government." The prime minister's appointments are in his discretion—no one tells him whom to appoint—but "discretion" is here an operative word. He selects his ministers for their competence in administering a ministry *and* because they are leaders of groups within his party. In selecting his ministers he must give a good deal of weight to selecting people who will be able to assure him of the continuing support of the members of his party in the House, for if he loses the support of his party's MPs he will be unable to function as prime minister and will have to resign (hence, ". . . so long as he retains the support of the House of Commons").

An important, a vital, attribute for a prime minister is the ability to get consensus among members of the cabinet who represent both different departmental interests and different positions in the political spectrum within the party. The prime minister both draws upon the cabinet for ideas for major government policies and attempts to persuade the cabinet of the virtues of his own ideas about policy. So far as his continuance in office goes, it really makes little difference whether he is a major source of ideas or whether he is effective at eliciting ideas and converting them into policy decisions which have the support of the whole cabinet. The important things are consensus and ideas. Without consensus the prime minister will lose office; without ideas the government will lose the support of its followers, both in Parliament and in the country.

In the formal constitutional system of Britain the prime minister stays prime minister until (a) he resigns of his own free will because he feels he has served long enough and would rather do something else; (b) his party loses a majority in Parliament at an election (which must be called at least once every five years); or (c) he loses a "vote of confidence" in the House, and realizing that he

no longer has the support of his party, asks the Queen to
appoint his successor as leader of his party in the House
to the prime ministership.

It the prime minister loses a "vote of confidence" he
must resign. He may ask (as in all such matters, in effect,
tell) the Queen to dissolve Parliament and call a new election, thus facing each MP with the possibility of losing his
seat. More important, the party might lose the election, so
MPs who in general want to keep the party in office will
support the prime minister in particular cases even though
they disagree with him. When the government has only a
small majority, to endanger that majority by voting against
the government on an issue will bring down the wrath of the
party's leaders upon the "rebel" MPs, whose prospects of
rising to office in the government will be much diminished
and who may find themselves deprived of the party's support
in the next election.

Governments do not resign every time they lose a vote
in the Commons. The government has the choice of making a
vote a matter of confidence, and if it loses such a vote it
does resign. But governments can also allow "free votes,"
which they will do when they feel that a true matter of
"conscience" is involved (e.g., capital punishment), when
they do not much care how the vote turns out, when the party
itself is badly split and the prime minister does not wish
to force the issue, and when discretion appears the better
part of valor (e.g., better that some unwanted changes in
the 1977 budget be accepted than that an election be held
which the Conservatives looked almost certain to win). However, a government will always ask for a vote of confidence
when what it regards as its "basic strategy" is involved,
and if a government is excessively flexible in modifying its
basic strategy in order to stay in office the opposition can
so tie up government business in the House and inflict so
many embarrassing defeats on the government that the government will be forced to make an issue a matter of confidence
and resign when defeated. Thus there is "play" and a limit
to "play" in the application of the principle that when the
government loses a vote it must resign.

In fact, as opposed to the stated principle of the constitutional system, prime ministers rarely leave office because they lose a vote of confidence--no prime minister in
the twentieth century had resigned because he lost a vote of
confidence until James Callaghan lost one in the spring of
1979. Because the loss of a vote of confidence can be anticipated a prime minister will ask for a new parliamentary election before he actually loses the vote. When, in 1951, Attlee
was governing with a very small Labour majority, constantly
threatened with losing votes in the House, he asked King

George VI to dissolve Parliament so that either Labour would
be returned to office with a larger majority or (as happened)
the Conservatives would become the majority. When the threat
to the prime minister comes from within his own party because
his followers have lost confidence in him, the elder statesmen of the party will persuade the prime minister to resign
as if of his own free will so that the party's position in
Parliament will not be endangered. The circumstances of
Callaghan's defeat in the Commons in 1979 were exceptional:
Labour had already lost its majority through defeats in by-
elections following deaths of Labour MPs and Callaghan lost
a vote of confidence when the minor parties, which had not
voted against Labour, sided with the Conservatives in order
to force an election. The formal constitutional system is
there to assure that prime ministers who are not wanted by
a majority of MPs do not stay on as prime ministers, but more
subtle and more courteous means of inducing resignation than
votes of no confidence are the rule.

During the twentieth century the power of the Commons
has become increasingly concentrated. The prime minister
and the ministers he appoints effectively make most decisions,
the party's Parliamentary majority ratifying them. The *de
facto* concentration of power in the leadership of the party
with the majority in the Commons has occurred partly because of the increased importance of party when one major
party is overtly socialist and the other overtly anti-
socialist: each party becomes in itself an over-riding
"principle." It is also partly due, perhaps mostly due, to
the increased burdens of governing as modern welfare governments have engaged themselves in influencing or managing
more and more activities. This has meant simply less time
to debate any particular issue. It has also meant that
more and more the business of government becomes administrative rather than legislative. The increasing concentration may also be exaggerated as a result of romanticising
the past and overstating the degree to which individual members of the House of Commons could or did influence legislation and the policies of government a half century and
more ago.

In any case, it may be said that the main function of
the House of Commons is to produce a government. "Producing
a government" means providing a working majority in the
House of Commons for the policies and legislation of the
Prime Minister and his ministerial colleagues. The true
power of the House is to withdraw its voting support for the
government of the prime minister, thus forcing him and his
ministers to resign.

The House of Lords has no real power (except in exer-
cising its judicial functions) but does have some influence

and a role of convenience. Most of its members inherit
their seats in the Lords, but since the mid-nineteen-sixties
it has become common to appoint "Life Lords" whose children
cannot inherit their seats. Also, as a rule, only a few
hereditary lords attend the sittings of the Lords.

The House of Lords cannot prevent the Commons from
appropriating money, but it does have the right to delay
legislation passed by the Commons for thirteen months after
its second reading in the Commons (the point at which the
Commons accepts the principle of a bill and then debates
and amends the particulars). However, the Lords seldom
exercise the right to delay. Since the fight over Parliamentary reform and social legislation between the Liberal
Commons and the Conservative Lords in 1909-11 it has become an accepted part of the constitution that the King or
Queen will, upon the request of the prime minister, appoint
enough new people to the House of Lords to give the government in power a majority if the Lords absolutely refuse to
go along with the House of Commons. Large numbers of additional Lords have never been appointed: the threat of
doing so has always been sufficient to bring the Lords into
line.

The House of Lords has four real functions. The first
is to act as a debating society of elder statesmen who can
bring up points or raise issues or consider aspects of
legislation that the rush of business in the Commons tends
to disregard. Debate in the House of Lords thus provides
a second opportunity to consider legislation. The second
function of the House of Lords is to provide a means whereby the government can amend legislation already passed by
the House of Commons, either because the government had not
thought of these changes at the time the bill went through
the Commons or because the legislative calendar did not
allow enough time to amend the bill in the Commons and it
would be easier to allow the Lords to amend the bill before
it returned to the Commons for a final vote.

The House of Lord's third function is to act as the
"supreme court" of the United Kingdom. It is the highest
judicial authority in the land. The full House of Lords
does not sit as the highest court; rather, only a few
lords, known as the "law lords," distinguished jurists appointed to the Lords for this purpose, hear and decide
cases brought to the Lords on appeal.

Finally, the Lords can be used to supply ministerial
talent to the government. If there is someone whom the

prime minister thinks would make a particularly useful minister and if this person is not in the House of Commons (either because he never ran for the House or because he lost his seat in the House), the Queen can appoint him to the Lords and he can then be appointed a minister.

The Labour Party has opposed the existence of the House of Lords as an anachronistic bastion of privilege. It is true enough that the great majority of Lords inherited their position from their fathers and are in the Lords by right of descent and not because they have earned the position on merit. It is also true that the great majority of Lords are Conservative. But neither of these facts are nearly so important as Labour speakers like to make out on the hustings. In the first place, most Lords-by-inheritance do not attend the sessions of the House of Lords, so that their deficiencies as legislators or representatives or their Conservative proclivities are irrelevant. In the second place, the real threat that the Queen will appoint additional Lords assures that the Lords will not behave in an unrepresentative or irresponsible manner. This has meant that most of those who participate in the debates and voting in the House of Lords are people who have themselves been appointed to the Lords because of their experience, distinction, or merit. If there are, on the Conservative side, a number of active Lords who have inherited their seats, most of them are people who would have been appointed to the Lords on merit had they not also happened to have been the eldest son of a Lord. It has thus become a forum for elder, more or less distinguished statesmen.

The Labour Party had opportunities to abolish the House of Lords in the late 1940s and in the late 1960s but did not do so. The House of Lords is in fact a convenience to Labour in several ways: besides helping the government to reconsider legislation, acting as a forum for elder statesmen, and acting as the highest judicial authority, the Lords, one strongly suspects, serve as a symbol of privilege about which left-wing speakers can be abusive.

In a formal, purely legal, ceremonial way, the Queen is the head of state. If she appoints the prime minister, if she signs bills into laws, if she addresses each annual session of Parliament with a "Speech from the Throne" setting forth the policies she would like to see followed and the bills she would like to see passed, she does so as she is told to do. She always appoints as prime minister the leader of the party with the majority of seats in the House of Commons. She signs all bills presented to her by

Parliament, without power of veto. The Speech from the
Throne is written for her by the government in office. Before the Conservative Party adopted a formal system of
selecting its leader in the 1960s the Queen (and the King
her father before her) may have exerted some influence on
the selection of Conservative prime ministers as they
"emerged" as leaders from a process of quiet, behind-the-
scenes common consent. But certainly her influence did not
extend beyond some weighting of the scales in close cases.
So, except for fun, horseracing, and sentiment, one can
largely forget the Queen.

"Her Majesty's government," which is responsible for
making the decisions of public policy and for administering
the departments of government, consists of the prime minister and the ministers whom he appoints, most of whom are
MPs. It requires upwards of 70 and sometimes over a hundred
MPs to man the various ministerial and sub-ministerial posts
(the number depending upon how many ministries are created
and how many junior appointments are made). This means that
one out of four or an even larger proportion of the MPs of
the governing party have a position in the government. A
much lesser number, however, have real power in influencing
government decisions, and an even smaller number are members of the "cabinet". The cabinet consists of those minis-
ters--usually about twenty--who have the most important
ministries or other important positions such as Lord Privy
Seal or Chancellor of the Duchy of Lancaster (honorific
titles: the duties will be oversight of several ministries,
or a general brief to look after and worry about a major
class of affairs). It is the cabinet that makes the major
decisions and gives character to the government. It is
"collectively responsible" and its discussions are secret.

Those ministers who head the largest departments bear
the title "Secretary of State for. . .," while those in
charge of lesser departments are called simply "Ministers."
Collectively they are known as "ministers." Serving under
and assisting the Secretaries of State and Ministers are a
large number of "junior" ministers, the most important of
whom are entitled "Ministers of State." Of less stature
are the Parliamentary Secretaries and Parliamentary Under-
Secretaries to the various ministries, and at the bottom of
the top are the beginners at governing, the personal assistants to the Secretaries of State and the Ministers, who
bear the title "Parliamentary Private Secretary."

British government departments do not have the relatively permanent form that government departments do in the

United States. They can be reorganized, amalgamated, abolished, and created at the discretion of the government, or their roles and power changed to suit the desires of the prime minister and his cabinet. Before 1965 there were often several departments assigned to one minister, but since that date there has been a good deal of combining of smaller departments into larger ones so that there is now a close correspondence between a department (the administrative unit charged with specific duties) and the ministry (the policy-making and responsible grouping of a minister and his subordinates).

A minister is in principle considered personally responsible for everything that his civil servants do. There is, of course, flexibility in the interpretation of this universal responsibility, but the inappropriate use of power by even a fairly low level subordinate may force the minister to resign. This is a rather brutal system: certainly no minister can in reality keep track of and control everything that goes on in his ministry; personal guilt is seldom his; but the doctrine does assure three things: (1) that ministers do exercise a good deal of care to make sure that things do not go badly wrong; (2) that civil servants are protected from political pressures; and (3) that MPs have a person (the minister) who is required to be able to answer their questions.

A politician rises to higher levels in government through the acquisition and effective employment of more and more power. This system contrasts with the American system, where the ability to get votes is vital. In Britain it is proving one's worth to party leaders and other MPs that is crucial to a successful career in politics. To rise a person first impresses members of his party with his loyalty, diligence, and perhaps with a potential for brilliant performance in high office. He will then be offered the opportunity to run for Parliament as the candidate of his party. He may, as a continuing proof of loyalty and diligence, run in a constituency where he will almost surely lose, but if his party wants him in Parliament the party leaders will eventually find him a safe seat, one where the voters almost always elect the party's candidate. (In Britain a candidate need not be a resident of the constituency in which he runs for office. In fact, many are not.)

Once elected a Member of Parliament he will be a "backbencher", serving on parliamentary committees, voting in the House, and sometimes delivering speeches to the House. If, after a period of service on the backbenches,

he is considered likely to make a successful minister he
will be offered a junior position in the government (such
as Under Secretary to the Minister for Overseas Development).
If good at the job the next step is to become a Minister of
State (a post assisting a minister or a secretary of state)
or a minister of one of the less important departments.
Successful performance in one or more of these roles may
lead to one of the major ministries: Chancellor of the Exchequer, Foreign Minister, Home Secretary (in charge of
police, justice, law, immigration), Secretary of State for
Defense, and finally the "top of the greasy pole"--the
prime ministership.

Many appointed to junior posts do not live up to expectations and return to the backbenches. Some who become
ministers prove less effective than desired and leave office.
It is a system which simultaneously trains and prepares for
higher office *and* tests for higher office by the grant of
increasing power and responsibility.

TABLE 3-1
MPs Elected and Government Majority

Date of election	Conservative	Labour	Liberal	Other	Government majority
July 1945	213	393	12	22	146
Feb. 1950	298	315	9	3	5
Oct. 1951	321	295	6	3	17
May 1955	344	277	6	3	58
Oct. 1959	365	258	6	1	100
Oct. 1964	304	317	9	0	4
Mar. 1966	253	363	12	2	96
June 1970	330	287	6	7	30
Feb. 1974	296	301	14	24*	-33
Oct. 1974	276	319	13	27*	3#
May 1979	339	268	11	17*	43

*Of which:	Feb. '74	Oct. '74	May '79
United Ulster Unionists	11	10	10
Scottish Nationalists	7	11	2
Plaid Cymru	2	3	2

#Majority later lost as a result of deaths of Labour MPs
and losses in the consequent by-elections.

TABLE 3-2
Parliamentary Elections:
Percent of Seats & Percent of Popular Votes

Date of Election	Conservative Seats	Conservative Vote	Labour Seats	Labour Vote	Liberal Seats	Liberal Vote	Other Seats	Other Vote
July 1945	33.3	39.9	61.4	48.5	1.9	9.0	3.4	2.6
Feb. 1950	47.7	43.4	50.4	46.1	1.4	9.1	0.5	1.4
Oct. 1951	51.4	48.0	47.2	48.7	1.0	2.5	0.5	0.7
May 1955	54.6	49.7	44.0	46.4	1.0	2.7	0.5	1.2
Oct. 1959	57.9	49.4	41.0	43.8	1.0	5.9	0.2	0.9
Oct. 1964	48.3	43.4	50.3	44.1	1.4	11.2	0.0	1.3
Mar. 1966	40.2	41.9	57.6	47.9	1.9	8.5	0.3	1.7
June 1970	52.4	46.4	45.6	43.1	1.0	7.5	1.1	3.0
Feb. 1974	46.6	38.8	47.4	37.4	2.2	19.4	3.8	4.4
Oct. 1974	43.5	36.5	50.2	40.4	2.0	18.8	4.3	4.3
May 1979	53.4	43.9	42.2	36.9	1.7	13.8	2.7	5.4

TABLE 3-3
Prime Ministers Since World War II
With Date of Taking Office

Clement Attlee (L)	26 July 1945
Winston Churchill (C)	26 Oct. 1951
Anthony Eden (C)	6 Apr. 1955
Harold Macmillan (C)	10 Jan. 1957
Alec Douglas-Home (C)	18 Oct. 1963
Harold Wilson (L)	16 Oct. 1964
Edward Heath (C)	19 June 1970
Harold Wilson (L)	12 Mar. 1974
James Callaghan (L)	5 Apr. 1976
Margaret Thatcher (C)	4 May 1979

L: Labour
C: Conservative

TABLE 3 - 4
Chancellors of the Exchequer Since World War II
With Date of Taking Office

Hugh Dalton (L)	27 July 1945
Stafford Cripps (L)	13 Nov. 1947
Hugh Gaitskell (L)	19 Oct. 1950
R. A. Butler (C)	28 Oct. 1951
Harold Macmillan (C)	20 Dec. 1955
Peter Thorneycroft (C)	13 Jan. 1957
Derek Heathcoat Amory (C)	6 Jan. 1958
Selwyn Lloyd (C)	27 July 1960
Reginald Maulding (C)	13 July 1962
James Callaghan (L)	16 Oct. 1964
Roy Jenkins (L)	30 Nov. 1967
Ian Macleod (C)	20 June 1970
Anthony Barber (C)	25 July 1970
Denis Healey (L)	15 Mar. 1974
Geoffrey Howe (C)	5 May 1979

L: Labour
C: Conservative

The rise to higher office is often quite rapid. Talent for both administration and parliamentary debate is rare, so that people who appear to have both talents are asked to run for Parliament and once in Parliament are soon asked to take on increasing responsibilities.

Not all MPs are "elected equal." Many are selected to run for Parliament because they are loyal and diligent, and backbenchers who vote for the government are always needed. One might say that it is a subtle, "two class" system--the troops and the officers and potential officers. But a trooper may rise to office, often by being unexpectedly effective in debate in the House. Conversely, an officer may be reduced to the ranks because he shows himself lacking in the hoped for Parliamentary and administrative skills.

THE SYSTEM OF LOCAL GOVERNMENT

The striking contrast, to an American, between the British system of local government and the American system of state and local governments is the lack of power of British local governments to initiate action or to develop and pursue regional or local policies. To an American the elected British county or district councillor appears to be virtually an administrator of national policy.

The system has two tiers: 65 county or metropolitan governments divided into 453 districts or boroughs. [Greater London, with 32 boroughs; 6 large English metropolitan areas with 36 metropolitan districts; 39 English counties with 296 districts or boroughs; 8 Welsh counties with 37 districts or boroughs; and 11 Scottish regions with 52 districts. According to the natives there are differences between the English and Welsh system, reformed by the Local Government Act 1972, and the Scottish system, reformed by the Local Government (Scotland) Act 1973, but the differences are not apparent even in the "moderately small-sized picture," let alone the "big picture." Similarly, the difference between metropolitan counties and counties, districts and boroughs, and even between the Greater London system and the others are minor, at least from the foreigner's point of view.] The upper tier governments (I shall hereafter call them all "counties") are in charge of police and fire protection, refuse disposal, weights and measures, and purity of food and drugs, major roads, and planning (which in Britain means something very close to what Americans mean by land use planning and zoning). Except in London and the metropolitan counties the county councils are

responsible for education (through the secondary level) and
for social services. District councils are responsible for
public housing (a large portion of housing in Britain);
hygiene, slaughterhouses, and smoke control; minor roads
and parking lots; and local planning. The metropolitan
districts outside London and the 20 outer London boroughs
are in charge of education (the 12 inner London boroughs are
united in an Inner London Education Authority). County and
district councils share powers over libraries, parks, bus
lines, museums, and baths (no joking matter in some city
districts and boroughs where numbers of houses were built
without baths as late as the 1930s--you pay a small fee and
are given a towel; an attendant draws your ration of hot
water; you add as much cold as you wish; and you do not have
to wash out the ring afterwards).

The combined powers and the county and district levels
approximate the powers of an American county or city government, less the judicial functions they enjoy in the U.S.
However, these powers are exercised under severely restrictive laws and rules laid down by the central government in
London. Salaries of teachers, for instance, are negotiated
at the national level. The national government lays down
the rules about what sort of social services should be provided; it subsidizes or forbids the establishment of industries in different areas (see "Regional Policy" in Chapter
4). The ministry of education decides a good deal of the
what and a great deal of the how of schooling. One forms
the definite impression that counties and districts decide
where to put public housing estates, where to site schools
and garbage dumps, what sort of offices social workers will
have, and whether to close a public bath. This impression
is inaccurate in some respects. The level of services provided by social workers--to the aged, the infirm, the distraught, the family in trouble--vary from district and
borough to district and borough. In social work--defined as
doing decent things for people--administration is probably
much more important than policy, and different attitudes
and intents in different places strongly influence the behavior of social workers. The quality as well as the amount
and siting of housing also depends on local government. The
arts and amenities--what J. H. and Barbara Hammond called
"public beauty and communal enjoyment," which is of large
but largely unrecognized importance in setting the tenor of
everyday life—do reflect the activities of local governments. However, always within restraints: of central policy
guidelines; of the terms of central government grants; or of
the power of a minister to intervene.

The total expenditures of all local governments combined amount to about a fifth of British GNP--a sizable sum
indeed--but the figure would be very misleading if taken as
an indication of economic or political power. In fact,
local governments might best be thought of, at least by
Americans, as agencies for carrying out the policies of the
national government and for administering the schools and
social services.

II. THE POLITICAL PARTIES

THE LABOUR PARTY

The British Labour Party is an amalgam of several
groups. The largest group, both in terms of membership and
of financial support, consists of the trade unions whose
members are also members of the Labour Party. (If a union
member does not wish to contribute to the Labour Party, and
thus be a member through his union, he may sign a card
stating that none of his union dues shall be contributed to
the Labour Party. However, members of unions do not as a
rule care to face down their shop stewards or other union
representatives in order to declare that they are not supporters of Labour; so that, while in a sense membership in
the Labour Party through the unions is legally voluntary,
it could be described as "not as voluntary as all that.")
The "constituency parties" are the second group. They are
the party organizations in each parliamentary constituency
and the organizations to which people attach themselves as
individuals. Membership in the constituency parties has
been declining over the years so that they are probably less
representative of those who consider themselves "Labour"
than are the unions. Cooperative societies (not including
the building societies) make up the third component of the
Labour Party.

The annual conference of the Party consists of delegates from the unions, from the constituency parties, and
from the cooperatives. The delegates have one vote for
every five thousand members whom they represent. The tenor
of the debates on resolutions tend to represent the views
of the constituency parties, often to the left of the main
strands of Labour Party thought; but because union membership constitutes about 85% of total Party membership the
votes accepting or rejecting resolutions represent the views
of the unions, each of which casts its total votes as a
block. However, a "union line" does not determine Labour
Party policy because there is a disagreement among the

unions, whose political outlook varies from far left to
just to the left of center. The National Executive Committee (NEC), which formulates Party policy about newly arising
issues between annual conferences and expresses the Party
view to Labour MPs, is elected by the annual conference:
twelve members by the trade union delegates, seven by the
constituency party delegates, and five women and a treasurer
by all the delegates to the conference. In addition, the
Leader of the Party in Parliament (who is also prime minister when Labour has a majority in Parliament) and the
Deputy Leader are members.

The Labour Party is "socialist." But precisely what
"being socialist" involves is not so clear. At least, what
is clear is not precise, and nothing precise is clearly
acceptable to all in the Labour Party. Perhaps the best
statement of what it means to be a socialist in Britain is
to be found in *The Future of Socialism* by C. A. R. Crosland.[2]
His argument is that it would be wrong to ask, "What is
socialism?" or, "What is the doctrine of socialists?" Rather, one should ask, "What are the aspirations of those who
call themselves socialists?" or, "What have been the re-
current themes of socialist thought?" The aspirations and
the themes have been several, some more important to some
people, some more important to others. Among the leading
themes of British socialism has always been the restraint
that it should be democratic, that government should be
responsible to an electorate consisting of the whole people.
In addition to that restraint Crosland distinguishes five
themes: "the appropriation of property incomes, cooperation,
workers' control, social welfare and full employment."[3] The
first may draw upon a long natural law tradition that all
value is created by labor, or it may be based more simply
on the view that the rich have much more than they deserve
and the poor far less. Cooperation expresses the idea that
competition is socially disruptive, reducing mutuality of
feeling and giving too little play to altruism; and also
that competition, as one of the elements of capitalism, has
been responsible for ignoring such needs as decent housing
and nutrition. The theme of workers control has drawn support from the insecurity of employment when workers had no
control over their employment, from the natural law view
that all value is created by labor and therefore labor
should control the creation of value, and from the proposition that in any case workers should have more to say about
what goes on. The aims of social welfare and of full employment are both rooted in ideas of humaneness, kindliness,
and human dignity. (Which is not to say that non-socialists
are inhumane, brutal, and enjoy denigrating people; it is,

rather, to say that this is how British socialists picture
themselves.) All these aspirations, aims, or themes have
in common the idea of "decency"--as opposed to ideas of
"economic growth" or of "economic efficiency" or of "just
reward to economic effort." This does not mean that
socialists are against economic efficiency or economic
growth or that they do not worry about reward to economic
input. Rather, it means that socialists have a different
ranking of priorities than are implied by these alternative
phrases.

While all that has been said about the socialism of
the Labour Party is true, there remains a strong strain of
not-so-socialist thought among a fairly large segment of
the Party. When the Liberal Party ceased to be a viable
route to influence or power in British politics, those
Liberals most strongly attached to ideas of reform and
equality joined the Labour Party. This group has reinforced Labour's attachment to the rights of individuals
but it has also restrained the tendency of Labour to
nationalize ever more industries. In addition, it is
rather favorably inclined toward the ideas of a moderately
large, private, competitive sector in the economy and of
free trade. This division of the Labour Party into what
might be called "liberal" and "socialist" wings became
important during the debate over joining the European
Economic Community (the EEC). On one side--including the
majority of the Labour cabinet--were those who supported
joining the EEC on the typical liberal grounds that
competition, comparative advantage, and larger markets
are beneficial. Those who wanted more nationalization and
much more discretionary intervention in the economy by
government campaigned against membership.

THE CONSERVATIVE PARTY

The Conservative Party has been more informally and,
one might say, more privately organized than has the Labour
Party. While the Young Conservatives and the Conservative
Trade Union Council are represented in the annual conference
of the Conservative Party, it is the delegates sent by the
party committees in each constituency who dominate that
conference. And while there are annual squeals from the far
right of the Conservative Party at the conferences, the
conferences are far more obedient to the Party's Parliamentary leadership than are the Labour Party conferences. It
might almost be said that the Labour party uses its annual
conference to let off steam and the Conservative party uses
its annual conference to assert its unity.

The National Conservative Association and its Executive
Committee serve as one conduit to present Conservative
feelings to the Party leaders but there appears to be no
tension between the Association (the formal organization in
the country outside Parliament) and the MPs and leaders in
Parliament. Much more powerful than the Association is the
Conservative Central Office. It is the center for political
organization, for propaganda literature on policy, and has
attached to it the Conservative Research Department. The
Chairman of the Party Organization and other important members of the Central Office are appointed by the Party's
leader in the House (prime minister when the Conservatives
are in office), so that the Central Office, while techni-
cally part of the Party in the country rather than in
Parliament, is an effective area of the leadership of the
Party in Parliament.

To define the Conservative political philosophy is impossible; to describe it almost equally difficult. Conservatives pride themselves on defending those values and institutions which have grown up slowly, whose origins reach
back in British history, and which (in the Conservative
view) represent the finest flowering of British civilization. Which means, pretty much, that Conservatives defend
the good aspects of the *status quo* and some of the bad aspects too. In contrast to the Labour Party the Conservatives stand for private property, but in a peculiarly limited way. Winston Churchill as First Lord of the Admiralty
nationalized 51% of the stock of British Petroleum in 1913
in order to assure the British Navy of a supply of oil. Although Churchill was a Liberal at the time, the point here
is that British who are conservative by temperament do not
mind a spot of nationalization in a good cause. (Earlier
Churchill had been a Conservative and later became a Conservative again. His comments on this aspect of his career:
"Anyone can rat on his party--it takes talent to re-rat.")
It was a Conservative government that nationalized the airlines in 1939. Between the two World Wars major elements of
the Conservative party wanted to nationalize the railroad
network, and a significant number of Conservatives were in
favor of nationalizing the coal mines. At various times
the Conservatives have liked to feel that they favor free
markets and competition--and compared to Labour they certainly do--but Conservatives between the Wars favored
"rationalizing" industry by reducing competition. Until
recently they strongly favored Imperial Preference, which
gave marked advantages to producers in Commonwealth countries over non-Commonwealth producers, and they have sometimes introduced their own schemes of price and wage con-

trols. To say that the Conservative view is that "whatever
is, is good" would be a caricature but perhaps a recogniz-
able one. Perhaps Conservative political and economic
philosophy could best be expressed as a set of attitudes:
sympathy for businesses and businessmen, sympathy for the
middle class, sympathy for the rich if not for the nouveau
riche, a strong but not overwhelming bias towards private
property, a deep respect for existing institutions as they
are, no particular distaste for class lines, and a distrust
of trade unions and the working class (not in principle, of
course, but a sublimated distrust which surfaces as a sensitivity to the dangers of trade union power and of working
class attitudes).[4]

Comparisons with American politics can be very misleading. It is true that the Conservatives are to the
right of Labour and that the Republicans are to the right
of the Democrats but that does not make Conservatives like
Republicans or Democrats like Labour. The traditions and
the rhetoric of the two countries are too different to permit easy identifications. One cannot conceive of a right
wing Republican joining the Labour Party but it is not impossible to picture a New England Republican as a Labour
Chancellor of the Exchequer; and if Senator Edward Kennedy
would make a decent Labour Minister of Health, so would he
also make a reasonable Minister of Environment in a Conservative government.

THE LIBERAL PARTY

The Liberal Party is a peculiar beast, beloved and
ignored. In the middle of the 19th century it was the party
of industrialists and other businessmen, the main opponent
of the Conservatives, who at that time tended to represent
the landed interest and the pre-industrial establishment.
Its political philosophy consisted of the 19th century
articles of liberal faith: free trade, free enterprise,
the belief that "that government which governs least,
governs best." In modern terminology one would call the
Party, as it then was, right wing. Toward the end of the
century, competing for lower middle class and working class
votes, the Liberal Party began moving to the left. By the
beginning of the 20th century it was forming an alliance
with the newly rising Labour Party and supporting legislation for social reform such as the rights of labor unions,
workmen's compensation, and old age pensions. It was the
Liberal Party which reduced the power of the House of Lords
in 1911 and enacted legislation which later became the basis
of the modern welfare state. The Liberal Party's decline

in the 1920s and later can be attributed to the competition
of the Labour Party. If one were working class, reform-
minded, or a socialist in the period around the turn of the
century, then it made a great deal of sense to vote for the
Liberal Party as the effective opposition to the Conservative Party; but once Labour began to achieve major party
status it became the obvious party for the working class to
support and so replaced the Liberals as the major opposition
to the Conservatives.

Liberal political philosophy is even less clear cut
than is Labour's, but it is clearly more reformist than is
the political philosophy of the Conservative Party. Liberals favor much greater social equality. They support worker
participation in the management of industry, but within a
context of private enterprise, and they are opposed to
nationalization. They favor all those reforms which all
good liberals throughout the world favor: abolition of
capital punishment, prison reform, legalization of homo-
sexuality between consenting adults. They are indeed far
stronger in support of civil liberties and civil rights
than are either of the two larger parties. In fact, a
primary emphasis on civil liberties and rights may be
modern liberalism's distinguishing trait. The Liberals
are also devoted to the cause of proportional representation.
They are undoubtedly sincere in believing that it is the
fairest system for electing a Parliament and that it will
assure individual MPs of a freedom to vote as they truly
think is best instead of feeling pressed to follow their
party's line all the time. But it is also true that the
Liberals stand to win a significant number of seats in
Parliament only if there is a system of proportional
representation.

In so far as sentiments go, there is probably a great
deal of friendliness toward the Liberals in Britain. The
problem for those who would like to vote Liberal is that
they feel they would be "throwing away their votes." Since
it seems virtually certain that either the Conservatives or
Labour will win every time, those who would like to vote
Liberal feel that the sensible thing to do is "to choose
the lesser of the two evils." The proportion of the total
1974 votes cast for Liberal candidates--19.4% in February
and 18.8% in October--probably understates the sentimental
support for the Liberal Party, although it is possible that
the large Liberal vote during 1974 expressed the view, "a
plague on both your houses," rather than a truly pro-
Liberal preference.

THE NATIONALIST PARTIES

There are now three "Nationalist" parties of some importance: the Scottish Nationalist Party (SNP), the Plaid Cymru (Welsh Nationalists), and the United Ulster Unionists. Each of these parties is devoted to only one over-riding aim. In the case of the SNP, it is independence for Scotland (although the SNP might settle for a very large degree of autonomy for Scotland). For the Welsh Nationalists, it is local autonomy for Wales. For the Ulster Unionists it is Protestant domination of Northern Ireland. Beyond these aims, none of these parties has a clear political program.

The nationalist parties became important in 1974 because Labour's Parliamentary majority was so slim (see Table 3-1). Labour did not actually have a majority after the February election and depended upon the support of the nationalist parties to outvote the Conservative opposition. The October election gave Labour a small majority, but in succeeding years deaths of Labour MPs followed by lost by-elections cost it its majority and Labour again had to depend on the votes of nationalist MPs. So long as the electorate is closely divided between the Conservatives and Labour the nationalist parties will be able to influence legislation by giving support to or withholding support from a major party; and so long as the nationalist parties can do this, sympathetic voters will feel that it is worthwhile voting for a nationalist party.

The United Ulster Unionists want to maintain Protestant majority rule in Northern Ireland (Ulster). Certainly a large number of Unionists are anti-Catholic. Certainly others, if not bigotedly anti-Catholic, are afraid of a Catholic government—a long-term possibility in view of the higher birthrates among the Catholic population of Ulster than among the Protestant. In part anti-Catholic, in part desirous to remaining part of the United Kingdom instead of becoming a part of the Republic of Ireland, all Unionists are united by a vested interest in the dominant position of the currently majority Protestants and in the subsidies that Ulster gets from the United Kingdom. Until recently the Unionists have supported the Conservatives (the full, proper name was the "Conservative and Unionist Parties") because they have felt that the Conservatives were more likely to preserve the position of the Ulster Protestants as the dominant group in Northern Ireland than was the Labour Party. Their ten MPs use their power to vote for or against the government in a very closely split Parliament to assure that Ulster will continue to have a special, privileged place within the United Kingdom, whether that Kingdom is ruled by a Conservative or by a Labour Party.

Scottish nationalism has a long history, there always having been some who never accepted union with England. In 1715 there was a quickly suppressed Scottish rising to put James Stuart (the Old Pretender) on the throne of Scotland (and perhaps of Britain). In 1745 there was the famous uprising under the Young Pretender, Bonnie Prince Charlie: suppressed, but not so quickly (following which there was a period of brutal repression in the Scottish Highlands). By the 19th century Scottish nationalism had become a matter of sentiment, balladry, and such local pride as one finds among Texans. There was not, until the 1970s, a serious movement for Scottish independence or even for greater autonomy for Scotland (the expression is "devolution"). While many Scots would have liked a greater degree of home rule, that desire was never strong enough to induce most Scots to vote for a Nationalist Party. There always appeared to be far more important policy issues for Britain as a whole. However, the 1970s have seen a change, and the SNP now gets the support of about one-third of the electorate. Two elements have contributed to this change. There is the long-felt feeling that Scotland is the "born loser" of the British Isles, always suffering from greater unemployment than does the English component of the Kingdom and never being a center for new and dynamic developments. But this feeling had never been enough to make the SNP a major political force. Rather, it made Scotland a very important element in the success of the Labour Party. In fact, Labour in 1964 and in 1974 would not have had a majority in Parliament if Scotland had not been part of the Kingdom. It is therefore, in a very real way, the second element--"Scotland's oil"--that has created the SNP. Were Scotland actually to become independent, the North Sea oil fields would provide a lot of oil revenue for an independent Scotland and it is this great prize that has induced a lot of Scots to support the SNP. If all revenue from these fields were to go to an independent Scotland, there would be an awful lot of income for the five million Scots and a great deal of foreign exchange with which to reorganize and to rebuild the Scottish economy.

How much oil would be Scotland's oil is not clear. When the line was drawn between England's share of the North Sea and Scotland's share, it was drawn due east from the English-Scottish border at Berwick-on-Tweed at the eastern end of the border. At the time the line was of no particular importance, simply a matter of accommodating some small

differences which still exist between Scottish and English
law. Were Scotland to become independent, the English would
have grounds for arguing that the line between the English
and Scottish oil fields ought to be drawn in a northeasterly
direction following the general tendency of the whole
English-Scottish border. If the line were redrawn, a lot of
the oil would become English instead of Scottish, but that
would still leave Scotland with a great deal of oil. But
there is another peculiarity. The Shetland and Orkney
Islands north of Scotland have always been considered a part
of Scotland. But the populations of Shetland and Orkney are
not sympathetic to Scottish nationalism and have made it
clear that, should Scotland become independent, or even
achieve a great deal of home rule, they would prefer to remain part of the English kingdom. The richest oil fields
are east and north of the Shetland and Orkney Islands, so
that if Shetland and the Orkneys did not become part of an
independent Scotland the Islands could claim, under current
international rules, that a very large portion of "Scotland's oil" was in fact "Shetland's oil" or "Orkney's oil."
It is, therefore, by no means clear how big a prize the SNP
could in fact bring to Scotland.

While North sea oil is a bonanza for Great Britain, it
would be a total economic revolution for Scotland alone,
provided Scotland got all of the oil fields which the Scots
nationalists now feel are Scotland's. To give some ideas
of the dimensions of the prize for Scotland: if all of the
value of the oil over and above the costs for extracting it
from the sea bed were to accrue to an independent Scotland,
the national income of Scotland would almost double for upwards of twenty years. If all this value, most of which
would be in foreign exchange, were used to purchase bonds
and stocks in Germany, France, Belgium, Holland, Switzerland,
and the United States, every Scot in Scotland at the beginning of the 21st century could retire at birth on an income
equal to the present per capita income of Scotland--and if
he wanted to work too, his income would be a good deal
higher. It should be little wonder, then, that many Scots
now see the SNP demand for Scottish independence as providing real rewards quite aside from sentiment and pride.

Like the Scottish nationalists, the Welsh nationalists
have existed for a long time, hoping for a degree of home
rule for Wales and working to preserve and revive the Welsh
language. There may be oil off the Welsh coast (or there
may not be), but the recent strength of the Plaid Cymru is
not a petroleum phenomenon but a result of the hope that a
few Plaid Cymru MPs joining with SNP and Ulster Unionist

MPs could get some decision-making power for a Welsh parliament.

In March of 1979 the Scots and Welsh voted on devolution. Autonomous but not independent parliaments were to be established in Scotland or Wales: (1) if a majority of those voting approved devolution; and (2) if this majority constituted more than 40% of all eligible to vote.   In Scotland only two-thirds of the electorate voted so that the small majority for devolution fell well short of the required 40%.   While the result was certainly a set-back to Scottish nationalism it was not a disaster and the Scots Nationalist Party may survive to wield influence in closely divided Parliaments.   In Wales only one of eight voted for devolution: the defeat may presage the end of Plaid Cymru.

ENDNOTES

1. A reader desiring more knowledge of this topic will find R. M. Punnett, *British Government and Politics* (London: Heineman, 1976) a detailed but clear and highly readable source.

2. C. A. R. Crosland, *The Future of Socialism*. London: Macmillan, 1956.   Later, when Crosland became an important minister in Labour governments, he was called Tony Crosland, doubtless to make him sound "working class."

3. *Ibid.*, p. 88.

4. Nigel Harris, *Competition and the Corporate Society: British Conservatives, the State and Industry, 1945-1964.* London: Methuen and Co. Ltd., 1972. Mr. Harris might object strongly to my citing his book as a source of these ideas, at least as I have so crudely stated them, but his book did help me to sort out my impressions and it did give me the courage to be so crude about Conservative ideology.

4

INDUSTRIAL STRUCTURE AND INDUSTRIAL POLICIES

British industrial organization differs from American in at least two important respects: first, the absence of a strong anti-monopoly policy; and second, public ownership of several industries and of a number of firms. In other respects the basic structure of British industrial organization is like that in the United States and in other industrialized capitalist economies: most firms are small and partnerships and proprietorships far outnumber corporations, but corporations, especially the large ones, dominate the industrial scene and produce the larger portion of output; corporations are legally owned by the stockholders but management is generally sensitive only to the wishes of large stockholders and of banking and other financial institutions.

I. CONCENTRATION AND MONOPOLY

One's general impression is that British industry is more concentrated in fewer large firms, and more monopolistic than is American. This is, however, a "general impression," not a measurement. It has been common practice among economists to measure concentration and market power by computing "concentration ratios": the proportion of an industry's sales or net output or employment contributed by the largest three or five or other small number of firms in the industry. Because industries are different, and industrial censuses define industries differently, precise comparisons cannot be made, nor do different measures (net output, employment) give the same results. Furthermore, comparative concentration ratios will vary depending on whether one uses the largest 3, say, or the largest 5 or 10. And in any case, no one knows exactly what each ratio implies about market power or probable effectiveness of competition.

In his review of the evidence as of 1968 Richard Caves concluded that "the distribution of concentration in British manufacturing trades in the 1950s did not greatly differ from that in the United States, although *situations of near monopoly seemed more common.*"[1] He also commented, "Roughly speaking, the chances seem higher that a small British industry will exceed its U.S. counterpart in concentration than will a large industry . . . ."[2]

Studies of industrial concentration have measured dominant firms' shares of output or employment within particular industries because economists' interest has focused on the degree of monopoly power in specific markets. While this focus certainly has great merits, it does not emphasize the importance of large firms in the total economy, where large firms produce goods for a number of different markets. Most of the world's largest corporations are American, and only three British corporations rank in the top fifty largest corporations in the world. But such comparisons as these may be misleading. Britain has only one quarter of the population of the United States and a per capita income only a little more than half that in the United States. Analyses of British and American firms in terms of capital employed and of total sales highlight the contrast between Britain and the U.S. As both Tables 4-1 and 4-2 show, large U.S. firms are almost four times the size of large British firms, a statistic that gives some weight to the British belief that British firms are too small to reap full economies of scale. (This line of argument does ignore those studies of U.S. firms which have indicated that the largest firms are often not the most efficient. It also overlooks the facts that the first, second, and tenth largest firms on the European continent are Dutch. The Netherlands' national market is but a fraction of the British, and the Dutch firms became large before the establishment of the EEC.)

On the other side of the contrast, the U.S. GNP is about eight times bigger than the British GNP. If one measures the size of firms in terms of the size of national markets, the comparisons of size are reversed. To compensate for the difference in the size of national markets, one can multiply the size of British firms by eight. The last columns in Tables 4-1 and 4-2 make this compensatory adjustment and show that large British firms are about twice as important in the British economy as are large U.S. firms in the American economy. Although individual market by individual market British industry may not be significantly more monopolistic than American, general economic power is

TABLE 4-1
50 Largest Firms by Capital Employed:
U.S. & U.K. Compared

Rank by capital employed	Average capital employed		U.K. firm's capital as percentage of U.S. firms' capital	
	U.S. (£mn.)	U.K. (£mn.)	Unadjusted %	Adjusted* %
1-10	6,424	1,879	29	232
11-20	3,124	687	22	176
21-30	2,011	463	23	184
31-40	1,554	363	23	184
41-50	1,294	302	23	184
1-50	2,882	739	26	208

* (Unadjusted) x (8), because U.S. GNP is approximately eight times larger than British GNP.

Source: *The Times 1000, 1976-77.* London: Times Newspaper Ltd., 1976, Tables 1 and 5, pp. 27, 29, 92, 94.

appreciably more concentrated in Britain. To the information given above should be added the facts that the British steel industry, the British shipbuilding industry, the British coal industry, and the British aircraft industry are all government owned and, were they included in the comparisons of concentration ratios (they are not), British industry might look a good deal more concentrated.

ATTITUDES ABOUT INDUSTRIAL STRUCTURE

Perhaps more important to understanding British industrial structure than the measures is the attitude in Britain toward industrial concentration and the existence or creation of monopolistic positions. Far from disapproving, the British are very much inclined to view industrial concentration as a good thing. There is no logical line or clear conflict in economic philosophy between the Americans and British on this matter. It is far more a visceral than an intellectual matter, an instinctive reaction rather than a

52

TABLE 4-2
100 Largest Firms by Sales:
U.S. & U.K. Compared

Rank by value of sales	Average sales		U.K. firms' sales as a percentage of U.S. firms' sales	
	U.S. £mn	U.K. £mn	Unadjusted %	Adjusted* %
1-10	12,830	3,787	29.5	236
11-20	5,093	1,268	24.9	199
21-30	3,328	940	28.2	225
31-40	2,809	751	26.7	213
41-50	2,492	658	26.4	211
1-50	5,310	1,481	27.9	223
51-100	1,661	452	27.2	217
1-100	3,486	966	27.7	222

* (Unadjusted) x (8), because U.S. GNP is approximately
eight times larger than British GNP.

Source: *The Times 1000, 1976-77*. London: Times
Newspapers Ltd., 1976 Tables 1 and 5,
pp. 27, 29, 92, 94.

considered judgement. The differences in attitude result
from the cumulation of a number of variations in emphasis,
in expectations, in history, and in those perceptions of
how the world works which people begin to acquire as soon
as they begin to learn their mother tongue. Both Americans
and British believe that large scale industry is often more
efficient than small scale industry; but Americans are inclined to attribute this efficiency to the physical, chemical, or engineering characteristics of large scale production while British are more inclined to attribute it to organization and management (this despite the fact that in
both American education and American society management provides a more prestigious career than in Britain). The British are also inclined to anticipate economies from scale in
more industries than are Americans.

The American position might be put this way: monopolies are bad; if they cannot be broken up into a more

TABLE 4-3

Share of 100 Largest Enterprises
in Net Manufacturing Output

Year	Percent
1909	16
1924	22
1935	24
1940	22
1953	27
1958	32
1963	37
1968	41
1972*	41

* Due to a change in statistical
methods, not strictly comparable
with previous years.

Source: *Financial Times*, May 11,
1978, p. 22.

competitive industrial structure, then they should be regu-
lated.   An American corporation arguing against being forced
to divest itself of some of its assets or against regulation
by the government always argues that it is competing vigor-
ously--and must compete vigorously--with a number of other
companies.   The British position might be put thus: monopolies may be bad--they do have opportunities to take advantage of customers or of suppliers--but many monopolies are
good because they do not abuse their dominant position in
the market and behave well.   When subjected to criticism a
British corporation will often respond with defenses of
"good behavior," "rationalization of the industry," or
"efficiency."   None of these are really proper defenses in
America: of course each are used by American corporations,
but only in conjunction with denials of a dominant position
and with insistence upon the competitive nature of their
businesses.

Although American rhetoric sounds more pro-capitalistic,
more in favor of private property rights, in fact British
sentiments are in some senses more pro-property than are
American.   The American's devotion to his property rights
may embrace his house and his car and his farm and his

family-owned business with a vengeance, but with distance
from self and from personal relations the American's feelings about property tend to weaken. From the Populists in
the late 19th century protesting at the railways' rights to
set rates to Ralph Nader criticizing General Motors or the
larger oil companies, America has been and is full of people
who feel that "*no* company has a right to be *that* large, to
be *that* powerful."

In contrast, British rhetoric is often abusive of private property and wealth while their actions indicate that
they are in fact very sensitive to the rights of property.
The government will sometimes forbid corporations to merge,
but corporations are not forced to divest themselves of
holdings although cases could be made that some divestitures
would increase competition and lower prices. Unauthorized
bullying by government leaders--called "jawboning" in the
U.S.--is rarer and raises more protests in Britain than in
America. The Stock Market, acting as an elite club, under
the aegis of the Bank of England and through its Take-Over
Panel, may or may not regulate the securities business more
effectively than the Securities and Exchange Commission does
in the U.S., but there is no authorized, legally empowered
SEC in Britain to enforce disclosure upon corporations.
(This situation may change in the near future.) The British
are much more hesitant to deprive corporations of the substance of their rights by changing the environment of laws
and rules than are Americans. The emphasis of the British
left on nationalization may be an evidence and a consequence
of this "property hang-up:" property rights may only be
altered by full-scale, legislative processes and not by
subtle changes.

A sampling of statements from and about the interwar
years will illustrate the kind of thinking shared by all
parties before the British decided to adopt a pro-competition policy after the war (I have added all italics):[3]

> . . . Labour members of the 1919 Committee on Trusts
> emphasized that the evolution towards combination
> and monopoly was both inevitable *and desirable*,
> provided it was controlled in the public interest. . .
> Conservative opinion showed a predisposition to
> favor regulation and controls *as opposed to free
> enterprise and competition*. (Swann *et al.*,
> characterizing the period.)
>
> *Production cannot be planned* in relation to estab-
> lished demand *while industries are organized on*

competitive lines.   (Harold Macmillan--(Chancellor of the Exchequer, 1955-57; Prime Minister, 1957-63--in 1932.)

. . . a tendency towards some degree of monopoly in an increasing number of industries is . . . inevitable *and even, quite often, desirable* in the interest of efficiency . . . . there is still room . . . for large-scale enterprises of semi-monopolistic character which are run for private profit and controlled by individuals. (The Liberal Party's *Industrial Enquiry*, 1928.)

After the war the British had a change of heart--or thought they had a change of heart. While moving toward an anti-monopoly, anti-restraint of trade position in some legislation, the pre-war (or simply British?) attitudes continued to run deep.

In the early 1950s Aneurin Bevan expressed a view which illustrates the continuing contrast between British and American attitudes.[4] Bevan was the leader of the left in the Labour Party in the late 1940s and early 1950s, the architect of the National Health Service, the leading opponent of any charges for prescriptions or for glasses, and a strong proponent of keeping living costs down with subsidies for food and housing. He proposed that *nationalized industries should* use their monopoly positions to *charge high prices.* He wanted to use the monopoly profits to finance socially worthwhile socialistic expenditures by government. Would any American radical propose that TVA should charge high electricity rates in order to finance re-housing slum dwellers?

As late as 1970 a leading British economist was saying, "No one in this country is likely to deny that there are 'good' and 'bad' mergers and 'good' and 'bad' monopolies . . . ."[5]

PUBLIC POLICY TOWARD MONOPOLY AND RESTRICTIVE PRACTICES

By the end of the war the British had come to feel that industry, both through monopolies or quasi-monopolies and through restrictive agreements between firms, might be limiting the growth of output and maintaining prices at a level higher than they need be. In 1944 both major parties had committed themselves to maintain full employment after the war and so it seemed less necessary to worry about industries having to defend themselves against the worst consequences of depression. So in 1948 the Monopolies and

Restrictive Practices Act was passed. The Act probably left American anti-trust lawyers wondering why the government had bothered to pass the Act at all. It set up a Monopolies and Restrictive Practices Commission to which the government *could* refer cases for investigation—*could*, not "were to." A monopoly situation was defined as one in which a third of the supply of a good was controlled by one company, by two or more interconnected corporations, or by companies acting in agreement. If the government felt that such a situation existed and if it felt that the monopoly was being abused, it could refer the case to the Monopolies Commission. The reference might only ask the Commission to determine if a monopoly existed, and what it did. It might also ask the Commission to decide if the monopoly's behavior was against the public interest, and if so asked the Commission would recommend remedial action if it concluded that the behavior was against the public interest. Whether any action was taken to change the behavior of the monopoly was then up to the government, which could decide to allow the practices to continue.

No practices were of themselves illegal. They became illegal only if the Commission concluded that they were contrary to the public interest and if the ministers agreed and if they decided to act. In effect the Monopolies Act of 1948 was not designed to end or even to reduce monopolization but rather to give the government the power to tell bad monopolies not to behave badly.

Over the following quarter century further acts were passed, making the laws somewhat tougher on companies engaging in restrictive practices. In 1956 a Restrictive Trade Practices Act established a Registrar of Restrictive Trading Agreements with whom all agreements setting prices or outputs or otherwise limiting competition had to be registered. Such agreements were presumed contrary to law unless they could "make it through a gateway." There were seven "gateways":

1. that the agreement protected the public;
2. "that the removal of the restriction would deny to the public . . . specific advantages enjoyed . . . by virtue of the restriction itself or of any arrangements or operations resulting therefrom;"
3. that the agreement counteracted the effects of third party restrictions;
4. that the agreement counteracted the effect of a monopoly supplier;

5. that the agreement protected against unemployment in an area;
6. that the agreement helped to maintain exports;
7. that the agreement supported other restrictions which had been found by the Restrictive Practices Court to be legal.[6]

If the parties to the agreement felt that it was legal the Registrar *had* to refer it to the Restrictive Practices Court set up under the Act. The Court consisted of both High Court judges and lay members. The Registrar presented the case for the Crown (the government: all the government's actions are taken in the name of the monarch). Most agreements taken to the Court were found to be illegal and the result was widespread abandonment of agreements. However, there were a number of ways around the law. Companies could have an agreement merely to exchange information on prices, output, costs, and sales—which could, of course, be a covert way of rigging the market. Each company in a trade could make an agreement with the trade association, legal because only one of the parties was agreeing to restrict trade, the trade association merely agreeing that the company would do so. Although an agreement struck down by the Court could not be replaced with another "to like effect," an agreement to abide by a minimum price could be replaced by one to abide by a maximum price, which would become "the" price. The courts did slowly strike down these means of evasion, but mergers continued to achieve the same results without "agreements."

A Monopolies and Mergers Act of 1965 empowered the Board of Trade to prohibit mergers which would create monopolies and even to dissolve monopolies on the recommendation of the Monopolies Commission. Any merger involving assets of ь5mn or more could be referred, and the Commission was empowered to control the prices of monopolies. However, there were few references to the Commission.

The 1968 Restrictive Trade Practices Act followed the courts in closing the loopholes of bilateral agreements and new agreements "to unlike effect" but with the same consequences. The Act prohibited all *collective* retail price maintenance—but made a resale price agreed between manufacturer and wholesaler binding upon a retailer if he were *informed, not* if he agreed. Information agreements had to be registered if the Department of Trade and Industry said a category of information agreements should be registered. The Registrar could ask companies if they had agreements (a strange omission for twelve years), if he had "cause to

believe" there were agreements (but not if he merely suspected). However, if the companies said "no" the Registrar
had no powers to seize documents to find out if they were
lying. In addition, the Department of Trade and Industry
could exempt an agreement from the prohibitions of the Act
if the Department thought that the agreement promoted a
project important to the economy, that the main objective
was to promote efficiency or improve capacity, that the object could not be achieved quickly without the agreement,
that the agreement created no restrictions other than those
necessary to achieve its main objective, and that it was in
the national interest. A further "gateway" (defense of an
agreement) was provided: to wit, the companies could argue
that the agreement did not discourage competition.

Then, in 1973, the Fair Trading Act replaced the Registrar of Restrictive Agreements with a Director General of
Fair Trading who added various consumer protection duties
to the anti-restrictive duties of the Registrar. A Consumer Protection Advisory Committee could investigate practices detrimental to the consumer. The Monopolies and Restrictive Practices Commission was renamed the Monopolies
and Mergers Commission, and the Director General could
refer cases; but the Secretary of State for Trade and Industry decided whether the referral went to the Commission
or to the Consumer Protection Advisory Committee. (The
Director General himself could also refer cases to the
Committee). As the official responsible for assuring com-
pliance with Act, the Director General tries to get the
assurance of the companies that they will comply with the
recommendations and only goes to the Restrictive Practices
Court for a ban if he cannot get the assurances.

There are almost no penalties involved. Until the
1973 Act a company had to defy the Court's decision and so
be in contempt before a penalty could be imposed. After
1973 evasion of an order approved by Parliament carried a
ł400 fine on summary conviction (hardly a threat to a large
company) and imprisonment only upon conviction after in-
dictment (ergo, confess before indicted?).

RATIONALIZATION OF INDUSTRIES

The British have long been taken with the idea of
"rationalization" as the route to greater efficiency. The
quotations above, from the interwar years, imply this attitude. The efforts to reorganize the coal industry between
the wars, the reorganization of the railways, and the 1939

TABLE 4-4
Merger References to Monopolies Commission

	1965–72		1973–77	
	No.	%	No.	%
Number of references	18	100	29	100
Merger offer withdrawn before report	4	22	12	41
Merger found to be against public interest	7	39	9	31
Merger found not to be against public interest	7	39	8	28

Source: Adapted from *Financial Times*,
            May 11, 1978, p. 22.

TABLE 4-5
Number of Mergers, 1963–77

Year	Number	Year	Number
1963	888	1970	793
1964	940	1971	884
1965	1,000	1972	1,210
1966	807	1973	1,205
1967	763	1974	504
1968	946	1975	315
1969*	907	1976	353
1969*	846	1977	482

* Data for 1963–69 based on company accounts; data for
  1969–77 based on "financial press and other sources."

Source: *Financial Times*, May 11, 1978, p. 22.

nationalization of the airlines are also indicative. During
the 1960s the attempts at planning (see Chapter 9) exempted
agreements designed to fulfil the plans. Programs to regulate prices and wages also make provisions to allow monopolistic or otherwise restrictive agreements where they might
further these policies.

"Rationalization"--the term itself connotes doing something reasonable--is thought to be desirable in many cases
in order to avoid duplication of plant or effort. Elimination of duplication obviously implies a belief that there
is excess capacity in an industry and that demand will not
grow to match capacity for some years--or that costs can be
reduced more by complete shutdowns of some plants during
periods of slack demand than they can be reduced by short-
time operation of all plants. Of course, cases can be
found--certainly easily imagined--in which this would be
true; but equally, there ought to be a number of cases of
excess capacity where complete shutdown would not reduce
total social costs. In addition to duplication of capacity
or effort, proponents of rationalization argue that combination will make management more efficient. This presumes
that in the process of combination the better managers will
emerge on top and that they will be a good deal better than
the managers who are eliminated. At first hearing this does
seem a reasonable argument, but further thought raises con-
siderable doubt. The Morris and Austin companies were manufacturing cars at a profit in the early 1950s. A series of
mergers finally created the Leyland company, which then pro-
ceeded to go bankrupt and after being taken over by the
government is still operating at a loss. Actually, there
is little evidence either to support or to refute arguments
for rationalization: by the very nature of the problem the
evidence can only emerge after the industry has been rationalized.

In any case, the British do incline to believe that
rationalization is often the best solution. In 1966 the
Labour government set up an Industrial Reorganization Corporation to help finance rationalization--which always involves mergers or agreements to divide markets--and to persuade the companies involved to merge themselves or some
parts of their businesses. The largest merger arranged by
the IRC was between General Electric and English Electric in
1968. This produced a company so large that one must call
it monopolistic if not an actual monopoly. It dominates
the British market in electrical engineering and electronics. On a smaller scale, scientific instruments and ball-
bearings were also rationalized, as were a number of other

industries.   When the Conservatives came to power in 1970
they abolished the IRC, but their objection to the IRC
seemed to be an objection to a large government corporation
arranging mergers and divisions of markets and not to mergers themselves if arranged by private companies and financial institutions.   The IRC illustrates the ambivalence of
the British toward competition.   It was established one
year after the same Labour government had empowered the
Board of Trade to forbid mergers which created monopolies
and even to dissolve monopolies.   The IRC arranged its
largest merger in the same year that Labour's legislation
closed loopholes in the criteria for deciding whether an
agreement was a restrictive practice and made collective
retail price maintenance illegal.

The tenor of the argument in the preceding pages has
probably implied that a stronger or more rigorous anti-
monopoly, anti-merger policy would have served Britain
better.   Actually, I am not sure that it would have.   Just
as "rationalization" is very largely an article of faith in
Britain, "competition" is an article of faith among Americans.   Both articles of faith depend far more on *a priori*
arguments about what must be the case if certain postulates
are true than on evidence that the postulates do in fact
reflect reality.   The pro-competition tenor of my argument
was an unavoidable consequence of the effort to show that
what the British mean by pro-competition policy is not what
Americans mean.   Which policy is better I do not know; it
is, however, certain that Britain is not following in the
footsteps of the United States.

Britain's entry into the Common Market (discussed in
Chapter 9) will make policy a bit tougher on monopolistic
behavior.   For instance, the Distillers Company had been
pricing their exported Black Label scotch a good deal higher
than it priced Black Label sold in Britain.   The European
High Court declared this to be illegal price discrimination.
However, Distillers response was to stop selling Black
Label in Britain and to maintain the high price for export--
which was not the result at which the Court was aiming.

A bit tougher is not, however, a lot tougher,   Europeans, like the British, rather admire an efficient or
"good" monopoly, and in 1977 and 1978 the European Economic
Commission, representing the Common Market, was busily engaged in trying to rationalize the shipbuilding and oil
refining industries by arranging agreed shutdowns.   Some
British practices may have to go because of Britain's entry
into the Common Market, but one should not anticipate any
great changes.

II. THE NATIONALIZED INDUSTRIES

There have been two distinct periods of nationalization.
Under the Labour government of 1945-51, nationalization of
industry was part of Labour's program to achieve socialism.
It was primarily a matter of principle, albeit strongly
supported by considerations which were quite independent of
socialist doctrine. The second period cannot be so clearly
defined but is roughly the 1970s. Recent nationalizations
have been largely forced upon the government, often by the
bankruptcy or incipient bankruptcy of firms and industries,
albeit Labour is able to find support for these cases of
nationalization in considerations of socialist doctrine.

Nationalization was an important part of Labour's program when it came to power in 1945. It was seen as the
means to achieve that "common ownership of the means of
production" which the Labour Party had adopted as its objective in 1919. The Party had no intention of nationalizing the whole of the British economy. The Party recognized that the government lacked the organizational means to
manage all the firms in the economy. Furthermore, despite
the traditional rhetoric of socialism, many in the Party
did not really wish to put an end to all private ownership
of the means of production--and this sentiment was certainly supported by a realization that such a thorough-going
program of nationalization was not desired by a majority of
British voters. But Attlee's government did wish to "seize
the commanding heights"--that 20% of the economy upon which,
it was believed, the other 80% depended. Labour believed
that if the "commanding heights" were nationalized, then
the government would be in a position to guide and to trans-
form the whole economy. The "commanding heights" were perceived as power (coal, electricity, gas), transportation
(railways, road haulage, airlines), steel, and the Bank of
England (through which the government could dominate the
banking and financial community). All industries are
directly dependent upon fuel and power and upon transportation and finance, and all industries depend indirectly if
not directly upon steel. Therefore control of these industries would give the government effective power to control
all businesses. As things turned out, the "commanding
heights" were not so commanding, but at the time it was
thought that they would be.

There were also strong non-doctrinaire reasons for
nationalization. It would be a means to "rationalize" industries. The coal industry, despite amalgamations between
the wars, had a multitude of firms and many high cost,

inefficient pits. Coal mining badly needed new equipment
and the industry had been so unprofitable that it could not
possibly arrange to finance new equipment through private
channels. Furthermore, labor relations had been so bad,
and wages so low, that everyone was agreed that "something
had to be done" to change the disposition of the miners.
An integrated, nationwide system of producing and distri-
buting gas would reduce costs. (Immediately after the war
"gas" meant the gases produced from coking coal; beginning
in the late 1950s it meant gas produced from petroleum; and
in the late 1960s natural gas from the North Sea gas fields.)

The railways had been running at a loss, as have railroads in most of the world in this century, and needed re-
equipping after thirty years of neglect. Also, it seemed
that a national authority could reorganize the railways into
a more efficient network. In the 19th century British railways had grown up--as they had in the United States--in a
rather helter skelter fashion. There were four major, un-
connected terminals in northern London and three more south
of the Thames, each originally built by a separate railway
company. There had already been many amalgamations and a
great deal of rationalization, an Act of Parliament in 1921
reorganizing the system into four main lines, but there was
a case for more rationalization. In road transport it
seemed wasteful to have competing companies running partly
empty lorries (British for trucks) because no organization
had the power to assure the maximum ton-mileage per gallon,
per hour of driver time, per lorry year, or per pound of
cost. A single, integrated system, it was felt, would reduce both real and financial costs appreciably. (The airlines had been nationalized by the Conservative government
in 1939 and government ownership was not in dispute.)

In addition to the particular problems of each industry,
and the hopes which nationalization held out for solving the
problems within each industry, Labour felt that there was a
large role for government in integrating the potentially
complementary character of different industries. Private
firms face many situations in which they can increase their
own profits by enlarging their markets, not only in successful rivalry with other firms in their own industry for an
existing market, but also in rivalry with firms in other industries (for instance, by inducing customers to substitute
electricity for gas, or oil for coal), or by enlarging the
existing market (for instance, persuading people to buy more
electrical home appliances). The Labour Party's view was
not that all such rivalry was wasteful--if electricity could
be produced by nuclear fission, fine--but that some rivalry

was likely to be wasteful, especially when existing capacity
still had a longish life before it and the capacities of the
construction and capital goods industries were strained by
other demands. Similarly, it seemed wrong to persuade people to buy electric heaters when the demands on the construction industry for needed hospitals were already competing with the demands of utilities to house generators.
In addition, because these industries were imperfectly or
monopolistically competitive, if they were not actually
natural monopolies, there were grounds in both experience
and economic theory for believing that they tended to create
excess capacity and hence to waste capital.

Labour carried through its program: quite successfully
in some respects, less successfully in other respects.
Electricity generation and distribution, gas, the railways,
road transport, coal mining, the Bank of England, and the
steel industry were all nationalized. Integrated systems
were established in electricity and gas; and, with some re-
organizations of management and the relationship between the
producing and distribution divisions, the systems created
by Labour in the late 1940s are still in operation. Integrated management of the railways was also achieved, as was
integrated management of coal mining. Road transport too
was organized by British Road Services (BRS) into a highly
efficient system, but was denationalized by the Conservatives
after they won the election of 1951. Steel was barely
nationalized before Labour lost that election and the Conservatives set about returning it to private ownership.
When Labour returned to office in the mid-1960s steel was
again nationalized and the renationalization was accepted
by the Conservative government of 1970-74. The nationalization of the Bank of England has been accepted without de-
murral.

The second round of nationalizations have been largely
forced upon the government. The firm of Upper Clyde Shipbuilders went bankrupt in the late 1960s and the government
nationalized it to preserve jobs: in part because it was
not obvious where else the skilled workers could find employment and in part because the area was a Labour strong-
hold and needed to be held if Labour was to continue to win
elections. (Labour probably cannot win a majority in Parliament without carrying most Scottish working class constituencies, which are concentrated around Glasgow and the
Clyde.) Then Rolls Royce (Aeroengines), having inadvertently
made a rather foolish contract with Lockheed, went bankrupt.
Again nationalization, but this time not only to preserve
jobs but because Rolls was (other than making a foolish con-

tract) an efficient firm and a major earner of foreign exchange. Rolls, it should be noted, was nationalized by a
Conservative government, not by the Labour Party. Then
British Leyland, the leading manufacturer of automobiles
and other vehicles, also found itself going bankrupt and in
need of large sums of money if it were to re-equip to become more competitive with other car manufacturers. So
Leyland became a government owned company, reorganized and
refinanced (and now called "BL").

In the mid-1970s a glut on the world's shipping market
meant lean profits or fat losses for shipbuilders all over
the world, and unemployment or parttime employment for its
workforce. Among Labour MPs shipbuilding always seemed a
prime candidate for nationalization: a basic industry, an
industry with poor labor relations, and one which, if not
actually mismanaged, had been losing badly to foreign competition. Financial difficulties plus socialist doctrine
thus combined to induce the Labour government to nationalize
shipbuilding in 1977.

Finally, the Labour government established the National
Enterprise Board (NEB) in 1975. The general idea for such
an organization goes back to the mid-1950s when Hugh Gait-
skell, then leader of the Labour Party in opposition, proposed that Labour should cease to nationalize industries
but should devise a system whereby the government—or, as
socialists would see it, the people—would share in the
rising capital values of private industry. Over the years,
and as it became apparent that British investment should be
re-directed toward export industries and modern, high technology industries, the idea was given more substance in a
proposal to create a government investment company which
would finance desirable investments and participate in the
resulting profits and capital gains. It was also increasingly believed, especially but by no means exclusively by
Labour analysts, that Britain's banking and financial markets did not provide enough finance to industry, and entirely too little to new and small firms which introduced more
productive methods and machines and developed new products.
The result was the NEB, which now lends to all sorts of
firms in all sorts of industries. (Regrettably, on government insistence, its first large acquisition was 95% of the
common stock of British Leyland, not quite the dynamic firm
the originators or managers of the NEB had in mind when
starting out.) In opposition the Conservatives said that
they would dismantle the NEB when elected to office, but

after winning in 1979 they announced that they would reduce the role of the NEB, not abolish it.

The nationalized industries have, by and large, been well run.[7] Errors of judgement have occurred, but they have not been of the foolish or unforgivable kinds. The worst may have been the decision in the 1960s to expand electricity generating capacity a great deal in a hurry. The decision was based on estimates of future growth in demand which proved to be too high. The bad problem which has resulted from the decision is that Britain now has over-capacity in the industries supplying boilers, generators, and other equipment, with associated financial pressures on the manufacturers of these items and unemployment and short-time working among the labor force in these trades. However, at the time the decision was made it appeared reason-able (and think of the outcries which would have been heard if demand had grown at the anticipated rate and the Central Electricity Generating Board had been too conservative).

In one respect the original intentions were not real-ized. The effort, if an effort there was, to achieve ratio-nal economic coordination between the various nationalized industries was abortive. The return of road transport to private ownership may account for the failure to integrate trucking with rail transport, but gas and electricity have remained in public ownership for twenty-five years, yet gas boards tout the virtues of gas cooking over electric, and electricity boards advertise the merits of electrical stoves and heaters over gas. Other than from the rather less flam-boyant tone of British advertising, the Martian visitor would have difficulty telling whether a private American utility or a nationalized British one was promoting its sales. Similarly, there has been little evidence of success in meshing the fuel policies in respect of gas, coal, im-ported petroleum, nuclear energy, and electricity generation. Such moves as have been made to get the Central Electricity Generating Board to use more coal appear to be responses to declining employment and profit opportunities in coal mining rather than the outcome of reasoned economic or social de-cisions about fuel policy. If the resulting problems for Britain are no worse than for the United States, they are no better, or only better because of the lucky discovery of oil in the North Sea.

Many criticisms have been made, in Britain as well as in the U.S., of the losses incurred by the National Coal Board, the railways, and more recently by the steel industry;

often accompanied by remarks about how much capital has been invested in these industries. The criticisms ignore the fact that demand for rail transport and for coal have been declining since the 1930s. Any contracting industry will have great difficulty making profits. Profits can sometimes be made by private firms in a declining industry as a result of bankruptcy proceedings. In effect the new owners make a "positive profit" while the "negative profits" (losses) are hidden in the capital losses of the creditors of the former owners. A nationalized industry's losses cannot escape the public eye in this way. On a couple of occasions the railways and the Coal Board have been forgiven some debt to the government, but far from hiding the losses the need to get Parliament's consent to forgiveness magnifies the matter in the public eye. A reasonable economic case could have been made at the time of nationalization that the proper compensation for the owners of firms with zero profit prospects was the scrap value of the property. The Labour government did not wish to be charged with failure to give "fair compensation" so they did not try to present this case, but had compensation been based on discounted present value of future profits very little compensation would have been paid for coal mines and railways and these nationalized industries would have had a far better financial record since.

In a contracting private industry the most efficient firms will make a profit while a large number, often the majority, will go bankrupt. In a contracting nationalized industry all the rail routes or all the pits are aggregated in striking up the accounts, so those which do make profits do not show up in the aggregated accounts. The difference between the two cases is not one of substance but rather one of the unit for accounting.

The criticism of failure to make profits after so much new investment in equipment also misconceives the logic of a contracting industry. Investment--say in new coal cutting machinery--can reduce the costs of getting coal by more than enough to pay for the equipment, including the carrying charges on the debt--and this is the criterion for a "profitable" investment. But the "profit" will not show up as a net positive profit for the industry but as a reduction in the losses which would otherwise occur.

A further problem faced the nationalized industries. On various occasions when the management wanted to raise prices--or when a strong economic argument could have been made for raising prices--the government has insisted that prices be kept down as a matter of public policy. This has meant that the nationalized industries have been deprived of revenues a private firm would have charged. While policies of price restraint can be criticized on a number of grounds, the resulting losses cannot be charged to the *inefficiency* of the nationalized industry's management or workforce. Again, there is an asymmetry in the public impression. The expanding electricity and gas industries made profits even though they were restrained in raising prices as costs and demand rose and thus gave no appearance of inefficiency (in fact, they were efficient). Railroads and coal, however, suffered larger losses as a result and so appeared to be inefficient (which they were not).

The tendency of government to restrain nationalized industries from taking actions they feel advisable is probably the strongest criticism which can be made of the way in which these industries are managed. Each nationalized industry has been set up on the following principles: (a) that a board will manage the industry on commercial lines (although not to maximize profits), taking responsibility for all day-to-day decisions; (b) each industry will pay its own way, "taking the good years with the bad;" and (c) Parliament will lay down broad guidelines of policy but will not interfere with day-to-day management. Two different problems arise in applying these principles. First, there really is not any way to draw a line between everyday management and high policy. The question of whether there should be large-scale expansion or contraction is high policy, and what kind of pumps to use is everyday management. But it is not apparent what the functions of a board are if they do not include specific pricing within the guidelines. "Taking the good years with the bad" implies that a board should respond to a bad year or two by taking actions in order to turn the next couple of years into good years, and, other than prayer and luck, pricing seems the way to do it. Several times the government has laid down rules about what rate of return each industry should achieve--perfectly appropriate as guidelines--but there is no way in which the government can both decide what the rate of return should be and, separately, what specific prices should be charged. The line is, however, hazy. Second, there is always temptation: given the ultimate power of Parliament and the haziness of the idea of general directives, a minister can be sincere and find it reasonable to view a decision about whether or not to raise prices as one involving higher public policy. In the early postwar years the price of coal to households--coal and coke were the fuels for many stoves and most heating of houses--was kept low as part of the program to keep all basic living costs down, and so could be considered a matter of higher public policy. But over the past three decades the frequency of government intervention with boards' pricing policies almost forces the conclusion that interventions have violated the spirit of the principles.

III. REGIONAL POLICIES

There are a number of schemes to encourage firms to build or to expand plants in the regions with more than average unemployment. These areas are called "areas for expansion" and are divided into three classes, from those worst hit by industrial change to those least damaged:

(1) *Special Development Areas*: around Cardiff in south Wales; northwest Wales; around Liverpool ("Merseyside"--just north and east of Wales); the west of the "Lake Country" (northwest England); around Glasgow and southward on the west coast of Scotland (Ayrshire); and around Newcastle-upon-Tyne (the very northeast of England). The whole of Northern Ireland is an area the benefits for which are even greater than for the Special Development Areas.

(2) *Development Areas:* Southwest England (Cornwall and north Devonshire); all of Wales not in a Special Area; all of Scotland not listed above; and all the rest of England north of an E-W line above Leeds.

(3) *Intermediate Areas*: the area south of the E-W line above Leeds and north of a jagged E-W line from N. Wales passing south of Liverpool and Manchester but north of the Midlands (well north of Birmingham and a little north of Nottingham) to the North Sea coast; two other small areas north and south on the Welsh border; and an area around Plymouth in south Devonshire.

In effect, all of Britain is classified as one or another kind of development area except for a rough rectangle of south England bordered on the west by Devonshire and Wales and on the north by the jagged E-W line south of Liverpool and north of Nottingham.

The schemes are numerous, the level and types of benefits are varied frequently, but fall into the following general classes:

(1) Subsidies for investment: provision for rapid

write-off of investment expenditures, including writing off
of all investment expenditures in the year in which they
were made; investment allowances, which permit more than
the actual amount of investment to be written off against
corporate income tax; outright grants to firms for making
specific investments; grants to defray part of the interest
costs of money borrowed to make investments;

(2) Employment subsidies: grants to defray the expenses of moving key workers to locations in the disadvan-
taged areas where new plants are being set up; a portion
of the wages paid to new, additional employees in these
areas; grants to defray the expenses of training new employees to man new plants in these areas;

(3) Licensing or planning permissions: forbidding
the building or the large-scale expansion of old plants
without prior permission so that the government can refuse
permission when the plants are not to be located in one of
the areas for expansion.

Some schemes for subsidization have been set up for
firms in particular industries; others have been open to
any firm which qualifies under general rules. Typically
the subsidies have been for investment in manufacturing
plant and equipment, with a bias towards equipment rather
than buildings. At times warehouses and office buildings
have not qualified; at other times they have, but at fairly
low rates of subsidy. Wholesale and retail establishments
which would serve the areas anyway have not been eligible
for investment subsidies.

The various regional subsidies do not appear to be
entirely consistent with the general policy aim of promoting
greater efficiency in British industry, and especially of
promoting investment in the most efficient firms in the
most efficient industries. While tending to shift economic
activity from regions with low to regions with high unemployment, employment subsidies may also preserve less efficient industries and firms and may even encourage some investment among the less efficient. At any rate these subsidies have no clear relationship to efficiency and still
less are they clearly designed to further investment in
those industries and firms with good export prospects.
Since they tend to reduce labor costs for the firm they may
even encourage intensive use of labor in lines of endeavor
which might prove more successful as capital intensive industries in the longer run. Similarly, the emphasis on sub-
sidizing industries with higher employment potential may

sometimes encourage firms which will not in the long run
be competitive in export markets or with imports.

To what degree these subsidies have served to increase
total investment or to maintain or increase employment in
the areas of high unemployment are indeed open questions.
If a business plans to invest in an area of expansion anyway it does not take sagacity on the part of management to
ask for the appropriate subsidies, and in such cases the
subsidies have not increased either investment or employment
but have merely shifted some of the financial burden from
the business to the government. When the effect of the
subsidies or the planning permission has been to site new
investment in the areas for expansion rather than in the
south and east of England, the effect on employment has been
the desired one but there has been no consequent net increase in total investment or in the efficiency of the
investment.

Regional policies can arouse local resentments.   In
1976 Toyota announced a plan to build a new automobile distribution center in Bristol but because Bristol was booming
--it had a high level of employment--planning permission
was not given.   Instead the Department of Industry offered
Toyota a grant of £1mn. to locate in a development area.
The offer was certainly consistent with the policy of shifting industries into areas with chronically high levels of
unemployment and the offer of a subsidy was well within the
law, but that hardly discouraged a Labour MP from Bristol
from calling his Labour government's offer a "bribe."

Regional development policies cannot always be en-
forced, especially when a company can locate abroad.   In
one case a company was denied permission to locate a center
south of London and asked to locate elsewhere.   It threatened not to locate the center in Britain at all--and eventually got its way.

It is difficult to estimate the effect of any or all
of these programs.   So much of the kingdom is now a special
development, development, or intermediate area that the
programs must have taken on much of the nature of a general
subsidy to investment.   In all probability they have had
some effect in delaying or reducing the movement of industry
from north and west to south and east, but no one can say
how much a reduction or how long a delay in what cases.

ENDNOTES

1. Richard E. Caves, "Market Organization, Performance, and Public Policy," Ch. VII in Richard E. Caves and Associates, *Britain's Economic Prospects*. Washington: The Brookings Institution, 1968, p. 285.
2. *Ibid.*, p. 282.
3. Dennis Swann, Dennis P. O'Brien, W. Peter J. Maunder, and W. Stewart Howe, *Competition in British Industry: Restrictive Practices Legislation in Theory and Practice*. London: George Allen & Unwin Ltd., 1974, pp. 42–44.
4. Aneurin Bevan, *In Place of Fear*. N.Y.: Simon and Schuster, 1952, pp. 112–126, but especially pp. 120–122.
5. G. C. Allen, *The Structure of Industry in Britain*. 3rd edition. London: Longman Group Ltd., 1970, p. 86.
6. Swann *et al.*, pp. 65–66.
7. Richard Pryke, *Public Enterprise in Practice: The British Experience of Nationalization over Two Decades*. N.Y./St. Martin's Press, 1972, p. 442: ". . . the public enterprise sector has had a significantly better performance in respect of technical efficiency than the private sector . . . [T]he operations of the nationalized industries have . . . .led to remarkably little misallocation . . . [T]he nationalized industries must. . . be judged an economic success, and it seems likely that they have had a favourable impact on the national welfare. What would have happened if they had remained in the hands of their former owners it is impossible to know . . . but in view of the quality of their performance it is difficult to believe that it would have been of the same standard had they not been transferred to public ownership."

5

INDUSTRIAL RELATIONS

LABOR UNIONS

The organization and traditions of British labor unions (generally called "trade unions" in Britain) and the situations in which they operate differ in important ways from those of American labor unions. First, they are closely associated with a political party, the Labour Party, for which they are the major financial support.

Secondly, almost all unions belong to the Trades Union Congress (TUC), whose advice and decisions are always seriously considered and often (but not universally) followed by the member unions. The TUC is a far more effective central directorate for British unions than is the American AFL-CIO; and, unlike the American situation where major unions such as the International Brotherhood of Teamsters, United Mine Workers, and the United Automobile Workers are not members of the AFL-CIO, all major British trade unions are members of the TUC. The association of most trade unions within the TUC has led to a view among TUC member unions that unions which are not members of the TUC are, somehow, not really unions. They are all suspected of being "company unions"--"sweetheart unions" is the popular British phrase. Even if they are not regarded as "company unions," nevertheless they are still thought of as deserters from the common working class front (and from the Labour Party).

Thirdly, industrial unions representing most of the work force in a particular industry are comparatively rare. The National Union of Mineworkers (NUM) is the rough equivalent of the UMW in the U.S., but generally one does not find unions defined by the industry. It is not that the British unions are all organized by skilled crafts but that the

unions representing the unskilled and semiskilled workers
recruit members from all industries. Recently the Amalgamated Union of Engineering Workers (AUEW), which formerly
recruited only skilled workers, has been recruiting the
semiskilled and unskilled. The General and Municipal Workers Union (the G&M) and the Transport and General Workers
(the T&G) each have memberships drawn from all sorts of
manufacturing and industrial occupations, service trades,
and government employment. Nineteen unions form an alliance
in shipbuilding and engineering (roughly, machine building
of all sorts). The allied unions meet as a group annually
at a convention, but retain their independence. There is
some tendency towards specialization of union organizations
by type of employer bargaining unit, but it is weak: the
National Association of Local Government Officers (NALGO)
tends to organize the more educated levels in government
service and the National Union of Public Employees (NUPE)
organizes mostly manual workers in government employment,
but there is a great deal of overlap. Across both cuts the
Association of Scientific, Technical, and Managerial Staff
(ASTMS) which also recruits university teachers. The co-
existence of several unions in the same industry is strongly
supported by a tradition of "no poaching" of members by one
TUC union from another TUC union. This tradition amounts
virtually to a moral law of the sort prohibiting the seduc-
tion of one's sister-in-law (and it may be no more effective). The Bridlington principles of 1939--that no union
should accept a member from another union without asking
the other union, and that no union should organize where a
majority of employees already belong to another union--are
overseen by the TUC's Disputes Committee.

Formally, legally, and often importantly, the Parliamentary Labour Party is independent of the National Executive Committee (NEC) of the Labour Party; but in addition
to the financial, electoral, and moral dependence of the
Parliamentary Labour Party on the Labour Party outside
Parliament, many MPs of the Parliamentary Labour Party (PLP)
are trade union members and many of the leaders of the
Party (fewer recently than in earlier years) have risen
through the trade unions. Thus the bonds among the TUC, the
NEC, and the PLP bind strongly.

Labour governments do not pursue policies opposed by
the TUC. However, this does *not* mean that the unions determine Labour government policies. By virtue of their intimate relationship with the Labour Party, the unions have
committed themselves to the success of Labour and so cannot
demand of the government whatever they wish whenever they

wish. If Labour cannot carry the country in an election,
then the power of the unions in the Party cannot be made
effective in the government. Therefore the unions must be
sensitive of the feelings of an electorate more broadly defined than their immediate working class constituency in
order to avoid finding themselves a very powerful element
in the formulation of opposition complaints rather than in
the formulation of government policy. The relationships of
the unions and the TUC to the Labour Party, and *vice versa*,
may be likened to the 50/50 relationship in a marriage: and
who knows when a marriage is "equal"?

        Another consequence of the way in which British labor
is organized is that there cannot be industry-wide bargaining. Often there cannot be company-wide bargaining by one
union because numbers of unions will have members in any
one company. For instance, it is even possible that there
will be members of the T&G (Transport and General Workers
Union), the G&M (General and Municipal Workers Union), and
AUEW (Amalgamated Union of Engineering Workers) on the same
assembly line. Joint Councils representing several unions
are often set up to represent labor in its negotiations
with management in a firm or an industry, but the union
members to whom the various negotiators must report are different and the times at which the contracts expire are
usually different.

        It would also be hard in Britain to arrange long-term
contracts. In the past couple of decades a majority of
American unions have moved from annual to triennial contracts; a similar change in Britain (should there be grounds
for thinking it desirable) would be difficult indeed because no single union could decide that it was a good thing
to do and then try to negotiate a three year contract. It
would not dare to do so for fear other unions would negotiate much better contracts before the three years were up.
Therefore, a three year contract would depend upon the
agreement of several unions, each of which, while not poaching on the others, does have an eye to its long run success
in recruiting and keeping members.

        To ask, "Why don't they do something about it?" is to
ask a specific variant of the hoary question, "Why isn't
this a better world in a differently organized universe?"
British unions, like American or French unions, like corporations anywhere, like golf clubs and universities, are ongoing institutions with their own traditions, their own
organizations, their own vested inverests, and their own
variants of political outlook. For instance, some aspects

of hospital management might be easier to handle if NALGO and NUPE were to amalgamate, but the bargaining position of women, immigrants and the unskilled who are now represented by the NUPE would probably become weaker--and one can certainly sympathize with the fear of NUPE workers that their position would worsen.

SHOP STEWARDS

The mixture of several unions representing workers doing the same or related work in the same plant contributes much to the peculiarity of the role of the British shop steward. As portrayed in the press--and not only in the careless or more sensationalist newspapers--he is a weird phenomenon.

In the press and among many who are not members of unions the shop steward is often considered a union official. In some union constitutions shop stewards are given official status, but commonly only as collectors of union dues. In many union constitutions there is no mention of shop stewards. Except as collectors of union dues, shop stewards are not members of the union hierarchy.

Shop stewards are seldom bound by tradition or by law or by moral obligation to carry out the policies of the unions. Rather, they are leaders and representatives of the workers among whom they work. They are responsible to their fellow workers on a particular assembly line, shop floor or larger unit and will remain shop stewards only so long as they have the support of their fellow workers. They derive their support from the immediate "consent of the governed" and in this sense shop stewards are a truly democratic institution. A shop steward may represent members of a number of unions because a number of unions have members in that particular shop. In these cases the shop steward as shop steward is not a member of any union (even though he is, personally, a member of one of the unions). Even when, as is more typically the case, a shop steward represents members of a single union only, he cannot be expected to carry out official union orders when those whom he represents do not want to follow union policy. Were he to try to carry out union orders in such cases the shop steward would immediately lose his power (if not his official designation) as a shop steward. In fact, his official designation often does not depend upon the union but upon the recognition by the employer that he is the shop steward for a particular group of workers.

A typical headline in a British paper will read "Rebel Shop Stewards Call Unauthorized Strike." Such headlines are doubly misleading and tendentious. The strike, it is true, has not been "authorized" by the union. Beyond that core of truth, there is no further sense to the headline. First, a shop steward could never call an "authorized" strike because given the terminology used in discussions of British union affairs, such a strike can only be called by the higher authorities of a union, never by a shop steward. So any strike led by a shop steward or a group of shop stewards must be "unauthorized" by the very definition of "authorized," but in another and meaningful sense they are authorized by the workers who elect and support their shop stewards. In fact, and by no means uncommonly, it is the workers who walk out on strike followed by their shop stewards who are often arguing, from the back of the line of workers marching out, the reasons for not striking. But at such a turn in affairs the shop steward must then join the strike, and as steward is obligated to lead it. What proportion of unauthorized strikes begin with shop stewards encouraging their followers to walk out, and what proportion begin with workers followed out by their shop stewards, it is impossible to ascertain. Data simply are not collected which would give us this information. Chance sampling from reading press accounts which do provide such information on particular cases indicates that shop stewards following may be as frequent as shop stewards leading--and leading may be a last minute dash to the front of the line.

British trade unionism thus has a dual organization: an official or "authorized" vertical system such as one finds throughout the world and unofficial or only quasi-official systems of shop stewards. Shop stewards and their constituencies should not be pictured as a gaseous mass of molecules bumping into each other and off the containing walls of management. Shop stewards have formed horizontal systems for communication and for joint action. Groups of shop stewards, sometimes from different operating divisions in a plant, sometimes from different unions in a plant, sometimes from different plants or unions in a company, sometimes from different companies or unions in an industry, will form joint committees chaired by an elected leader called the "convener." The stewards inform each other of what is going on in their particular bailiwicks and, when issues arise, try to gain the support of the other stewards. They hope to be able to present a united front representative of more than one shop floor or union. More often than not each steward gets sympathy but not much action. On the other hand, if the issue is "victimization" (usually

dismissal) of an employee by management, more solid forms
of support are likely: resolutions sent to union headquarters asking that a strike be authorized, and occasionally even joining a strike. This network of shop stewards
does not and, within the system of British industrial relations, cannot be made to fit with the vertical system of
union organization.

The case of Derek Robinson illustrates in extreme form
how complex a shop steward's roles can become. He is a shop
stewards' convener of conveners. A shop steward in a Leyland car plant in Birmingham, he is also convener of all
the shop stewards in that plant. He is convener of T&G
shop stewards in Leyland plants all over Britain and the
convener of the shop stewards' joint committee for the British automobile industry. Whom does Derek Robinson represent? T&G workers at Castle Bromwich? G&M workers at
Solihull? AUEW workers at Ford's Dagenham plant? Or maybe
the TUC? But he was not elected to any office in the TUC,
nor was he appointed to any office in the TUC. Derek Robinson's position is unique, but any convener of shop stewards is almost bound to be acting with and for members of
more than one union. Quite a few will be acting for employees in more than one plant; others for employees of more
than one company.

Against, whom, then, are shop stewards rebelling?
Against their unions? No, for they are not officers of the
union. Against their constituency of co-workers? No, for
they have their co-workers' active consent and often their
active insistence that they lead the strike. A properly
informative translation of the exciting headline, "Rebel-
lious Shop Stewards Flout Union Bosses" might read "Elected
Stewards Disagree With Union's Leaders."

LABOR LAW

Industrial relations in Britian lack the formal legal
structure of industrial relations in the United States.
There is no extensive list of "unfair labor practices."
There is no equivalent of the National Labor Relations Board
to decide whether actions are "an unfair practice," nor to
determine the legitimate bargaining agent. The law protects
the right to strike and forbids employers to discriminate
against union organizers. Unions cannot be sued for damages
caused by their members or officers, nor for losses arising
from breech of a collectively bargained agreement. Beyond
that, the law is rather vague.

The recently created Advisory, Conciliation, and Arbitration Service (ACAS) is rather like the Federal Mediation and Conciliation Service in the U.S., but how effective it will be, and what its powers actually are, were still open questions in 1979. It has arbitrated a fair number of minor disputes and sorted out some potential disputes, but when feelings run high and one side asks its help its intervention may be more exacerbating than conciliatory. In one case (the Grunwick strike of 1976-77), there was a strike for recognition of ASTMS (Association of Scientific, Technical, and Mangerial Staff) as the workers' bargaining agent. The owner of the company fired all the strikers--evading the legal prohibition on discriminating among employees in labor disputes by firing everyone indiscriminately--and hired a new workforce. (Ordinarily this would be very difficult to do in Britain, working class feeling about "blacklegs" being what they are. However, the employees fired at Grunwick, and the new employees hired, were immigrant Asian women. Thus, on the one hand, the strikers were not Englishmen; and, on the other hand, the low wages paid and the limited opportunities open to Asian women created some sympathy for the women who took the strikers' jobs.) The union asked ACAS to intervene. ACAS could not force Grunwick to rehire the strikers, but it could make recommendations. It tried to poll all employees, but the company would not provide the names and addresses of its current employees, so ACAS recommended recognition of the ASTMS and rehiring the strikers. The company sued, arguing the ACAS had exceeded its powers. The company lost in the lower court but won on appeal. What was at stake was not entirely clear. The owner and some Conservatives said it was matters of principle: management's prerogatives and the worker's right not to join a union. However, since ACAS could not issue binding orders but only make suggestions, one is left wondering what the suit accomplished.

There appear to be several reasons for the lack of a clear legal framework for labor relations. On the employers' side, a formal legal procedure enacted by Parliament would almost certainly restrict the powers of employers where unions appeared to be weak or when employers wished to be particularly anti-union. On the union side it is feared that a clear demarcation of union rights will limit union powers in what are now gray areas. Unions also fear that if they accept the precedent of a formal legal structure, then Conservative governments will rewrite the law of industrial relations to limit the power of unions far more stringently than they are presently limited by the informal system. In this respect, union fears are also a legitimate expectation. After the Conservative electoral victory of 1970 the Heath government passed the Industrial Relations Act, 1971. The Act was designed to establish a new system of industrial relations in which

1. Unions would have to register themselves and their union rules with a registrar who could deregister unions which did not comply with the law.
2. Collective agreements were to be legally binding and breach of collective agreements actionable at law for damages.
3. Union rules could not provide for restrictions on output and "the basic functions of shop stewards would be laid down in union rules."
4. Pre-entry closed shops were prohibited, many inter-union disputes could be disallowed as legitimate "industrial disputes" by the Commission on Industrial Relations; and "cooling-off periods" and "employer's last offer" ballots could be required by the government.

In the event most trade unions refused to register and in the face of this massive union resistance the government made no effort to enforce the Act.

Finally, the working class has long distrusted the law, the courts, and all men with attaché cases. The legal profession is part of The Establishment, its practitioners members of the upper and middle classes. Certainly judges are all these things. In addition, the law and lawyers are thought to be "tricky." Britain has changed in forty years. Many distinguished solicitors and barristers are members of the Labour Party. Not all judges are Tories. It would be hard today to argue that leaders of the Labour Party and of the TUC are not members of The Establishment. The effective rejection of the 1971 Act by almost total non-compliance is hardly consistent with a view that unions can be victimized by tricky Tory law. Nevertheless, on these matters working class feeling runs deep. In its history the working class has not had many pleasant experiences before the courts and has had many unpleasant ones (see Chapter 2 for some illustrations). The working class has done best when and where the courts could not interfere. So even if British society and its Establishment are changing, experience has taught the workers and their unions to avoid law and legal action whenever possible. It is not an entirely reasoned position--not that it is an irrational position; feelings need be neither rational nor irrational: they are often just felt--but if not entirely reasoned, it is not unreasonable. If the British world has changed, the working class

may be right in thinking that "it hasn't changed all that
much," so that discretion may still be the better part of
legislation.

LABOR AND MANAGEMENT

The relationships between hourly paid workers and industrial managements are bad. Reading the British press
(which is, by and large, right wing in its politics) one
gets the impression that the British labor force is strike
happy; only too eager to down tools. But by international
comparisons the total number of strikes in British industry
is not great, and man-days lost in labor disputes are not
many. In contrast with the other nations of Europe and
North America, major strikes by large groups of workers for
extended periods are less frequent in Britain and one, two,
and three day local strikes more common. It is not the
strikes which are particularly harmful--they do not reduce
man-year productivity any more than do strikes in France or
the United States--but the underlying perpetual disgruntlement and mistrust on both sides which shows up as a pattern
of short, "wildcat" strikes unauthorized by the unions. It
is the mistrust which reduces cooperation and therefore
productivity all day every day. Whatever management does,
workers are conditioned to assume that management is trying
to "rip-off" the workers. Whatever workers suggest, management assumes a plot to reduce productivity or to invade
management prerogatives. The belief of one side that the
other side is doing evil tends to make each side do evil in
self-defense or in revenge. If workers think they are being
ripped-off they will, quite naturally, want "to get back at"
management and will try to cause management trouble, including trying to work less or to work less effectively or
to take over powers of management. If managers think that
the workforce is uncooperative, is trying so to reduce
management's powers that management cannot operate effectively, then managers will, quite naturally, anticipate trouble
and try to force workers, by threat, or by trickery in
speeding up the work schedule, to get what they can out of
labor. When relations get this bad in families spouses can
divorce each other, children at least grow up and leave
home; but British management and British labor are caught
in perpetual rounds of distrust and recrimination.

Two instances from late July, 1976, will illustrate
the distrust. If they are in some respects almost funny,
they are not unusual: a month of reading the labor columns
of the *Financial Times* will provide several cases as point-
less or foolish.

SORRY IS THE HARDEST WORD TO SAY

On a Thursday afternoon during the summer of 1976 the
workers on the assembly line in a Scottish plant of British
Leyland were sent home 20 minutes earlier than the usual
end of their shift. The workers left, and the next Wednesday when they received their pay for the previous week they
discovered that they had been docked 20 minutes pay for
leaving early. The workers walked off the assembly lines,
demanding that they be paid for the 20 minutes. It was a
day and a half before management agreed to reimburse them
for the missing 20 minutes.

During the same summer a wildcat strike occurred at a
foundry in Wales. The union contract had provided that,
whenever the temperature rose above 80° on the foundry
floor, management would serve orange juice to the workforce.
At 3:00 one afternoon the temperature rose above 80°. No
orange juice appeared. At 3:30 the workforce walked off.

Who thought they were doing what, to what purpose?
This is indeed a difficult question to answer. Press reports do not give the information one would like to have.
One can only guess. Perhaps, in the Scottish case, whoever
dismissed the workers early forgot to tell the payroll department what he had done. Perhaps someone in the payroll
department forgot that he was told. Perhaps a computer did
not understand. Perhaps whoever told the workers to go
home wanted "to get even" with them. Perhaps someone higher
in management wanted "to get even." Or perhaps someone in
management thought that people should never be paid if they
were not working, no matter what. Or perhaps the local
management wanted to pick a fight with the workforce. Certainly the typical working class reaction in such situations
is that management is trying to pick a fight and workers
respond with the feeling, "OK, if management wants to pick
a fight, then let them have a fight they'll remember."

However, whether it was oversight by local management,
a computer error, or a willful challenging of the workforce,
it is difficult to understand what the higher levels of
management in British Leyland thought they were, or were
not, doing. And equally difficult to understand what the
executives on the National Enterprise Board (the NEB, which
owns 95% of British Leyland stock) thought. Of course, the
outsider, including the press, would not be told if there
had been irate telephone calls from the head office to
Scotland, bawling out and threatening the local management;
but one senses--from somewhere in the atmosphere--that there

were no phone calls to Scotland, and no phone calls from
the NEB asking what Leyland management thought it was doing.
Such events happen so often that one cannot believe other
than that higher management does not discipline lower
management for mishandling labor relations.

It is hard to believe that higher management at British Leyland, let alone the NEB, wants to pick silly fights
with labor--"Why? Oh why would they?"--but it is puzzling
that the person who had been in charge of labor relations
before the NEB took over British Leyland was still in
charge of labor relations a year later. He may well have
been a very good man (he is reputed to be very good), but
since bad labor relations had been one of the reasons for
the bankruptcy of Leyland as a private concern, the new
ownership might have moved the person to some other position, just to show "good will" toward a disgruntled labor
force.

In the case of the Welsh foundry, again one does not
know just what happened. But suppose that management had,
without malice, simply overlooked the orange juice clause:
why didn't a someone from the floor go upstairs at ten past
three and say, "Hey, did you know it's eighy-two on the
floor?" Maybe there wasn't any orange juice available. Why
didn't someone from management go to the foundry floor and
say, "Hey, mates, sorry, we're out of orange juice. Can we
get you some lemonade or a nice cold drink of milk?" Con-
sidering how nasty labor relations can get, why wasn't
management careful, down on the floor within two minutes
after the temperature went over eighty to say, "Orange
juice is coming," or to offer milk? And after the workforce started to walk off, why didn't someone in management
go running after the workers to say, "Do come back. We're
awfully sorry we goofed. Lemonade is on its way"?

And similarly, back in Scotland, why didn't someone
apologize for docking twenty minutes pay, for which management was, obviously, blameworthy?

Neither case reflects well on the courtesy of any side.
Both cases illustrate a poor sort of human relationship.
If management was the proximate cause of each walkout (and
both *The Socialist Worker* on the far left and the *Financial
Times* on the right were agreed on this point) one can still
wonder why no one in either workforce pointed out that
trouble was coming if something was not done promptly.
Part of the answer may be that the workers did not expect a
civil reply; but one may also suspect that part of the

answer is that any "pointing out" would have been (perhaps
was) done in such abusive terms as to assure a fight. Apparently "sorry" is a very hard word to say; and "excuse me,
but" almost as difficult.

In contrast with what is generally true of industrial
relations in the U.S., in Britain there is no joint willingness to abandon relative bargaining strength as the means
of dispute resolution.[1] In contrast with the situation in
the U.S., one could describe British grievance procedures
as rudimentary. There is rarely a provision for a neutral
arbitrator to determine the meaning of an agreement where
the interpretation is in dispute, and in many cases where
there is provision for an arbitrator his decision is not
binding. Arbitration is even rarer when the matter in dispute is a question of equity, decent treatment, or the cus-
tom of the trade or plant. Normally disputes are handled by
negotiation between union officials and representatives of
the employers, sometimes involving appeal through two or
three tiers above the plant (the British call it the "works")
level to the national level. But this system is really a
process of continuous renegotiation rather than of interpretation or of application of mutually accepted rules.
Only infrequently does an "outside" conciliator participate.

While for disputes involving everyone in a plant--say,
the application of rules for piece-rates to new machinery--
union-management negotiations may be suitable, the negotiating machinery is peculiarly unsuitable for disputes involving one or a few men. Only union officials may participate, which often bars participation by the shop steward
who may not be an appropriate official under the union's
constitution but whose knowledge, leadership, and interpersonal relationships are crucial to the resolution of
such conflicts. Managements always refuse to negotiate
while an unauthorized strike continues, which means that
many cases in which the sides might begin to achieve "sweet
reasonableness" are fought over but never discussed. These
positions make it almost impossible to develop a mutually
accepted tradition of grievance procedures and binding
arbitration. The result is that intra-plant and intra-firm
relationships between management and labor are unstable.
An aggrieved worker feels no assurance that his complaint
will be treated as a matter for just as opposed to politic
decision. His "mates" feel the same way. Managers too
have the same fear. This leads, on the one side, to unauthorized strikes: the belief that "only a walkout now"
will achieve justice; that justice delayed through negotiation will never be justice. On the other side, it rein-

forces management's insistence upon its "prerogatives." To
questions about why the British have not developed grievance
procedures or systems of arbitration, the answers are the
attitudes just discussed, plus the distrust and lack of
understanding between classes and the dislike and even fear
of courts and formal procedures.

"INDUSTRIAL DEMOCRACY"

The phrase lacks precise meaning, but the objective,
the reasons therefore, and the issues are clear. The aim
is to assure that employees of a firm have an effective
role in all managerial decisions which affect their lives
in their work or because of their work. A moment's consideration and one realizes the implication: since every decision will affect some employees, in every decision there
must be a voice for some group or other of employees. The
justification is that employees as much as anyone, more than
most stockholders, more than many suppliers or customers,
have committed themselves to, and have to some degree, often
a very large degree, built their lives around the firm.
While not so interested as owners in the profitability of
the firm, nor so interested as buyers in the pricing policies of the firm, employees are more interested than any of
these groups in wage policies, working conditions, seniority,
security, promotion policies, and retirement policies--and
because of these interests, as great an interest as anyone
in decisions about expanding or closing plants, about where
to site new plants, about what sort of machinery is to be
used in what kinds of plant layouts, and about hiring, re-
training, and reassigning the workforce. The reasons for
industrial democracy can be summed up in the rhetorical
question: "If so much of what I do and how I do it--and
where I live and who my spouse knows and where my children
go to school--depends on decisions by the management of my
firm, why shouldn't I have a major voice in reaching these
decisions?" The issues are how to achieve the objective
while protecting the interests of stockholders and stimulating technological change. Curiously, an answer in the
negative to the rhetorical question--the answer, "No, you
shouldn't"--is not an issue. The basic objective, stated
in a most general way, is acceptable to the Conservative
Party and to the Confederation of British Industry (the CBI,
representing the interests of management and owners in the
private sector).

The roots of the idea go deep in British tradition: at
least as far back as Robert Owen's vision of self-governing

economic communities and the cooperative movement (which also owes much to Owen). Guild socialism—the management of each industry by the workers in each industry—was espoused by G. D. H. Cole, a leading socialist theoretician, in the 1920s. Between the wars the Liberal Party adopted the idea of worker participation in ownership through profit sharing. Its modern manifestation, however, is of very recent origin. In the middle 1970s it suddenly became a widely acceptable idea, among many managers as well as among others. The government appointed a Committee of Inquiry under Lord Bullock. In January 1977 his Committee published its report approving the idea of having workers on the boards of directors of firms. The proposal of the majority of the Committee became known as the "2x + y formula." An equal number of directors would be appointed by the owners (present management) and the unions (x directors for each group) and additional, "neutral" members (y directors) would be appointed to hold the balance of power when the owner and the worker directors could not agree.

There is general assent to the idea of some form of "industrial democracy," but general assent has not meant agreement to any specific proposal. The Bullock Report was not welcomed by management and criticisms came thick and fast. The TUC at first gave a general blessing to the Report, but after a while a number of union leaders also expressed grave reservations. The Labour government welcomed the Report but did not commit itself to any of the proposals. In the months following the Report numbers of alternative schemes were proposed. One of the most popular was "two-tiered" boards: a higher, very general policy making board which would include the worker directors and a lower level board consisting only of managers who would run the business from day to day and give specific content to the general policies approved by the higher tier board. But so far all these proposals have been opposed by the CBI and other spokesmen for private industry, and a number of union leaders have now said that they would rather the unions employ their power outside the formal framework of management.

Meanwhile the post office, which was reorganized in 1969 as a government corporation to manage mail, telephones, and telegraph, changed the membership of its board to include representatives of the unions. The British Steel Corporation has been examining ways to introduce union members to its board and has committed itself in principle. However, since both of these are government owned businesses, they are not representative of British private industry.

The objections to the proposals are various. First, and most obviously, the "2x + y" formula would make the neutral directors the effective directors whenever there were divisions in which worker and owner directors lined up against each other. The problem then would be two-fold: neutral directors are not apt to be as expert as either the owner or the worker directors, and the neutral directors would certainly not be as committed to the firm as either the owner or worker directors (that is, they would not have to live the results of their decisions in the way that both owner and worker directors would). Then the division of powers between upper-tier and lower-tier directors could not be made clear. The problem is analogous to the relationship of the boards of nationalized industries to ministers and to Parliament: any general policy becomes meaningful only when it is given concrete expression in day-by-day management, and day-by-day management cannot avoid creating general policies through the cumulative effects of apparently minor decisions. Further, there is the fear that worker directors will put the interests of the union ahead of the interests of the company as an on-going concern. There is also a fear that worker directors will betray company secrets. And then, there is, on management's side, probably the simple reaction: "workers are there to work and management to manage, and to put workers on the upper-tier of directors is just all topsy-turvy."

Very strong objections have been made to the proposal that the worker directors be appointed by the unions. There are several aspects to these objections. One stems from the idea of the liberty of the individual: that a man should have the right not to join a union if he does not wish to, and to allow unions in which such a person is not represented to appoint the worker directors would deprive that person of his powers in an industrial democracy. This has led to the counter-proposal that the worker directors be elected by the employees of the company. Another objection is that middle managers are not often members of unions and that their views ought to be represented on the board. A further worry is that, if the worker directors are appointed by the unions, they will represent the national interests of the union, which will have members in other industries as well as in other companies, and will not represent the precise and local interests of the employees of that firm.

The TUC position--that all worker directors must be appointed by the unions--appears on its face to be a simple power play, even an assertion of union power as against

local interests. It is almost impossible not to agree.
However, the TUC position is perhaps not quite so gross as
it seems. Again, one must consider the history of trade
unionism in Britain and the importance of class. They have
resulted in a view that unions are *the* representatives of
workers. A person who is not a member of a union is, in
this union view, "not in favor of the workers." "What,"
the loyal trade unionist will then ask, "do we want with
directors elected by people who are not in favor of workers?"
To this is added the fear that there are many ways, or that
many ways will be thought up, to frustrate the spirit of the
system if non-unionists can vote. The brief account of the
Grunwick strike could serve to illustrate that the fear is
not totally unwarranted. Furthermore, the union view is
that if a person wants to influence the selection of directors, he can always join a union. Except for a few people
with rather peculiar religious views, to whose existence
and whose rights the unions admit, trade unionists do not
see any respectable reason why a person would not join a
union. As for middle management, if middle managers do not
want to join a union, it is presumably because they will be
properly represented by the owner directors. So it is not
all simple greed for power. But still, the TUC position is
not thoroughly democratic and one returns to the proposition
that there is a good deal of "taking care of the unions
first" in its stand. The Labour government itself did not
appear to be wholly convinced that it should adopt the TUC
demands.

The idea of industrial democracy does not require that
there be worker directors. Another line of development,
which appeals to some trade unionists, is to require that
companies consult with the unions before major decisions are
made. This would allow the unions to continue to represent
the interests of the unions and their members without putting
themselves in the ambivalent position of being responsible
for looking out for the company as well as for the workers.
Embellishments may be added to this rough idea. Consultation
will not achieve the aims of industrial democracy if, having
consulted, the company can go its own way. Conversely, an
absolute power of union veto on company plans would make the
union the effective board of directors. So it seems likely
that developments along the line of joint consultation will
include some procedure for reference to arbitration. Reference to arbitration would itself be a new development in
British industrial relations.

What exactly will emerge from the debate over industrial democracy is not at all clear at present. Whether

some system of worker involvement in the decisions of management will begin to take concrete form in a year or two or whether a decade will elapse before one can begin to speak with confidence about a "system of industrial democracy in Britain" is a question best left to inveterate gamblers. What does seem sure is that some system will develop. (Perhaps an emerging system of industrial democracy will also provide institutional mechanisms to help in the formulation and administration of a national incomes policy--a problem discussed in Chapter 11.)

ENDNOTES

1. I am indebted to Professor J. Fred Holly of The University of Tennessee for this perception of the British situation.

6

BANKING, FINANCE, AND THE CITY OF LONDON

THE CITY OF LONDON

The City of London is *the* center of banking and finance in the United Kingdom, and, along with New York, one of the two major centers in the world. The City of London (also called, simply, the City) is an area of one square mile, chartered as a city in the middle ages, and now virtually without residents but containing the headquarters of almost all British financial institutions from commercial banks through merchant bankers to insurance companies and branches of many foreign banks. The City--its institutions, its streets, its telephones and telex machines--is the money market *par excellence*. The City, presided over by its Mater Familias, the Bank of England, has been the model for money markets for nearly two centuries. It has also been the model from which economists have derived their theories of money and banking.

The basic principles of banking, finance, and money markets are the same in London as they are elsewhere in the western world, but there are a number of uniquely British traits in the organization and functioning of British financial markets.

Commercial banking is dominated by the "big four:" Barclays, National Westminster, Midland, and Lloyds (not related to the groups of insurance underwriters famous as Lloyds of London). Of total deposits in 1971 of ₤37.9 billion, ₤33.2 billion (or 87.5%) were with these banks. The Scottish banks--the second largest group, consisting of the Royal Bank of Scotland, the Bank of Scotland, and Clydesdale Bank--do less than 10% of the business done by the six London "clearing banks" (members of the London

Clearing House; beside the "big four" there are Coutts & Co.
and Williams and Glyn's Bank). Wherever one goes, where-
ever one lives in Britain, one goes to a branch of one of
these banks; and usually to a branch of one of the "big
four." These "clearing" or "deposit" banks, as they are
called, are like banks on the continent in that they are
huge, but unlike continental banks in that they do little
long-term lending. In fact, they are even more given than
American banks to lending on short-term in quickly and
easily liquidated form. This has contributed to the be-
lief--it is not clear how well-founded the belief is--that
British banks do not lend enough to British industry.

At the center of the short-term money market are the
"discount houses," members of the London Discount Market
Association. In the 19th century discount houses dealt
largely in the commercial or trade bills with which the
City financed trade the world over. Today their main business is with 91-day government bills. Discount houses
borrow from the commercial banks and use the borrowed sums
to buy (discount) trade bills and government paper. This
borrowing is usually "at call," meaning that the banks can
demand repayment at any time, and when the banks are short
of liquidity they do demand repayment. The discount houses
are the major link between the banking system and the Bank
of England, Britain's central bank. In this respect the
British system differs markedly from the American. In
America it is the member banks of the Federal Reserve System
who deal directly with the Fed. In Britain the commercial
banks only deal with the Bank of England when the Bank (as
it is also called) requires "special deposits" (a bit like
reserve deposits in the U.S.). The rest of the time it is
the discount houses who deal with the Bank. When a discount house finds itself short of cash because a bank has
called its money at call, the discount house rediscounts
bills with the Bank of England. This is the origin of the
characterization of a central bank as a "lender of last
resort." The rate the Bank charges on these rediscounting
transactions--it used to be called "Bank rate" and is now
called Minimum lending rate (MLR)--thus strongly influences
the rate of discount charged by the discount houses, which
rate in turn largely determines the interest rate on the
call money they borrow. Thus is the Bank of England's MLR
linked to the interest rates charged by commercial banks.

Another major feature of the City is the group of
financial institutions known as "merchant bankers." There
are perhaps one hundred such institutions (the definition
of a merchant bank is not entirely clear). Of these the

seventeen most prestigious constitute the Accepting Houses
Committee. The seventeen have also joined with another
thirty-nine to form the Issuing Houses Association. The
Committee and the Association formulate standards and over-
see each other's behavior--not as of legal right, nor even
(as a rule) by formal procedure, but by something akin to
that continuous informal contact which regulates a regimen-
tal mess or a well-disciplined fraternity. The other merchant bankers are either small and highly specialized, not
recognized (or not yet recognized) as proper merchant banks
by the Committee and Association members, or just starting
up.

The two branches of merchant banking are "accepting
and issuing." The former means that a merchant banker adds
his highly respectable name to discountable commercial
paper and thus makes it easily marketable. This is a service of great use to foreign firms and banks desiring finance from the City. "Issuing" means organizing and under-
writing new issues on the stock exchange. This business in
turn involves the merchant bankers as advisors to all sorts
of businesses and in this role they become closely involved
in arranging mergers and take-overs among Britain's industrial and commercial firms. Merchant bankers are also
"wholesale" bankers, accepting large deposits (in the
millions of pounds) on fixed term and finding borrowers who
want very large sums for exactly the same period. [In this
business a day less or more is not to be ignored: one day's
interest on Ł30 mn at 7.5% per annum is Ł6,250--about two-
thirds of a doctor's annual income.]

MONETARY POLICY

Just as the basic principles of banking are the same
in the countries of the western world, so too is the
logical core of monetary policy: the use of interest rates,
bond sales and prices, and the manipulation of the liquid
reserves of banks. As mentioned above, the Bank of England,
operating through the discount market, influences short-
term interest rates. It affects long-term rates and the
liquidity of the system by selling (or not selling) government bonds. The treasury will issue bonds which the Bank
sells "at the tap"--offering more or fewer bonds at lower
prices (higher interest rates) or higher prices (lower
interest rates).

Traditionally the clearing banks kept an equivalent of

30% of their demand deposits in the form of cash or highly
liquid short-term paper. In 1971 there was a "reform" of
the system. Like so many British "reforms," they appeared
far more revolutionary to the British than to foreign observers. The banks were required to hold "eligible reserve
assets" equal to at least 12.5% of "eligible liabilities"
(all deposits payable in sterling with less than two years
to maturity). "Eligible assets" are deposits at the Bank
of England (other than special deposits, see below), British government securities with less than one year to maturity (including Treasury bills), some local government paper
of short maturity, and (up to 2%) commercial bills of the
sort which the Bank of England will accept for rediscount.
So far it would appear that a slightly less stringent legal
requirement has replaced a slightly more stringent tradition.
"Tap sales"--the counterpart to U.S. Federal Reserve open
market operations--are still the most important means to
affect the liquidity and therefore the willingness of banks
to lend.

The 1971 reforms continued the system of "special
deposits" started in the 1950s as a supplement to other
means available to limit bank liquidity. The Bank of
England can call upon the banks to make deposits with the
Bank equal to a percentage of their "eligible liabilities."
Unlike the American system of reserves, the Bank pays interest on these deposits at the current rate on Treasury
bills. Calls are rare and the percentages are small: one
or two percent.

After 1971 the Bank's MLR (minimum lending rate) was to
be set by formula a half percent above the rate of Treasury
bills, rounded up to an even one-fourth percent. The idea was
that the MLR should reflect rather than guide the market.
However, so soon as the Bank had reason to think the market
needed guidance, in the crisis years after 1974, it began
to set the MLR independently of the market, indicating the
short-term rates it thought should be charged.

Before 1971 the Bank had controlled the amount and
direction of credit by "requests"--which no banker would be
crazy enough to ignore. It was felt that "requests" were
too clumsy a method, and insufficiently responsive to the
market, so the Bank was asked to desist from the practice.
But it remains true that the Bank (and the Chancellor) can
make their wishes known, and the wishes of the "authorities"
will not be ignored whatever the principle officially
enunciated.

The bank of England was privately owned until nationalization under the Attlee government, but from the middle
of the 19th century, if not actually from the beginning of
that century, it had acted as a responsible central bank--
it was the original model for central banks--and nationalization hardly made a difference. Labour had felt that the
Bank had been anti-working class during the interwar years,
and so insisted upon nationalization; but it was not the
private nature of the Bank but the beliefs of those years
which made the Bank harsh on the subject of unemployment.
It is true that the Governor of the Bank must now consult
with the Chancellor of the Exchequer, and the Chancellor
can give the Bank orders, but Governor and Chancellor consulted frequently before nationalization and it is difficult
to believe that the Bank would have refused to take the
government's advice if the government had felt strongly.

BUILDING SOCIETIES

The major form of savings for most people in Britain
is investment in the shares of building societies. These
societies are rather like savings and loan associations in
the U.S. but much larger, several having branches all over
the country. Almost all house purchases and family construction of private homes is financed by the building
societies, the borrower almost always being someone who has
already been saving with the society which makes him the
loan.

The building societies do not compete with each other,
nor do they try to maximize their earnings. They regard
themselves as a kind of public servant. They have a tradition, rooted in their origins in the early cooperative
movement, of extending as much credit as cheaply as they
can for purchases of homes and restrict their lending very largely to home mortgages (except for the investment of surplus funds in government bonds). In a peculiarly
British arrangement they pay the income tax on shares for
their members at "the standard rate" (the rate which most
Englishmen pay: it has varied from 30 to 35% in the 1970s),
the "dividends" (i.e., interest) then being tax-free. The
managers of the societies meet in their national association
to set mutually agreed policies in respect of interest rates
charged and share dividends paid.

They are major competitors with the clearing banks for
deposits. The clearing banks resent the fact that the
building societies have not been brought within the ambit

96

of Bank of England credit controls and lobby for a change
in policy. So far the societies have retained their
independence and recognition as a privileged agency to
serve the savings and mortgage needs of the less well-to-do
segments of British society.

NATIONAL PRODUCT: PAST AND PRESENT

For the past thirty years, and even for the past century, the British economy has not grown as rapidly as have some others. Before World War II the annual rise in the productivity of labor in industrialized countries ranged around two percent, with Britain trailing the U.S., Germany, and France. Since World War II figures around six percent have become common in continental European countries, and in Japan the figure has been almost ten percent. In Britain the figure has more than doubled since the pre-war years but is still a third under the new continental "norm," and far below the new Japanese "abnorm." (Comparative figures are given in Table 7-1. Note that U.S. performance has been even worse than British performance.) Being next to last among developed countries has been a disappointment to the British and a basis for many criticisms of both industry and labor and of British government policy.

Several aspects of British economic history go some way toward explaining Britain's relative economic decline. First, and by no means least important, Britain started out at the head of the league--which meant there was no way to go but down. In 1850 Britain was the only industrialized country in the world and could justly call herself "the workshop of the world." This long lead at the middle of the 19th century meant that Britain would necessarily be at or near the top, both in total industrial output and in per capita income, for many years to come. When one adds to its industrial lead its political power and the extent of its empire, one can understand why not only the British but many other people came to think of Great Britain as *the* "top dog" and became accustomed to expecting to find Britain in that position. There has thus been a vague, almost unarticulated, but pervasive view that Britain should somehow rank high--should somehow perform better than Italy or France or

TABLE 7-1

Average Annual Rates of Growth of Output Per Manhour

	1870–1913 (%)	1913–1950 (%)	1950–1960 (%)	1961–1974 (%)	1960–1977# (%)
France	1.8	1.6	3.9	4.0	5.7
Germany	2.1*	0.9	6.0	5.4	5.5
Japan	–	–	–	9.6	8.8
Italy	1.2	1.9	4.1	6.8	6.3
U. S.	2.4*	2.4	2.4**	3.5	2.6
U. K.	1.5	1.7	2.0**	4.0	3.4

* 1871–1913

** From 1950 to 1955 the U.S. rate was 2.8% and the British rate 1.6%; but from 1955 to 1960 the U.S. rate was down to 2.0% and the British up to 2.3%.

Manufacturing industry only.

Sources: Data for 1870–1960 are adapted from Angus Maddison, *Economic Growth in the West* (London/N.Y.: Twentieth Century Fund, 1964), p. 37. Data for 1961–1974 are computed from Robert Bacon and Walter Eltis, *Britain's Economic Problem: Too Few Producers* (London: Macmillan, 1976), p. 161, where they computed total growth from 1961 to 1974 at 1963 prices. Data for 1960–77 are from Congress of the United States, *Notes from the Joint Economic Committee* (March 2, 1979) V:7:1.

Spain or India or Mexico. Once, however, this view is plainly articulated, one asks, "Why should not Italy or France or India or Mexico perform better than Britain?" And once this question is asked, one must, bigotry aside, admit that there are no obvious answers. Since nations and cultures are not identical, one should not only expect differences between them at any particular time but also differences in their pasts and futures. We do not feel that Italy's lead in learning in the 14th century or Portugal's lead in discoveries in the 15th century are grounds for believing that there is something wrong if Italians do not win all the Nobel prizes for literature or if the Portuguese are not the first people on the moon. In short, it should not be surprising that the world's leading industrial nation of the period 1790-1870 is not the world's leading industrial nation in the latter half of the 20th century. It does seem likely, therefore, that some of the disappointment with British economic performance during the past 100 years is based on a feeling that somehow Britain should violate the "historical law" that "nobody can be first all the time." This much said, a number of other comments can be made upon possible reasons for Britain's relative loss of position.

"Being first" is likely to have contributed to Britain's relative decline in several ways other than the logical one that the only way was down. The new technologies of the industrial revolution in the first half of the 19th century did not require large aggregations of capital. When the technologies of the latter part of the 19th century came along, a structure of small firms already existed in the industrial sector. Iron and iron products—major elements in the British industrial revolution—were produced efficiently by small firms in 1850. Later, as they became available, the Bessemer and open-hearth processes for making steel were adopted by the British firms. However, the great virtue of these technologies was that they reaped the economies of ever increasing scale and the smaller British firms did not, perhaps could not, amass the capital, integrate vertically, and expand horizontally so as to match the rapidly increasing productivity of American and German steel-makers. Merely to suggest that this was the case raises an interesting question in economics: if existing firms did not or could not take full advantage of the new technologies, why did not new firms arise to do the job? The contrast between Britain and the United States or Germany implies that a Carnegie who did not leave Britain could have founded a firm to take advantage of the new technologies and drive the smaller firms out of business, or absorb them and reorganize them into a more productive organization. Alternatively, it implies that British investment bankers or other financial institutions could have, with profit, arranged for the amalgamation and reorganization of the smaller firms. Economic logic implies that some such changes as these would have taken place, but in fact they did not. Why not? Again, we do not know. There was already capital "sunk" in the older, small-scale units of production but, as any economist can explain, "Sunk costs are spilt milk." Sunk costs should always be ignored if new arrangements are more profitable. The existence of many small firms operating profitably may have served to divert attention from the opportunities for greater profits from reorganized and re-equipped industry, but even this suggestion does not really explain why no industrial or financial entrepreneur saw or seized the opportunity. To some degree, one must always leave economic logic aside. Once a person or the executive of a corporation becomes involved in one line of endeavor or another he is likely to see what he is doing as a good and proper way to carry on. Self-respect, self image require that a person believes in and admires the things that he does. It is relevant here to note that it has been said that Carnegie "did not give a damn" about iron or steel but was fascinated with organization and so could reorganize the American steel industry without qualm about what his reorganization implied about the people who had been running the industry.

The 20th century provides another case. At the beginning of the century the British cotton textile industry was still a large and successful industry, exporting its products all over the world. It too was an industry consisting of many firms. In the course of this century competing industries have arisen in Japan, then India, and later in Hong Kong, South Korea, and in many other nations because the manufacture of cotton goods requires neither technological sophistication nor skilled labor. But textile firms, just as other firms, do not voluntarily go out of business so long as they can limp along, even on very low margins of profit. Even when firms go bankrupt their spindles and looms are not destroyed but are taken over by other firms which can buy them very cheaply. Again we have a problem of "economic logic". Why did not the industry run down, scrapping plant as it wore out, but not replacing it? Partly the answer is, of course, tariff protection by the government and later various forms of subsidy: for instance, in 1977 the textile industry was the major recipient of the £20 per worker per week "temporary employment subsidy." British policy in respect of textiles in this cen-

tury has certainly reflected the fact that a great many
workers, who are also voters, not only work in the textile
industry but live in towns and areas where there are few
alternative employment opportunities if they lose their
jobs in textile mills. The case of British textiles may
also be an excellent example of a kind of gap in economists'
reasoning--the tendency to think of the "long run" without
attaching actual numbers of years to the "long run." It
may take half a century to run down and eliminate a declining
industry. The British textile industry, especially the
cotton textile branch, has been contracting for many years
and is much smaller than it was twenty-five years ago, let
alone fifty years ago. But it should be noted that the
productive life of a spindle is twenty years or more and if
only three-quarters of worn out spindles are replaced each
time, it takes more than forty years to reduce the spindlage
by a half. If each time the worn out spindles are replaced
by improved models, total output will decline even more
slowly.

Another possible, indeed likely reason for Britain's
relative decline was her pattern of investment. Throughout
the 19th century and until the First World War Britain invested a good deal abroad. Of total savings generated, between a quarter and a half were spent on creating capital in
foreign lands. British capital was important in the development of the United States. (Those who watch late-night
"westerns" made years ago may wonder why there was frequently a silly young Englishman as the butt of humor. The
answer is that British financial houses provided much of the
finance for the development of American cattle ranches and
the silly Englishman was a young partner-to-be of a British
firm, learning his trade by visiting his firms' American
clients.) British capital built the railway network in
Argentina. British capital was important in constructing
the transportation networks and port facilities of New
Zealand, Australia, Canada, India, South Africa, and British
colonies elsewhere. Certainly these investments abroad were
profitable, but profits are only a portion of the gains from
investment. Investments in infrastructure (railways, ports)
and in plant and machinery increase productivity--the net
value added (NVA) in a country, but NVA accrues not only as
profits but also as wages and other incomes. A rule of
thumb--a very rough rule of thumb indeed--is that an investment of five pounds (or dollars) will give rise to a
perpetual increase of one pound (or dollar) in the income
stream of net value added (a capital:output ratio of 5:1).
With profits for the investing firm of 10% and a capital:
output ratio of 5:1 the investing firm will reap only one-
half of the total gain from the investment. If the investor

supplies the funds for the capital projects by buying bonds paying 5% per year, then the investor will reap a fourth of the total increase in NVA. Thus British investment in a well-stocked ranch in Texas, in a tramway system in Buenos Aires, or a tin mine in Malaya will do even more to increase the income of the United States, Argentina, or Malaya than it does to increase the income of Great Britain. By contrast, had, say Ⱡ100 been invested in capital equipment in Britain instead, the British people would have enjoyed an increase in British GNP of Ⱡ20 instead of an increase in interest and profits of Ⱡ5 to Ⱡ10. Britain's tendency to invest abroad instead of at home may be contrasted with the American, Russian, German, and Japanese tendency to invest capital at home. In the case of America the tendency was probably a result of the inward-looking character of America before 1914. In the case of Soviet Russia ideology and necessity are sufficient to explain events there. In the cases of Germany and Japan, chance, opportunity, and a nationalistic outlook were certainly reinforced by definite and often not so subtle government pressures to invest at home. It should also be noted that the British were the only nation which really-truly believed in free trade and the associated ideas of the free flow of finance and capital. But whatever the reasons, the fact is that Britain invested much more abroad and much less at home than did other industrializing nations.

The answer to the question--"Why would Britain invest abroad if the total return to the British economy would have been greater if she had invested at home?"--lies in the structure of a capitalist, free enterprise economy. From the point of view of the individual investor, whether someone buying a bond for the interest or a firm building a plant for the profit, the meaningful return is the income that actually goes to the investor. From his point of view, what looks like an assured return of 5% on an Argentinian bond or of 10% from the operations of a Malayan rubber plantation is obviously to be preferred to 4% interest on the bonds of a British company or an 8% return on the manufacture of iron skillets in the English Midlands. The rest of the net value added by the investment is simply unavailable to the investor in the capitalist system. Instead, the capitalist market system spreads the increased NVA in the forms of higher wages for people in the country (not only the industry or town) where the investment is made and of more products available more cheaply to people everywhere. A decision to direct investment funds toward the creation of capital structures and equipment in the domestic economy may be a wise one for a nation as a whole but it is by no means necessarily wise or rational for a single individual, firm, or investment banking house.

This line of argument should not be understood to mean that it is always better to invest at home rather than abroad. As Britain became more industrialized and as her population grew it certainly made sense to open up sources of supply for foodstuffs which could not be produced in sufficient volume at home as well as sources of supply for other industries using raw jute from Bengal or cocoa from West Africa or cotton from India or the Sudan (just as to-day it makes sense for the United States to help open up supplies of North Sea oil or West African iron ore). It would therefore be wrong to say that British investment abroad before 1914, and the continuing investment abroad on a much smaller scale up to the present, was or is a complete mistake. All industrialized nations are highly dependent upon supplies from abroad, both as essential inputs to their industrial output and as essential elements in their standard of living. If foreign areas have not or will not or cannot develop as sources of supply to the industrialized nations, then these industrialized nations must of necessity participate in developing these regions. But if British growth depended in some part upon the development of ports in Argentina or West Africa or upon tin mines in Malaya, it is by no means so clear that it depended upon there being rice mills or teak mills in Burma, or railways to exploit the diamond and gold mines of South Africa. That Britain needed rubber is certain, but that British investment in Malayan rubber plantations was necessary is not. Britain could have induced more Malay small-holders to cultivate more rubber trees or bought rubber from Dutch plantations and small-holders in Sumatra.

It is impossible to say how much British economic growth has been retarded by the tendency to invest overseas but it does seem reasonable to conclude that less foreign investment and greater domestic investment would have given Great Britain a larger GNP today.

Another strong possibility, which is not subject to quantitative or other economic analysis, is that the British have not been doing productive things as well as other peoples, or have been doing wrong or less worthwhile things. The suggestion is that the Japanese make the best and the most of each new technological development, the Germans and French follow behind them, and the British just miss out on a number of possibilities. This argument is a variation on the observation that some people do some things very well

[Chinese and table tennis, Italians and opera] and some do
not do some things so well [Americans and soccer, French-
men and distance running].

Tables 7-2 and 7-3 give some (but not overwhelming)
support to this hypothesis. During the thirteen years before World War I the productivity of British investment at
home compared very unfavorably with that of other industrialized countries, and during the decade 1950-60 all the
major industrial countries of western Europe and North America enjoyed lower capital:output ratios. Furthermore, one
normally expects investment in machinery to have a lower
capital:output ratio than investment in construction, yet
the proportion of total investment devoted to machinery and
equipment by Britain has been relatively large (see Table
7-3). Thus, although one would expect the relatively low
ratio of investment of GNP to cause total output and productivity in Britain to rise more slowly than elsewhere, one
would expect the productivity of what was invested to be
relatively high. This issue of why Britain has not done so
well as her competitors is discussed further in the section
on "Exports, Imports, and Quality" in Chapter 8.

In addition to the fact that Britain's total output is
lower than it would have been had productivity grown more
rapidly, the relatively slower growth in British productivity has had at least two further troublesome consequences.
First, for the balance of payments: at pre-1971 fixed exchange rates the more rapid rises in productivity in other
countries made their goods relatively cheaper on international markets, with a resulting tendency for their goods to
undersell and replace British goods. Simultaneously, the
cheaper foreign products appeared increasingly attractive to
British buyers who therefore imported more. Britain's exports and invisible earnings were enough to permit her to
withstand the pressure on the pound from 1949 to 1967 at a
value of $2.80 and from 1967 to 1971 at a value of $2.40.
When exchange rates were allowed to float--that is, to sink--
after 1971, the effect was to drive down the value of the
pound in terms of all important currencies--even the 1979
dollar-pound ratio was higher than the 1971 ratio. The
relatively slow increase in British productivity contributed
to Britain's international economic difficulties, but it
has been far from the whole story (see Chapter 8).

Secondly, the more rapid rise of productivity abroad
produced more rapidly rising real incomes in those countries
and observing these more rapidly rising real incomes
probably had a "demonstration effect" upon the British--

TABLE 7-2
Capital:Output Ratios*

(1)	(2)	(3)	(4)	(5)
	1900–13	1913–50	1950–60	1950–60
Range**				
Low	3.3	4.1	3.2	2.1
High	6.4	10.4#	7.5	6.2
Median	4.9	5.1#	5.7	4.1
U. K.	6.4	4.6	5.9	4.3

*For Columns 2, 3, and 4, defined as average ratio of gross
domestic investment to G.N.P. divided by rate of growth
of output in real terms. For Column 5, defined as average
ratio of fixed non-residential investment to G.N.P. divided by the rate of growth of output in real terms.

**For 1900–13: Canada, Denmark, Italy, Norway, Sweden, U.K.,
U.S.; for 1913–50; same plus Germany; for 1950–60: same
as for 1913–50 plus Belgium, France, Netherlands.

#10.4 for Italy inconsistent with earlier and later data
for Italy and with all other figures. If we assume
Italian data faulty, then the high was Sweden (7.0) but
median falls only to 5.0.

Source: Adapted from data in Angus Maddison, *Economic
Growth in The West*. (London/N.Y.: Twentieth
Century Fund, 1964) pp. 77–78.

TABLE 7-3
Investment in Machinery and Equipment, 1950–60

	As percent of GNP	As percent of Gross Domestic Investment
France	8.1	42.4
Germany	11.1	46.3
Italy	9.0	43.3
United States	7.2	37.7
United Kingdom	7.4	48.1

Source: Adapted from Angus Maddison, *Economic Growth in the
West*. (London/N.Y.: Twentieth Century Fund, 1964)
pp. 76, 80.

that is, it encouraged them to spend more, at home and abroad, on foreign as well as domestic goods, in an effort to keep up with the joys of the Joneses (who in this case were not Welsh).

THE USES OF NATIONAL PRODUCT

The tables in this section present some major measurements of the quantitative aspects of the British economy and of the uses to which the British have put their national product over the past three decades. Detailed information on foreign trade is presented in Chapter 8, and on welfare state expenditures in Chapter 11. Tables "speak for themselves," so I comment on them individually only to relate them to current arguments and to the discussions which follow in this book.

Many of the tables express the data as percentages of GNP. I present the statistics in this fashion because numbers make sense only when related to other numbers and proportions seem the best way to express relationships. Numbers of pounds can be misleading, partly because as national income grows, each component also grows, and partly because inflation, especially in the 1970s, makes comparisons of numbers of pounds over the years virtually meaningless.

To the question, "How much is a 1979 pound worth?" the simple answer is "About two dollars." In the free markets which have existed since 1971 the exchange value of the pound has been as high as $2.64 and as low as $1.55, a range which tells a lot more about the effects of speculation on the value of a currency than it does about the domestic purchasing power of the pound. During 1978 the pound fluctuated around $2.00 and this is about as good an estimate as can be made. For the period from the end of the Second World War to the mid-60s a figure of $3.00 is a reasonable estimate (the actual fixed exchange rate was $2.80), and for the following decade the slow decline to $2.00 reflects the relative change in domestic purchasing powers of the pound and dollar fairly well. Because relative prices within any two countries vary and because the composition of national output varies one can never make precise computations of relative purchasing powers. In comparing British national product with American national product four variables are involved: the composition of British output, the composition of American output, relative British prices, and relative American prices.

Any combination is equally legitimate: U.S. national product computed in U.S. prices and British in British prices,
using the current rate of exchange to compare; both national products computed at U.S. relative prices; both national
products computed at British relative prices; both national
products computed as if Britain produced goods in the same
proportions as the U.S. does--using British or U.S. prices;
both national products computed as if the U.S. produced goods
in the same proportions as Britain does--again using British
or U.S. prices. There are thus at least seven legitimate
ways to compare GNPs and the purchasing power of dollars and
pounds. The range of variation between any two results often
exceeds 25% and may be appreciably higher.[1] Thus the statement, "a pound is worth about two dollars," must be taken to
mean, "within a large margin or error:" but it is as good as
any other statement.

    In reading about the British economy one often sees
"gross *domestic* product at *factor* cost" used as the measure
of Britain's national product. I use "gross *national* product at *market prices*" instead. In the United States the
commonly used figure is that for gross *national* product, so
using British gross *national* product allows more accurate
comparisons between the two countries.

    Gross domestic product at factor cost understates "all
that is available" to the British because, by the conventions
of national income accounting, the "value paid for" which
flows to the government in indirect taxes is not counted, and
neither are net British earnings from investments abroad.
Thus British gross *national* product *at market prices* exceeds
British gross *domestic* product *at factor cost* by 15 to 20%.
Many statements about the proportion of British product
absorbed by the government make the British figure seem
comparatively high because G*D*P has been used in the denominator. Much more misleading is the occasional use of after-
tax, before-transfer payments "personal income" in the denominator, a practice which overstates British proportions
by as much as 40% in comparison to U.S. figures using G*N*P.
The Moral Lesson: always look closely to find out what
measure of national product is being used.

    If one does look closely at the numbers in this book
he will discover that I have made one change from normal
national income accounting practice. In computing GNP I
have not subtracted subsidies from "taxes on expenditures"
(indirect business taxes) to get a net figure on the grounds
that most subsidy payments are as much a collective valu-
ation of the worth of an activity as are other government

payments (e.g., the payment of an "employment subsidy" to
firms in northeast England is no more and no less a positive
collective evaluation of those firms' products than are
wages paid to tax inspectors or to social workers).

While I present a few times series for each year since
World War II, I frequently average figures for three years
to represent the state of affairs for "representative"
periods. I have usually avoided including those election
years in which one party replaced the other on the grounds
that neither the outgoing nor the incoming government could
be considered effectively in charge during those years. The
reader is free to use the periodization to blame or praise
Labour, or to praise or blame the Conservatives. I cannot
see that the talents in economic management of one party of
the other have been clearly superior. The periods are:

1946-48: Years of postwar recovery and legislation to
achieve Labour's prewar aims of economic and social reform.
Clement Attlee was Prime Minister. If not the dominating
figure during these and the next three years--"dominating"
is not the word for the man, and there were certainly other
very strong ministers in the Labour government of 1945-51--
he was the man who "put it all together."

1949-51: Years in which Labour began to administer
their reformed or welfare state. These years spanned an
election in 1950 which left Labour with a very small majority (see Table 3-2). Here I have included the election
year of 1951 in order to average three years instead of
only two years.

1953-55: Although Winston Churchill was Prime Minister,
economic policy was probably most influenced by the views of
R. A. Butler, Chancellor of the Exchequer until December,
1955. These years represent the state of affairs during the
early years of the long (1951-64) period of postwar Conservative government.

1961-63: Years which represent the results of Conser-
vative government. Harold Macmillan was Chancellor of the
Exchequer from December 1955, until he became Prime Minister
in January, 1957, serving until October, 1963 Although
Anthony Eden was Prime Minister from April, 1955, until
January, 1957, he was not one of the strong personalities in
Conservative politics. While Macmillan's four Chancellors
of the Exchequer (Thorneycroft, Heathcoat-Amory, Lloyd,
Maulding) were influential, the tenor of the years 1956-64
reflected Macmillan's personality and attitudes.

1967-69: Harold Wilson was Prime Minister from October, 1964, until June, 1970, and set the tone for the entire period. Selecting the years 1967–69 allows comparisons between the later years of the second postwar Labour government and the later years of the long postwar period of Conservative government and between both and the early 1950s.

1971-73: Again, it was the Prime Minister (Edward Heath) rather than his Chancellor of the Exchequer (Anthony Barber) with whom one associates policy. 1971 was the first full year of Heath's Conservative government. 1973 was the last year of "normalcy."

1973--: It would be difficult, and perhaps dangerously misleading, to make judgements about Britain's long run prospects on the basis of performance since 1973. It has been a peculiar period for all of the industrialized nations. The OPEC price rise was made especially difficult for the British to handle because it came on top of a large upswing in the prices of many of its other imports (although, as North Sea oil comes on stream, the British become net beneficiaries of the price rise). The reactions of the international money market and of foreign and international monetary authorities made it particularly hard for Britain to handle the situation (see Chapter 8).

Periods such as "1953–56" or "1967–70," which the reader will find in a number of the tables, represent the same periods. Statistics about government activities are supplied for fiscal years which run from April 1st through March 31st, so that, for instance, April 1, 1953, through March 31, 1956, is the period for statistics about the government which corresponds most closely with the calendar years 1953–55. Where the fiscal year data are expressed as percentages of GNP, which is supplied for calendar years, the GNP data has been adjusted by weighting the overlapping years: e.g., fiscal 1953–54 data are divided by the sum of 0.75 times 1953 GNP plus 0.25 times 1954 GNP.

In analyzing the tables which follow it is important to recognize that the shares of GNP spent by government or paid in social security benefits have increased almost inevitably: that is, not because of new policy decisions but because of wage inflation during a period of depression. Merely "carrying on as before" in the public sector, but at wages and salaries more-or-less matching rising wages in the private sector, means that government expenditures--the numerator in computing percentages--will rise more rapidly than will GNP (the denominator by which one divides). In addition,

depression has meant that unemployment and other social
security transfer payments rise disproportionately (see
"Income Maintenance in Britain" in Chapter 11). Add to these
considerations the unusually rapid rise in the prices of food
and housing since 1970 and it is easy to account for the rise
in welfare state expenditures.

The data for Tables 7–4 through 7–15 and for most of the
tables in Chapters 8 and 11 have been drawn from many issues
of the U.K.'s Central Statistical Office, *Annual Abstract of
Statistics* (London: HMSO), and very occasionally from recent
issues of the *Monthly Digest of Statistics* (London: HMSO).
Because I have used so many tables in so many issues in the
Annual Abstract, I simply cite *"Annual Abstract of
Statistics*, various issues" for these tables.

Tables 7–4, 7–5, and 7–6: there was continuous growth
in GNP and GNP per capita from 1946 through 1973, except for
1952 when both fell and for 1958 when GNP hardly rose and
GNP per capita fell. Stagnation since 1973 is a consequence
of the world price upheaval of 1973–74 and of British efforts
to defend the external value of the pound and to find a
suitable incomes policy (see Chapters 8 and 12). The average
compound rate of growth in GNP per capita since the end of
postwar reconstruction (1948) to 1973 was 2.51% (mid–year
population grew from 49.2 million in 1948 to 55.9 million in
1977). If the period is extended to 1976 the rate is down
to 2.34%. As pointed out in the previous section, these
rates are "not good" in comparison with postwar rates in
most other industrialized countries, but they are respectable
by historical standards. Investment has maintained a
respectably high level. Whether it has been well–employed
is discussed above and in Chapter 8.

Table 7–7 shows one of the consequences of the post–OPEC
depression: the profits of private businesses have fallen
drastically. Inflation has much reduced the purchasing
power of the flow of funds from allowances for depreciation
and the reduction in profits makes the job of finding funds
for investment even more difficult. (It should, however, be
noted that Britain is moving toward a system of "current
cost accounting" so that allowed depreciation will match
current replacement costs).

Tables 7–8 and 7–9 show why I usually express values as
percentages of GNP: absolute values in pounds would not
allow comparisons over time.

TABLE 7-4
Index of Real GNP

(1970 = 100.0)

Year	Index	Year	Index	Year	Index
1946	51.2	1957	69.7	1968	95.9
1947	52.6	1958	70.1	1969	97.5
1948	54.7	1959	72.9	1970	100.0
1949	56.4	1960	76.5	1971	102.6
1950	59.2	1961	79.1	1972	105.2
1951	60.4	1962	80.0	1973	113.0
1952	60.2	1963	83.3	1974	111.7
1953	62.7	1964	87.5	1975	109.5
1954	65.6	1965	89.5	1976	113.7
1955	67.2	1966	90.6	1977	114.3
1956	68.3	1967	93.0	1978	117.5

Source: computed from *Annual Abstract of Statistics*,
various issues, and *Monthly Digest of Statistics*,
March, 1979.

TABLE 7-5
GNP Per Capita at 1970 Prices

Years	₤s	Years	₤s	Years	₤s
1946	479	1957	690	1968	897
1947	500	1958	691	1969	908
1948	532	1959	714	1970	929
1949	539	1960	743	1971	950
1950	561	1961	762	1972	970
1951	575	1962	764	1973	1,040
1952	571	1963	794	1974	1,027
1953	595	1964	834	1975	1,008
1954	616	1965	847	1976	1,047
1955	631	1966	855	1977	1,053
1956	641	1967	873	1978	1,083

Source: computed by chain–linking from *Annual Abstract of
Statistics*, various issues, and *Monthly Digest of
Statistics*, March, 1979.

TABLE 7-6
Gross Domestic Fixed Capital Formation
As a Percentage of GNP
(Annual Averages for Selected Periods* and Intervening Years)

Years	Percent	Years	Percent
1946	8.9	1961–63	16.3
1947	10.7	1964–66	17.7
1948	11.6	1967–72	18.1
1949–51	12.3	1973	18.8
1952–54	13.8	1974–75	19.5
1955–56	14.5	1976	18.6
1957–59	15.0	1977	17.6
1960	15.7	1978	18.2

* Periods selected so that maximum exceed minimum percentages by 0.5% or less.

Source: computed from *Annual Abstract of Statistics*, various issues.

TABLE 7-7
Before Tax Profits
(After Allowing for Depreciation and Stock Appreciation)
(Averages for Selected Periods)

	1949–51	1953–55	1961–63	1967–69	1971–73	1974–76
Profits as a percent of GNP	16.7	17.3	14.8	12.5	11.6	6.2

Source: computed from *Annual Abstract of Statistics*, various issues.

TABLE 7-8

Year to Year Growth of GNP
In Current Market Prices

Years	Percent	Years	Percent
1946–1969	6.9*	1973–74	14.9
1969–70	9.8	1974–75	24.2
1970–71	11.7	1975–76	18.6
1971–72	10.6	1976–77	13.2
1972–73	15.3	1977–78	11.0

* Average for period. In only two cases [1947–48 = 11.6% and 1951–52 = 10.0%] did the annual increase exceed 9.0%, and in only six other cases did it exceed 8.0%.

Source: computed from *Annual Abstract of Statistics*, various issues, and *Monthly Digest of Statistics*, March, 1979.

TABLE 7-9

Retail Price Index

1973 = 100

Year	Index	Percent change on previous year	Year	Index	Percent change on previous year
1946–67	–	3.8*	1973	100.0	9.2
1968	69.7	4.7	1974	116.1	16.1
1969	73.5	5.5	1975	144.2	24.2
1970	78.1	6.3	1976	168.1	16.5
1971	85.5	9.5	1977	194.7	15.8
1972	91.6	7.1	1978	212.9	9.3

* Average for the period.

Source: adapted from *Annual Abstract of Statistics*, various issues.

Table 7-10 gives some, but only some, idea of the distribution of income among classes. One cannot equate "Wages and Salaries" with working class incomes, for the figures include the salaries of management. "Income from Self-Employment" includes both professional incomes (i.e., of doctors, dentists, lawyers, consultants) and incomes which are largely "working class wages" (e.g., of retail butchers, tobacconists, barbers, publicans). "Rents" and "Dividends" certainly accrue in much greater part to the upper classes; but they also accrue in some small part to the less well-off, especially through insurance policies. "Interest" obviously goes to the well-to-do, but also to others: from small holdings of government bonds bought at post offices and, more importantly, from shares in building societies. The distribution of income is not especially skewed toward the rich, and certainly less skewed than it was immediately after the Second War. Note that these shares would be reduced by more than a fifth expressed as percentages of GNP since depreciation and indirect business taxes do not accrue to anyone as income (see Table 7-11).

The effect of the tax system on income distribution is mixed. About one half of central government revenues come from progressive and proportional direct taxes: personal and corporate income taxes, inheritance and gift taxes, and social security taxes. The other half comes from regressive taxes: VAT, customs duties, and taxes on tobacco, beer, and liquor.

Table 7-11: welfare state expenditures have risen markedly since the late 1940s. It is commonly said that the British economy is in a parlous state because the government takes such a large share of the GNP. A common inference is that "the government" spends this money and therefore that "people" do not. Actually, as a perusal of Table 7-11 will show, about a half--sometimes a bit more, sometimes a bit less--of direct taxes return to consumers in cash benefits from social security (pensions, unemployment compensation, sickness and disability benefits). As the last column shows, consumer decisions about how to spend their money incomes determine the composition of over two-thirds of the national product.

Table 7-12 shows that individuals and families directly and personally enjoy three-quarters of the GNP. While political processes rather than consumer choice determine the composition of benefits in kind, one doubts that consumers

TABLE 7-10
Factor Shares in Total Factor Incomes Before Taxes
(Annual Averages for Selected Periods)

Years	Wages & salaries %	Income from self-employment %	Rents, dividends & interest %
1946–48	71.5	14.1	14.5
1949–51	74.6	13.6	11.8
1953–55	77.2	12.0	10.8
1961–63	77.8	9.7	12.5
1967–69	77.4	9.5	13.2
1971–73	77.4	11.3	11.4
1975–77	78.8	10.5	10.7

Source: computed from *Annual Abstract of Statistics*, various issues.

TABLE 7-11
Disposable Money Incomes as Percentages of GNP
(Annual Averages for Selected Periods)

Years	Total factor incomes before taxes	Factor incomes after taxes	Social security benefits*	Total disposable money incomes
1949–51	74.2	63.4	4.8	68.2
1953–55	72.7	63.1	5.0	68.1
1961–63	75.1	63.0	6.1	69.1
1967–69	73.3	58.1	7.4	65.5
1971–73	74.4	58.7	7.6	66.3
1975–77	78.0	57.8	8.9	66.7

* Social security benefits computed for fiscal years so that
  periods start and end three months later than periods for
  factor money incomes: e.g., social security for 1971–73
  is actually for April, 1971, through March, 1974.

Source: computed from *Annual Abstract of Statistics*, various issues.

116

would be in any way happier if that portion of GNP (4+%) devoted to health care "in kind" were left with consumers in cash (see "The National Health Service" in Chapter 11). The other benefits in kind help only some people directly and personally, but many feel that they do make for a better society for all (see "The Rest of the Welfare State" in Chapter 11).

Table 7-13 presents the same data from the point of view of the government's accounts. If one considers Table 7-13 along with Table 7-14, one notes that of the percentage of GNP spent directly by the government (21 to 26%) a significant portion accrues as real benefits to people.

In presenting data on welfare state expenditures I have not included "Education," which the British often include in their classification "Social Services," because public education long antedates the welfare state and is regarded throughout the developed world as a "normal" expenditure of government.

TABLE 7-12
Percentages of GNP Enjoyed Directly by People
(Annual Averages for Selected Periods)

Years	Disposable money incomes %	Incomes in kind* %	Total real incomes %
1949–51	68.2	6.5	74.7
1953–55	68.1	6.2	74.3
1961–63	69.1	5.7	74.8
1967–69	65.5	6.9	72.4
1971–73	66.3	7.6	73.9
1975–77	66.7	9.9	76.6

* Incomes in kind computed for fiscal years: see note to Table 7-11.

Source: computed from *Annual Abstract of Statistics*, various issues.

Table 7-14 shows the "real" role of government as a user of the nation's productive resources. The figures are evidence of the falsity of the wide-spread view that government in Britain absorbs an enormous portion of the nation's resources or product. The proportion is higher than in the U.S., where it has been running at slightly over 20%, but is hardly grossly higher. Note also that about a fifth of government expenditures on goods and services are devoted to capital investment, which increases Britain's productive efficiency (e.g., roads, and schools as training centers) and her ability to supply consumer benefits (e.g., hospitals and schools as humanizing influences).

Taking Tables 7-11 through 7-14 together, it is clear that a major function of the British government is to transfer purchasing power from earners and other income recipients to the beneficiaries of the welfare state--two classes which overlap a good deal, especially over people's lifetimes (see Chapter 11 and "The Fundamental Problem" in Chapter 12).

Table 7-15 provides evidence of the small but not tiny role which government plays in financing investment for the production of marketed goods (see next section). It actually understates the role because government allows many deductions and rapid write-offs against taxes for investments in capital equipment. It is not clear what the effect of these programs on the national budget are. An investment grant will show up as an expenditure by the government; an investment allowance will not show up in government accounts because it is a permission not to pay taxes on a portion of profits and so will make its presence felt only by its absence from the revenue side of the national budget. Accelerated write-off of depreciation shifts government revenues from the near to the farther future and results not only in lower current government revenue but also in higher current government expenditures on servicing the national debt.

Table 7-16 provides the basis for the frequent complaints that local council governments are becoming "bloated." That their expenditures have grown is beyond question; whether it is "bloating" is another question (see "The Rest of The Welfare State" in Chapter 11). Over 40% of the increase in local spending since 1953-56 has been on education (from 2.8% to 5.9% in 1974-77)--and much of this increase is a result of agreements with teachers negotiated by the central government and of the decision by the central government to turn all schools into comprehensive schools (see "Education and Equality" in Chapter 2). It might also be noted that the *increase* in spending on

TABLE 7-13
Welfare State Expenditures
As Percentages of GNP
(Annual Averages for Selected Periods)

Years	In kind* (%)	Social security (%)	Total (%)
1949–52	6.5	4.7	11.2
1953–56	6.2	5.0	11.2
1961–64	5.7	6.1	11.8
1967–70	6.9	7.4	14.3
1971–74	7.6	7.6	15.2
1974–77	9.9	8.9	18.8

* National Health Service; Personal Social Services;
  School Meals, Milk and Welfare Food; Housing. And see
  note to Table 7–12.

Source: computed from *Annual Abstract of Statistics*,
         various issues, with annual data for GNP adjusted
         to fiscal years by weighting.

TABLE 7-14
Total Government Expenditures on Goods and Services
As Percentages of GNP
(Annual Averages for Periods)

Years	Public authorities' current expenditure on goods & services (%)	Gross domestic fixed capital formation by central & local governments (%)	Total government expenditures on goods & services (%)
1946–48	17.3	–	–
1949–51	15.4	–	–
1953–55	16.8	4.2	21.0
1961–63	16.5	3.4	19.9
1967–69	17.1	4.8	22.9
1971–73	17.7	4.5	22.2
1975–77	20.2	4.1	24.3

Source: computed from *Annual Abstract of Statistics*,
         various issues.

TABLE 7-15

Direct Financing of Investment by Government
(Annual Averages for Selected Periods)

Years	Fixed capital formation by public corporations (% of GNP)	Capital grants to private sector (% of GNP)	Net lending to private sector (% of GNP)	Net expenditure on company securities (% of GNP)	Subsidies* (% of GNP)
1961–63	3.22	0.36	0.37	–	1.98
1967–69	3.60	1.39	0.19	0.06	1.93
1971–73	2.91	1.20	0.42	0.05	1.84
1975–77	3.54	0.85	0.15	0.07	2.82

* Some to agriculture. See "The Common Agricultural Policy" in Chapter 9.

Source: computed from *Annual Abstract of Statistics*, various issues.

education was three times the *total* expenditure on those
social services which have become the object of so much
criticism (see Table 11-7). Finally, the figures in this
table exaggerate the local government drain on real resources because a quarter of total expenditure are transfer
payments (interest, grants, subsidies).

TABLE 7-16
Local Government Expenditures
As Percentages of GNP
(Annual Averages for Selected Periods)

Years	Total expenditures
1946–49	11.5
1949–52	10.4
1953–56	10.8
1961–64	12.5
1967–70	15.6
1971–74	18.3
1975–77	18.9

Source: computed from *Annual Abstract
of Statistics,* various issues.

Welfare state expenditures as a proportion of GNP have
increased greatly during the 1960s, by about 50%. The
causes and consequences of this increase are discussed in
the next section, but it should be recalled that the rise
since 1973 is a result of rising wages and salaries and of
stagnation and unemployment in the rest of the economy--
events which have raised the financial costs of government
relative to national product but have not meant that more
real resources are devoted to government activities.

PRODUCTIVITY AND THE GROWTH OF
THE GOVERNMENT SECTOR

While rising productivity *is* material progress, it
should not be thought that increasing productivity fits
easily and smoothly into an economy. As the productivity
of labor in any firm, industry, or larger sector of the
economy grows, the sales of that firm, industry, or sector

must grow at the same rate as or more than productivity grows *or* some of the labor force must be laid-off. Of course, everyone in the industry is happy if the market for the product grows faster than the increase in productivity: existing employees have greater job security and more opportunities to earn overtime; the firms make larger profits; and those newly added to the work force become more cheerful. But there can be redundancies (lay-offs) if the market is expanding less rapidly than is productivity. If manhour productivity increases at, say, 4% a year--and that is approximately the annual rate at which labor productivity in British industry increased from 1961 to 1974--while sales increase at, say, 2%, then 2% of the workforce must be laid off each year.

Historically the economic growth of the industrial economies has been sufficient--by and large, over the years, and forgetting periods of depression--to absorb those made redundant by technological advance. For some industries the rate of growth of the market far exceeds the rate of growth of productivity, absorbing more and more workers: air transport and electronics are recent examples. For other industries the market grows more slowly; and for some it shrinks; but the total effect has always been the reabsorption of labor made redundant in one industry by other expanding industries *or employments*.

This latter point is important. By no means has all the reabsorption been into other industries. As an economy becomes highly industrialized all sorts of expanding services tend to replace industries as the new employer for those made redundant (laid-off) or newly joining the labor force: first more ushers in more movie theatres, then more TV cameramen, and so on. There are also more doctors and nurses and hairdressers and plumbers and lawyers and psychologists and termite eradicators. And there are more public servants: policemen, firemen, schoolteachers, social workers, auditors, sanitarians, and administrators and their clerical staffs. It has been, to a very large degree, to the constantly increasing productivity of labor in industry that we owe our constantly expanding and more varied services.

Three words of warning are here in order. First, the process of reabsorption can be long and painful. A whole generation of handloom weavers and their families suffered enormously during the first half of the 19th century. The long, slow contraction of the textile industry in this century is another case in point. Secondly, the process does not work at all, or at all well, during periods of depression, or even during periods of only slowly increasing demand. Thirdly, and related to the first two, the process is always easier for the unskilled or semi-skilled than for the skilled. The case of the handloom weavers is the classic case of the problem for the skilled, but a much more recent contrast illustrates both the second and third points. The unskilled and semi-skilled labor made redundant by the shrinkage of railway traffic during the 1950s and 1960s shifted fairly easily into other employments, but the skilled workers in shipbuilding had no place to go when it became apparent in the late 1970s that the shipbuilding industry would have to contract a lot and quickly.

What has been happening in Britain is that industrial productivity has been rising at a respectable rate by historical standards--and not all that badly by international comparisons (see Tables 7-1 and 7-2)--but that the markets for the output of British industry have not been increasing nearly so rapidly. The consequence has been a shrinking number employed in industry, a shrinkage much greater than the shrinkages in other countries and much greater than that to be expected from the long-term tendency for services to expand. Britain's public sector (especially local government services) has absorbed the redundant labor, including the "excess over to-be-expected." This has meant that the proportion of *non-marketed output* as a proportion of GNP has grown a great deal.[2]

A shift into non-marketed services requires a sizable increase in the burden of taxation. The wages and salaries of the additional government employees and the incomes generated as the private sector supplies more equipment for the use of the additional public employees compete for marketed output with the incomes generated in the marketed sector. The result would be increasingly rampant inflation if the government did not tax away an additional amount of income larger than the additional expenditure by government on non-marketed services. Increased taxation would not necessarily be a disaster. In fact, taxes have been increasing for many years as the roles of governments have expanded, and this expansion has had its merits. Thus

> . . . almost all the civilized activities of a
> modern society are wholly or largely non-marketed.
> Both Convent Garden [ballet, opera] and Glyndebourne
> [opera] cover only a fraction of their costs by
> selling tickets, and universities, schools, art
> galleries, libraries, and hospitals produce out-
> puts which are almost entirely non-marketed.

Defense is also non-marketed. . . It can almost
be said that a country with a larger non-market
sector will be either militarily stronger or
more civilized. . . There would, of course, be
no adverse response to a diversion of resources
of this kind if the increased social spending
was a direct and exact response to workers'
preference. . .[3]

It may be that the shift from private goods to public services has been greater than the British population wants--
Bacon and Eltis feel that this is the case, and this is why
there have been constant inflationary pressures and why
British imports of manufactured goods are constantly on the
rise. However, the case may be somewhat different, and more
complex. Perhaps it is an incomplete realization of how
much is in fact required to accomplish the aims of the welfare state--compounded on the one side by feelings that the
poorer are paying for the civilization of the richer (and
for the Glyndebourne Opera, they are) and by feelings that
the richer could pay the whole of the additional burden
(they plainly, arithmetically cannot); and on the other
side by a feeling on the part of the economically secure
that social security benefits are generous (they are not).
Further experience, not only of inflation but also of what
public services must be given up and with what consequences
may induce people to accept a higher burden of taxation--
but then again, further experience may convince people that
what they really do want is more goods and fewer services.
At present one cannot say whether the logic of Bacon and
Eltis' view is or is not the psychologic of the British
people.

ENDNOTES

1. For two examples of such comparisons, see Angus
   Maddison, *Economic Growth in the West*. N.Y.: 20th
   Century Fund, 1964, p. 140.
2. The argument in this and the following paragraphs owes
   much to Robert Bacon and Walter Eltis, who have spelled
   out the relationships among productivity, markets,
   British policy, and public sector employment in *Britain's
   Economic Problem: Too Few Producers*. New York:
   St. Martin's Press, 1976, *passim*. However, other arguments of mine in this book--about international and
   domestic markets, prices and quality--should not be
   blamed on Messers. Bacon and Eltis.
3. *Ibid.*, pp. 31 and 100.

8

THOSE FOREIGNERS: BRITAIN AND THE INTERNATIONAL ECONOMY

Foreign trade and the balance of payments--or, more precisely, their consequences--are intimately entwined with all of Britain's domestic problems and policies. Table 8-1 indicates one reason why international trade is so important to Britain. She imports more than any other of the larger developed economies and only Italy's and Germany's exports are as large or larger a proportion of GNP. Her situation is more precarious than Italy's because Britain is also an international financial center (see Chapter 8). Britain's dependence on foreign trade has been increasing. The years since 1973 reflect disruption in the world economy and depression at home, but the percentages were rising before 1973. It has not been a matter of "irresponsibly" increasing imports while failing to pay for them: exports have been rising as well, recovering rapidly from the 1974 slump (see Table 8-2).

The first, immediate consequence of the dependence upon imports is that the British price level is very sensitive to changes in world prices. The necessary and immediate effect of a 5% rise in the prices of Britain's imports is a 1% rise in her domestic price level (since about a fifth of her GNP is spent on imported goods). The situation is actually a bit worse because Britain imports an unusually high proportion of raw materials and foodstuffs, whose prices have tended to rise more than world prices in general during recent booms. Since raw material imports are important to many British industries there is also an immediate upward push on the prices of British exports. This effect is much exacerbated when the exchange value of the pound declines. Then the prices of all imported goods rise by an amount proportional to the fall in the value of the pound.

TABLE 8-1
Imports & Exports as Percentages of GNP
for Selected Developed Countries
(Annual Averages for the Years 1974–76)

Country	Imports (%)	Exports (%)
France	18.3	16.3
Germany	18.3	22.6
Italy*	24.6	20.1
Japan	12.4	11.9
U.S.A.	7.3	6.9
U.K.	25.7	20.1

* 1974 and 1975 only.

Source: computed from U.N., *Statistical Yearbook, 1977*, Tables 151 and 194.

TABLE 8-2
Exports as Percentages of Imports
(Calendar Years or Annual Averages for Selected Periods)

Years	Percent	Years	Percent
1946–48	70.3	1971–73	86.5
1949–51	74.4	1974	71.6
1953–55	76.6	1975–76	82.4
1961–63	86.3	1977–78	90.6
1967–69	83.7		

Source: computed from *Annual Abstract of Statistics*, various issues, and *Monthly Digest of Statistics*, March, 1979.

The second and associated effect is indirect. The standard economic argument is that a devaluation of a currency (or a rise in prices abroad) will make the prices of goods and services produced in the devaluing country relatively cheaper and therefore more attractive to foreigners. However, this argument assumes that British prices are set independently of foreign prices, which is a most doubtful proposition indeed. British suppliers of goods to the British market in competition with similar imports will quite naturally--after all, British suppliers do read the newspapers and do learn what their competitors are doing--

these British suppliers will raise the prices of their own goods to match the higher import prices. Similarly, firms which supply both the domestic and export markets will raise their prices in pounds to match the prices expressed in foreign currencies. Thus a 5% devaluation of the pound can be expected to raise British prices by a good deal more than 1%. The prices of many British goods will soon rise by the full 5%.

A third effect is that Britain is somewhat more subject to wage-push inflation than are other large countries. It is not a difference in kind--rising prices create demands for higher wages everywhere--but in degree. A rise in world raw material and food prices has more effect in setting off a wage-price spiral in Britain than in these other countries because world prices have a greater effect on British prices. It is true that some smaller countries-- e.g., The Netherlands or Denmark--are even more heavily engaged in foreign trade. It may be, however, that they have learned better than the British to live with the problem. But it is also true that they do not suffer from the associated financial problems discussed below.

The fourth, and perhaps the most important consequence-- a consequence which stems not only from the importance of foreign trade but at least as much from the importance of international finance--is that domestic fiscal and monetary policies must often be made subject to the exigencies of Britain's international economic position no matter what other policies may seem more appropriate from the points of view of domestic aims or internal development.

Since it is a common view--as common in Britain as elsewhere--that Britain has done badly on the foreign trade front, it may be best to address that issue before discussing more of the complexities. If one compares Britain's performance with that of Japan or Germany, Britain does come out badly, but their performances have been remarkable by any standards. No other, non-oil-exporting countries have been in the league with Japan and Germany. Tables 8-2, 8-3, and 8-4 show a respectable, even an improving record for Britain. While the value of imports increased by 249% between 1953-55 and 1971-73 the value of exports increased by 288%. 1974, the year of the fourfold increase in oil prices and of the 3-day work week due to the miners' strike, should be taken as exceptional--and was, in fact, no worse than the immediate postwar years. Table 8-5 provides an answer to the charge that, even if there has been improve-

TABLE 8-3
Values of Imports & Exports
(Calendar Year or Annual Averages for Selected Periods)

Years	Imports (c.i.f.) £mn	Exports (f.o.b.) £mn
1946–48	1,725	1,212
1949–51	2,927	2,177
1953–55	3,516	2,695
1961–63	4,719	4,074
1967–69	7,550	6,334
1971–73	12,266	10,460
1974–76	26,288	20,862
1978	40,969	37,363

Source: computed from *Annual Abstract of Statistics*, various issues, and *Monthly Digest of Statistics*, March, 1979.

TABLE 8-4
Indices of Volume of Foreign Trade

1970 = 100

(Averages for Selected Periods)

Years	Imports (Index)	Exports (Index)
1946–48	36.6	34.8
1949–51	43.9	50.2
1953–55	50.8	52.9
1961–63	67.4	67.1
1967–69	91.4	87.9
1971–73	117.8	115.7
1976–78	137.5	151.2

Source: computed from *Annual Abstract of Statistics*, various issues, and *Monthly Digest of Statistics*, March, 1979.

TABLE 8-5

Balance of Payments as Percentages of GNP
(Annual Averages for Selected Periods)

Years	Percent	Years	Percent
1946–48	−2.26	1971–73	+0.29
1949–51	−0.11	1974	−4.15
1953–55	+0.25	1975–76	−1.30
1961–63	+0.28	1977–78	+0.18
1967–69	−0.13	1949–73	+0.30

Source: computed from *Annual Abstract of Statistics,*
various issues, and *Monthly Digest of
Statistics*, March, 1979.

ment, the record is still very poor. There have been good
years and bad years since the end of postwar reconstruction,
but over the whole period from 1949 to 1973 Britain ran a
surplus on her current balance of payments of +0.3% of her
GNP. Even if one includes 1974 and 1975 in the period, the
27 year balance is still positive, although only at an
average of +0.06% of GNP.

However, another aspect of Britain's problem is implied by Table 8-5. The margin between surplus and deficit
on current account is small. With imports and exports each
running at about a fifth of GNP and the annual surplus on
the current balance at +0.3% of GNP, a rise in imports or
a fall in exports of as little as 5% can swing the current
balance from a surplus of +0.3% of GNP to a deficit of −0.3%,
which, on the record, appears to be enough to cause strong
downward pressure on the value of the pound in the international exchange markets.

Another common view is that Britain has been pricing
herself out of international markets. A proof or disproof
of this view would require an item by item comparison of
British prices with the prices of her foreign competitors,
but insofar as gross figures can be revealing, the numbers
in Table 8-6 lend little support to view. The prices of
British exports have risen roughly in line with the prices
of the goods she imports. However, the numbers cannot show
"over-pricing" when the over-priced good loses its markets
abroad and so disappears from the prices of exported goods.
British motorcycles might be a good example, except that
they became not so much over priced as under qualitied.

TABLE 8-6
Unit Values of Imports and Exports
(Annual Averages for Selected Periods)
1970 = 100*

Periods	Imports (c.i.f.)	Exports (f.o.b.)
1948–50	61.4	53.5
1953–55	80.4	66.4
1961–63	76.2	74.6
1967–69	90.4	89.7
1971–73	117.7	114.2
1978	331.9	303.9

* Chain-linked at 1977, 1970, 1964, 1954, and 1950.

Source: computed from *Annual Abstract of Statistics*, various issues, and *Monthly Digest of Statistics*, March, 1979.

The problem of the weakness of the pound in foreign exchange markets stems largely from Britain's important position in international finance. The British started the postwar period with a markedly over-valued pound (Ł1 = $4.02), with war-worn industrial equipment, and with a high domestic demand competing against export markets for limited British output. Devaluation to Ł1 = $2.80 followed fairly shortly in 1949. The British managed to maintain this value until 1967 when another devaluation, to Ł1 = $2.40, was forced upon them. After exchange rates were floated in the early 1970s continued pressure on the pound reduced its exchange value further so that it fell to $1.55 in 1976. In the late 70s the pounds "trade-weighted" value (an average of its exchange value in other currencies, each currency given a weight in averaging proportional to that nation's importance in British trade) was only slightly more than 60% of its 1971 value. [Please see "Postscript" at the end of this Chapter for changes in the situation in 1979.]

There are several--by no means consistent--considerations which bear upon the value of a nation's currency. One is its balance of trade. The more that Britain imports relative to the amount it exports, the more British businesses are demanding foreign currencies relative to foreigners' demands for pounds, thereby forcing down the value of the pound in terms of other currencies. However, Britain had an adverse (negative, imports exceeding exports) balance

of trade for many years without suffering pressure upon its
exchange rate because it had a favorable balance of payments for invisibles (earnings from shipping, from financing
international trade, and from insuring foreigners, their
ventures, and their property). Foreigners' demand for
these services translated into foreign demand for the pound.
Also, previous investments abroad by the British earned interest and dividends in foreign currencies and when these
were repatriated to Britain there was further demand for
pounds. Finally, the pound sterling--the traditional name
for the Britain's national currency, dating back to the
days when the pound was a silver currency, before Britain
became the first gold standard country in 1821--the pound
sterling served as the international reserve currency for
the colonies and commonwealths of the British Empire and for
a number of other countries, and hence, like gold, was always in demand. The pound has retained this status, albeit
for a decreasing number of countries, to the present day,
and Britain is still, along with the U.S., a major "bank"
for Arab "petro-dollars." Until 1914 these other demands
for the pound were more than sufficient to maintain the
pound at $4.86. Furthermore, they not only covered the
adverse balance of trade, they allowed British businesses
and finance houses to demand foreign currencies in large
quantities to pay for British investments abroad (that is,
to export capital). In fact, after 1914 the invisible
earnings and the role of the pound sterling as an international reserve currency kept the pound the second strongest currency (after the dollar) until the Second World War
and were the reasons why the British could maintain the
pound at $2.80 for eighteen years after the devaluation of
1949.

Even with a "floating" pound whose dollar value fluctuated from $2.10 to $1.55 to $2.30 in the late 1970s, London
remained, along with New York, one of the world's two centers of finance. It may still be larger than New York in
strictly international terms. This means that at all times
Britain has a large volume of short-term debt owed to
foreigners. That the short-term debt is more than balanced,
in ultimate accounting terms, by the long-term assets she
owns abroad does her no good during the short periods of
international speculation against the pound. Britain's
position can be likened to that of a bank which has some
very good assets due later and customers clamoring to have
their demand deposits paid now. As a center of international finance London is where many foreigners will invest their

temporarily surplus funds in short-term assets which they
can liquidate in a hurry should they decide to sell pounds
and buy some other currency. Also as a center of finance,
Britain is subject to speculation against the pound by importers and exporters, and the large volume of imports and
exports increases the effects of speculation. If it is
felt that the value of the pound is likely to fall soon,
importers will try to buy foreign currencies now while the
value of the pound is still high, to pay for their imports
later. Exporters will try to delay collection of payments
owed them so that they can exchange the foreign currencies
they earn later, when the foreign currencies will buy more
pounds. These considerations mean that the British are much
less able to withstand speculation against (or in favor of)
their currency than are, say, the Germans or the Japanese.
In addition to the fact that these countries are not so
deeply involved in international finance, their lesser involvement also permits them to exercise more stringent
exchange controls.

In addition to providing finance for international
trade, the City of London is also a major center for arranging financing for firms all over the world. Although
not providing all the funds, by any means, the merchant
bankers of the City sell their services as arrangers and
underwriters to foreign banks and firms. It was the City
which created the Eurodollar market. Then, London is still
the largest international center for insurance. Table 8-7
shows how important to Britain's balance of payments are
the services it provides foreigners. The gross amount
earned from private services amounts to about a third of
the amount earned by merchandise exports. While net invisible earning are much less, they are appreciably larger
than the small surpluses typical of the current balance of
payments. It has been suggested that Britain get out of
the business of being a world financial center, the longer
term benefits in the form of a lessened sensitivity of the
pound to international speculation outweighing, in this
view, the small net addition to GNP from earnings on invisibles. But for such a policy to succeed not only would
Britain have to get out of the business, she would also
have to get foreigners to stop using the services of British firms--and it is not clear how she could do this and
still abide by the rules for good members of the western
international community or the European Economic Community
(the Common Market). A first step in the direction of with-
drawal from a primary position in international finance was
made in December, 1976, when Britain agreed with the International Monetary Fund, as part of an arrangement for a

TABLE 8-7

Current Balance of Payments:
Selected Invisibles* as Percentages of GNP
(Calendar Years or Annual Averages for Selected Periods)

Years	Private services credits only (%)	Net private services (%)	Net interest profits & dividends (%)
1954–56	5.39	0.74	1.11
1961–63	4.94	0.75	1.10
1967–69	5.46	1.19	0.90
1971–73	6.54	1.46	1.19
1975–77	7.53	2.16	0.69

* Excludes Government Services and Government and Private
  Transfers.
Source: *Annual Abstract of Statistics,* various issues.

large standby credit, to cease financing the trade of "third
countries" (e.g., trade between, say, Australia and Japan).

The situation presents Britain with unpleasant alternatives. Being a center of finance, financial services,
and insurance weakens her ability to maintain the value of
the pound, but not being a center would cost her dearly.

INTERNATIONAL ECONOMY AND DOMESTIC POLICY

For the past twenty-five years the British response to
pressure on the pound has been essentially two-fold: interest rates in the City are raised in an effort to induce
foreigners to buy short-term sterling assets to tide over
the crisis; and government expenditures have been limited
or taxes raised in order to reduce aggregate purchasing
power and thus demand for imports.   The methods have worked
fairly well in the crises--from 1949 to 1967 there were no
devaluations of the pound--but the long-term effects have
not been so happy.   "Stop-go" policies--dampening down
domestic demand when there has been pressure on sterling
and stimulating domestic demand when the pressure has been
met--have tended, in the long-run, to reduce investment
rather than consumption or government expenditure on currently produced goods and services; and this goes some way
toward accounting for the slower rate of economic growth in
Britain than on the continent.   While the reduction in

domestic demand (not absolutely, until 1974, but relative
to what it would otherwise have been) may have "released"
some goods for export which would have been bought at home,
the lower rate of investment has probably reduced the longer
term level of exports below what it might have been. The
"high interest rates,dampened demand" of "stop" policies
have thus not been a happy choice--but, as pointed out
above, they are a consequence of Britain's international
financial role. And, of course, a necessary consequence of
Britain's efforts to be part of an increasingly free international economy.

There has been, and is, an alternative set of policies.
The British could meet pressure on the pound by limiting
imports and limiting British investment abroad.   Imports
could be limited by requiring importers to get a license to
import and then limiting the number of licenses, granting
them generously for imports of food and of raw materials
and semi-processed goods necessary to the functioning of
British industry but very stingily for imports of goods
produced in Britain or goods which do not seem so necessary
to the welfare of the British people. This would allow the
British to maintain a higher level of domestic investment
and its consequent high level of domestic aggregate demand
without having to devalue the pound and thus import an even
higher level of inflation. Other consequences would be a
less free trade, a reduction in the role of the City in international business, and an increased role for government
decisions about patterns of output and consumption. The
Conservatives regard these consequences as too high "costs,"
as do many on the right and into the center of the Labour
Party. The left wing of the Labour Party, however, does
not think of these latter consequences as "costs" but as
additional benefits from the policies. Although only a
rather small minority now favors controls as a means of
handling the problems presented by foreigners, continuing
pressure on the pound and continuing inflation may lead
others to change their minds--or might, except that the
savings in foreign exchange costs and the foreign exchange
revenues from the exploitation of North Sea oil are likely
to solve (or postpone) Britain's problems with foreigners
for some time.

Two sets of events of recent years are changing Britain's international position, and in opposite directions.
On the one side, Britain is losing out not only in competition for international markets but in competition with
foreign companies in her domestic markets. On the other
side, the discovery and development of North Sea oil is both

reducing British dependence on imports and increasing her export earnings. Up until 1978 the worsening competitive position dominated. Beginning in about 1980 the gains from oil should dominate--for how long, it is hard to say. The North Sea oil fields have been given lives of about twenty years, but a continued worsening of the competitive position could overtake the gains from oil before then. Or the gains from oil could be the foundation of more competitive domestic industries. [A colleague has suggested to me that the determining factor will be plain luck, and that British luck is plain bad.]

EXPORTS, IMPORTS, AND QUALITY

Britain's deteriorating competitive position in international markets is often illustrated with figures showing that her share of world markets is shrinking. However, these numbers do not prove much because a shrinking share is a necessary algebraic consequence of the rise of other countries into the group of industrialized nations. Table 8-8 is therefore probably a better indication of what has been happening. If one asks oneself the question, "What sorts of goods would one expect Britain to produce most competitively?" a plausible answer seems to be, "Modern or high technology goods." At least, such appears to be the case from reading the British economic and financial press: both its analyses and its reports on what public, industrial, and trade union leaders say. Consideration of Britain's natural endowments and her contributions to science and technology would lead to the same conclusion. The four industries for which data are presented in Table 8-8 fit the class of goods in the manufacture and marketing of which one expects Britain to be competitive. But since the early 1960s foreigners have been remarkably successful at penetrating Britain's domestic market in three of these industries. Motor vehicles could be described as a disaster industry. It is curious, and perhaps significant, that of the four industries the one requiring the least technological sophistication--iron and steel--performed best in competition with foreigners.

It is a puzzling picture and no one really knows why so much of Britain's domestic market in these and other industries has been lost to foreigners. Inefficiencies, reflected both in cost accounting and in manning levels, have been thoroughly documented in recent studies, but the same inefficiencies were found by productivity teams comparing British and American industries just after the Second War,

TABLE 8-8
Trends of Imports as Percentages of Exports:
Selected Industries
(Calendar Years or Annual Averages for Selected Periods*)

Chemicals			Motor Vehicles (includes chasses; excludes tractors)	
Years	%			
1962	49.9		Years	%
1963	55.3			
1964–66	61.5		1962–65	7.1
1967–72	67.1		1966–69	12.6
1973	70.5		1970	19.1
1974	73.9		1971	32.9
1975	64.7		1972	63.1
			1973	70.5

Machinery & Transport Equipment			Iron & Steel	
Years	%		Years	%
1962–63	22.8		1962–65	54.1
1964–66	29.9		1966–69	52.9
1967–71	43.3		1970–73	61.5
1972–75	61.8			

* Where there has been little year to year variation, or
  no apparent trend, the figures for these years have been
  averaged.
Source: computed from *Annual Abstract of Statistics,*
          various issues.

15 to 20 years before import penetration began to become so
large. If it is true that British manning levels and unit
costs are higher than German, French, or American, and have
fallen less than German, French, or Japanese, it is also
true that the pound has declined in value over the years so
that one might expect the increased cost of imported goods
to make up for the relative inefficiency of British industry.
Also, the 4% per year increase in manhour productivity in
Britain from the early sixties to the mid-seventies should
have done a good deal to limit import penetration.

    In the discussion of performance in Chapter 7 I sugges-
ted that the British just do not make a number of things
well, or do not make the right things. This may be an

important reason for rising levels of import penetration
and the less-than-hoped-for rise in the volume of exports.
This is not so much a matter of costs and prices as a matter of producing goods with traits or qualities which potential buyers find inferior to the traits or qualities of competing goods. A scene in a CBS "60 Minutes" program a few
years ago amply illustrated the point. A British business-
man was showing the differences between the British and the
foreign motorcycles he had for sale. Pump, pump, pump, he
went at the pedal of the British cycle: it finally started.
Then he put a key in a Japanese cycle, turned the key, and
off the motor roared. The cost difference, and therefore
the price difference, between the two models could not have
been large: the weight of the raw materials was about the
same; the labor involved in fitting the parts was about the
same; British engineers are certainly capable of designing
a self-starting motorcycle. What appears to be the case is
that the British were just continuing to make what they had
been making, perhaps 4% per year more efficiently--but making something no one particularly wants these days. If one
has driven British, German, American, and Japanese made
cars one has experienced the CBS show on a lesser level:
British made cars are just more trouble to keep running
smoothly. If they sold more cheaply, one might well decide
to face the troubles and save the cash; but ill-designed or
ill-fitted equipment is no cheaper to make and to fit than
well designed and well fitted equipment.

Or take modern airplanes. The British invented the
jet; the first commercial jet airliner (the Comet) was British. But the Comet fell apart in the air three times too
often and a long time passed before the British sorted out
the problems. Rolls Royce (Aeroengines) is still a leading,
perhaps the world's leading manufacturer of jet engines, and
the British make good aircraft wings, but the rest of the
market was lost to the Americans, and now to the Europeans.
It was not incompetence: a decade after the demise of the
Comet the British produced the BA 111, as nice a mid-sized
commercial jet as one could find at the time. But then no
more.

The puzzle, the mystery remains. Arrogance? Possibly,
but in the circumstances, one would think unlikely. Stupidity? Not by any usual measure of stupidity. Bullheaded-
ness? Possibly. How does one find out? And if one could
find out, what could one--Chancellor of the Exchequer or
Secretary of State for Industry--do about it? Perhaps as
good a guess as any about why the British just do not produce the right things at the right time is that British

society attaches prestige to the higher levels of the civil
service, to law and academia and pure science and to banking
and finance and not to engineering and marketing and listen-
ing to what others want--with the result that the better
natural talents do not enter careers in industry. But whatever the reasons, the solution is not so much more investment as better investment; not so much a new "industrial
strategy" as more imaginative (or effective) management.
Governments can redirect funds, subsidize, even give orders;
but there is no content to the order, "do something else,
or do it differently." It may be the greater emphasis on
technology among German and Japanese bankers and managers
and among French civil servants that helps account for their
countries' greater success. A problem remains, however, for
it is the less technologically sophisticated British leaders
who must be asked to become more sophisticated or to recruit
people more sophisticated in technology. It is by no means
a question of whether the leaders are willing to do so: if
a leader does not understand what technological sophistication is, how does he acquire the sophistication to identify the sophisticated?

NORTH SEA OIL

Natural gas was discovered in the southern portion of
the North Sea in the early 1960s; oil fields in the northern
portion several years later. In the earlier years the price
of oil was low, the costs relatively high, and the technology was in its infancy. But after OPEC '73 the situation
changed: the price of North Sea oil became double and more
the cost of recovering it.

Sinking wells, pumping oil, and selling it are not of
themselves a royal road to wealth. Benefiting from the exploitation of oil has its peculiarities. The major virtue
of oil finds is that the price of oil far exceeds the costs
discovering and pumping it. The difference is a costless
windfall gain to whomever has the property rights in the
oil.[1] Table 8-9 allows one to appreciate the magnitude of
the windfall. North Sea oil commands a quality premium
over Persian Gulf oil so that--with OPEC prices rising to
$20 and more--the windfall from North Sea oil is approaching
$15 per barrel.

At one extreme, if foreign oil companies were allowed
to exploit the fields for a small license fee, most of the

TABLE 8-9

Costs Per Barrel of Producing North Sea Oil

Range of Costs for the Fifteen Established Fields

	Lowest costs ($)	Median costs ($)	Highest costs ($)
Capital costs	0.80	1.80	3.60
Operating costs	1.40	3.00	4.80
Total costs	2.40	5.00	8.40

Estimates of Costs for Future Fields[@]

	Capital costs* ($)	Operating costs** ($)	Total costs ($)
Fields yielding			
200,000 bbls. per day	2.58	4.70	7.28
300,000 bbls. per day	3.36	3.68	7.06
400,000 bbls. per day	3.10	3.66	6.74
700,000 bbls. per day	3.92	3.88	7.78

[@] See source for details of how estimates were made.
* Undiscounted total outlays, including discovery.
** Allowing for inflation. Assumed rate of inflation declines from 16% in 1977 to 6% in 1981 and continues at 6% through 2000.

Source: Computed from Colin Robinson and Jon Morgan, *North Sea Oil in the Future: Economic Analysis and Government Policy* (London: Macmillan Press for Trade Policy Research Center, 1978), pp. 75-83. Costs in pounds converted into dollars at Ⱡ1.00 = $2.00.

benefits of the oil would accrue to the companies and almost none to the British or to the British balance of payments. At the other extreme, if all the oil companies were wholly British owned, all the windfall would accrue to people in Britain and to the balance of payments. Since British oil companies had neither the capital nor the expertise to exploit the North Sea, it was necessary to encourage foreign companies to search for and pump the oil. However, to make sure that the lion's share of the windfall does not go to foreigners, the international oil companies (mostly American) must bid for licenses to search, must pay royalties on the oil, must incorporate a subsidiary in Britain to serve as the legally responsible producer and thus pay corporate profits tax (the current rate is 52%), and now must pay a special tax on oil profits. They must also give the government-owned British National Oil Corporation (BNOC) a 51% share in each field. The rate of development of the fields has slowed somewhat, but the system of recouping the windfalls for Britain means the prospect of perhaps as much as Ł5 billion improvement in the balance of payments by the early or mid-1980s, extending to the end of the century or beyond.

While the largest gain by far is the windfall, there are profits to be made in supplying the drilling and pumping equipment and the human expertise. There are also large savings in the balance of payments to be had by doing so. When the North Sea fields were first being opened up the British had neither the manufacturing plant or the expertise to make the equipment, nor the expertise to do the discovering and drilling themselves. The main source of expertise and equipment was and is the United States. However, the British have been learning the technologies and constructing the needed plant. They prefer to delay the full exploitation of the oil fields until they can provide much of the equipment and expertise themselves. Developing such British capabilities is one of the roles of BNOC.

Just how much oil will be produced when are impossible questions to answer. It is a guessing game; but while the difference between, say, Ł600mn and Ł200mn in two years is important for the balance of payments in the short run, a Ł400mn not realized in the 1970s will be realized at the end of the century in a longer life for oil fields. It was this reasoning which caused the government to forbid the oil companies to pump from one field, already brought on stream, until they made provision to recover the associated natural gas rather than flare it.

POSTSCRIPT

Suddenly, in June, 1979, the pound jumped in value by 15%, reaching $2.30 in the summer. It then fell back to the range $2.15 to $2.20, while the trade-weighted index of the value of the pound rose to about 70% of its 1971 value. It is, as usual, impossible to account for the specific timing and amount of the increase. To some degree it reflected the fall in the value of the dollar, but more importantly

it was due to increasing receipts from the export of North
Sea oil. Much of the analysis of this Chapter is based on
historical experience to date, and the pound may well
suffer from over- rather than under-valuation for another
decade or two. However, all that has been said in this
Chapter about the rest of Britain's foreign trade and role
in international finance remains largely unaffected. Just
as a declining pound did not protect her domestic markets,
a rising pound should not be interpreted as the root cause
of her failure to compete in international markets. And as
North Sea oil begins to give out at the end of the century
the pre-1979 situation will recur unless there are other
major changes in the meantime. The "green currency"
problems described in the next Chapter will become less important, unless the German Mark continues to rise, but the
rest of the analysis of agricultural pricing and the
Common Market also remains substantially correct.

ENDNOTES

1. D. I. MacKay and G. A. Mackay, *The Political Economy
    of North Sea Oil* (London: Martin Robertson, 1975) is
    an excellent, unusually clear introduction to the
    economics of oil, to the rationale for British policies,
    and to the specific issues which arise from North Sea
    oil.

BRITAIN
AND THE EEC

The EEC (the European Economic Community, often called the Common Market or the Community) is a free trade area with a common customs on imports from non-EEC countries. In 1957 France, Germany, Italy, Belgium, Luxembourg, and The Netherlands signed the Treaty of Rome, founding the EEC. Fifteen years later Great Britain, Denmark and Ireland joined.

Member countries must follow common "constitutional" (Treaty of Rome, as amended) policies. They are also required to abide by decisions made by the Council of Ministers (a Minister representing each country). In the Council of Ministers Britain, France, Germany, and Italy each have ten votes, Belgium and The Netherlands five votes each, Denmark and Ireland three each, and Luxembourg two. In matters of "fundamental importance" (such as amending the Treaty or admitting new members to the EEC) unanimity is required, but on other decisions only a "qualified majority" of 41 votes from at least five states (in effect, the four major powers must have the support of at least one minor power, and all the minor powers together would have to persuade three major powers to support them). The Council can make "decisions" or "regulations" which are immediately binding upon all members, with the effect of law in each country. Such decisions must be about matters on which the Council is authorized to "legislate" by the Treaty. Where the Treaty so authorizes, the Council can give "directives" to the member states, requiring them to pass appropriate laws or make appropriate regulations. Finally, it can express "opinions" which are not themselves binding, but can give rise to further action if ignored--such as diplomatic bullying and cajoling if not actual decisions and directives. A High Court adjudicates disputes over the meaning, applica-

bility, or interpretation of the Treaty and of decisions by
the Council of Ministers. There is also a European Assembly.
Until 1979 its members were appointed by the national governments but beginning in June of 1979 its members are
elected by the citizens in each country. Whether the Assembly will tend to take on powers as a result of its popular
mandate from election is not known.

There is an EEC Commission, headquartered in Brussels
and with a President. The Commissioners (each with responsibility for an area of policy: e.g., industry, agriculture,
competition) and the Commission's employees are civil servants acting above and without regard to the national interests of their home countries. They have in fact been remarkably successful in being impartial. Their jobs are to
carry out the joint decisions of the ministers and to enforce EEC rules on all member states: first by reminding;
then by prodding; and finally, if necessary, by bringing
legal action before the High Court. In doing their jobs the
Commissioners and their civil servants effectively influence
ministers' decisions by the way they formulate issues and
prepare proposals for consideration by national ministers.

The major sources of funds for financing the common
policies of the EEC are the receipts from customs duties
and a 1% Value Added Tax (VAT: an *ad valorem* tax on the
difference between a firm's receipts from sales and what it
pays for inputs other than salaries, wages, rents, and
interest). The 1% VAT is collected by each country and
turned over to the EEC. If these funds are not sufficient,
"contributions" are levied upon the member states.

There are fairly continuous discussions designed to
"harmonize" policies among the member states. ("Harmonize"
is a favorite EEC word.) The Community takes action in
response to various problems as they arise. For instance,
in 1977 it set minimum prices for a few steel products. It
has engaged in negotiations with the Japanese to open Japan
to greater imports from the EEC and to limit Japanese exports to EEC countries. In 1978 it was trying to reach
agreement with the oil companies and the members states to
reduce petroleum refining capacity. It sets limits on the
amount of fish which each country can catch in the North
Sea. Such policies are not, however, "constitutional rules"
but joint agreements arrived at by the Council of Ministers.
The ministers do not always arrive at their agreements happily. Limits on North Sea fishing, for instance, were only
agreed after the British barred all fishing within British
waters. (In this case, the "constitutional rules" forbade

Britain to discriminate against non-British fishermen, so
Britain had to forbid British as well as non-British fishing
in British waters.) The EEC has a common "competition"
policy prohibiting restraint of trade and dual pricing in
different markets within the EEC and limiting the rights of
member governments to subsidize industries. EEC competition
policy could be described as harder on monopolistically inclined firms than policy in Britain but not so stringent as
American anti-trust policy. There is a regional policy to
help develop the lagging regions within the EEC. Finally,
and for Britain very importantly, there is the Common Agricultural Policy, referred to as "the CAP."

For years the members of the EEC have been trying to
reach agreement on a common monetary system. In late 1978
all but Britain had agreed to join in the EMS--the European
Monetary System--but with Italy and Ireland agreeing only
reluctantly. The EMS is designed to keep the exchange rate
of each currency in stable relationship to each of the
others, the EMS currencies floating as a group. Britain
refused to join because she feared that the policies required would limit her choices of domestic policies and
might lead to additional pressures on the pound as well as
to higher food prices in Britain (see below, under "CAP").
Just before the EMS was to start operations in January,
1979, France insisted upon a delay until Germany agreed to
terms which would lower the incomes of German farmers and
raise those of her own. As I write this passage the outcome is uncertain, but unless the British change their minds
about joining the EMS as currently organized, it will not
have much direct effect upon the British economy.

BRITISH ATTITUDES TOWARD THE EEC

Just why the British joined the EEC is not entirely
clear. The British attitude toward the EEC was and still
is ambivalent. In a referendum in May of 1975 the British
electorate approved joining the EEC by a 2 to 1 majority,
which seems pretty overwhelming for such votes. However,
despite an enthusiastic campaign by most leading Conservatives and the majority of the Labour cabinet to persuade
people to vote "Yes" on joining the EEC, and an equally
enthusiastic campaign by a few Labour ministers, the Labour
left, and the Conservative right for a "No" vote, an ob-
server may be justified in feeling that for a large proportion of voters the decision to vote "Yes" was, if not a
marginal decision, then one without great emotional content.
Opinion polls since 1975 indicate that a vote in 1977 or

1978 might have gone the other way and certainly would not
have been so large.

There is a good deal of evidence that the British have
been less than fully cooperative with the other members of
the EEC, and that they lack a strong commitment to take on
their fair share of the burdens (this is certainly the
French interpretation of British actions and motives).
Evidence of "footdragging" has been accumulating for twenty
years. When the "Six" (France, Germany, Italy, Belgium,
The Netherlands, and Luxembourg) began negotiating the Treaty of Rome to establish the EEC, the British view was that
the negotiations would collapse. When the Treaty was signed
in 1957, the British suggested a special arrangement whereby
the British would join the customs free area of the EEC
without undertaking to abide by many of the other rules or
to share major costs. They were, of course, turned down.
They then founded EFTA (European Free Trade Area), consisting of Britain, Norway, Sweden, Denmark, Switzerland,
Austria, and Portugal (with Finland as "associate member").
EFTA was not an important step because it largely tended to
reinforce existing patterns of trade. One suspects Britain
sponsored it as much to "thumb its nose" rudely at the Common Market Six as for any other reason. When Harold Wilson's
Labour government entered negotiations to join the EEC in
the late 1960s the British gave the impression not only
that they wanted the rules revised to suit themselves but
also that the continental members of the EEC should wel-
come Britain on whatever terms the British felt appropriate.
The British did give in on many points but, not surprisingly,
De Gaulle vetoed the British application. With De Gaulle
departed from power in France and the British willing to be
more conciliatory, British along with Irish and Danish membership was successfully negotiated under Heath's Conservative government. The Labour Party, then in opposition,
objected to the terms, so when Wilson's government came to
power the terms were renegotiated still another time. Since
1975 British ministers have rather irritated their European
colleagues in EEC ministerial conferences. Several times
the European Commission and the High Court have felt com-
pelled to tell the British to change domestic policies to
bring British procedures within the rules of the EEC.

WHY JOIN THE EEC?

The reasons why Britain joined the Common Market are
rooted in the traditional economic thought of the western
world. Among economists, liberal Conservatives, Liberals,

and rightish Labourites there is a good deal of faith in
the virtues of free trade and of large national markets
such as are found in the United States. Several elements
appear to contribute to this faith: (1) a belief in the
doctrine of comparative advantage; (2) a belief in the beneficial effects of competition; and (3) a belief that there
are economies of scale to be gained in a large market.
Whereas quite plausible arguments can be made that these
reasons for favoring common markets are founded upon more
than hopeful belief, they are not entirely persuasive and
may be even less persuasive in the case of Britain than they
are in some other cases.

(a) According to the doctrine of comparative advantage,
a good will be produced by those nations most suited to
specialize in its production. In which nations a particular
good is produced depends upon which nations are relatively
most efficient in its manufacture. With the resulting international specialization there will be "gains from trade:"
that is, the total output and consumption of all goods rise
for all the trading nations taken together and for each
trading nation separately. The freer the trade, the greater
the gains, because the greater the specialization in the
nations with the greatest relative efficiency.

Where the comparative advantage for each good lies is
determined by underlying conditions generally thought to be
pretty lasting. These advantageous conditions are mostly
natural or God-given and fixed, so that a nation's comparative advantage is regarded as unchanging. Generally, climate, soil, natural resources, the amount of labor and
capital, and the technology of production are perceived as
sources of cost advantages, the emphasis varying somewhat
from economist to economist. Such advantages are gained
independently of conscious national policy and there is
something rather permanent about a nation's specialization
in a good.

The theory presumes a good deal of reciprocal international cooperation to reduce trade restrictions, and a
good deal of competition among producers of traded goods.
But these assumptions are not its greatest weakness as a
guide to policy. Historically, the permanence of comparative advantage is questionable, and national policies have
clearly influenced specialization. Four and five centuries
ago England was an exporter of raw wool. She then brought
weavers over from the continent and became a leading producer of woollen cloth. In the 1840s Lancashire had an
overwhelming comparative advantage in manufacturing cotton

textiles. Years ago I was taught that this advantage was
in part due to Lancashire's cool, moist climate. In the
1970s Punjab State in India has a comparative advantage in
cotton textiles--and a hot, dry climate (and no air condi-
tioning). England, it has been said, experienced the Industrial Revolution first because it was an island of coal
and iron ore. Today the Japanese, without coal or iron
ore, are the world's most efficient steel producers. Artis-
tic traditions and geography are equally poor guides to
existing comparative advantages. Why the English Midlands
should have a comparative advantage in the production of
fine chinaware or why The Netherlands (with only 30 frost-
free nights a year) should have a comparative advantage in
nurseries for semi-tropical plants are aesthetic and geo-
graphical mysteries. Policy and effort can change relative
costs. An existing apparent comparative advantage may be
a poor guide for deciding upon long run specialization.

The doctrine also ignores the processes of change from
the pre-free trade situation to the ultimate reaping of the
advantages. If adjustments take many years--a generation
or more with bankruptcies and unemployment or short-time
work, as there may be in some industries--it is by no means
clear to the current sufferers from the adjustment process
that the long run benefits for another generation are worthwhile. And it is, of course, quite possible that during
that period of adjustment other events and new technologies
may have so altered circumstances that the adjustment called
for by comparative advantage may not be all that good when
seen from the vantage point of a later time.

(b) From the point of view of a particular nation,
the generally beneficial effects of competition may not be
specifically so beneficial. Certainly competition does
discipline firms producing for a market, forcing high cost
firms to become more efficient *or* driving them out of business. If less efficient firms become more efficient, that
is fine for the economy. But if the less efficient firms
are driven out of business and their business is taken over
by foreign firms producing in foreign lands, then the result
is not so good for the national economy. Proponents of
competition go on to argue that new lines of endeavor will
replace the old, inefficient lines. Perhaps new lines will
emerge, but it may take a long time indeed.

A variant, or perhaps a reinforcement, of the pro-
competition position is the "shock argument:" when plunged
into the new, more competitive situation the less efficient
firms, which have been going along happily behind some

protective barrier, will react quickly to the new threat
and change their ways. One cannot deny that this may sometimes occur--dire threats do have a way of concentrating the
mind--but one cannot help doubting. It there *clearly* was a
way to increase productivity significantly, why was not the
means adopted sooner? A lazy or a "live-and-let-live" attitude is probably not conducive to rapid response to the
new "shock." If there was a way to increase efficiency but
it was not clear to the inefficient firms, why should shock
alone make the mysterious clear? Finally, it does not seem
likely that managements which have fallen behind are ones
which are likely to be particularly adept at adapting and
catching up. If the "shock treatment" fails, the entire
nation may become a "lagging region."

(c) The idea that there are large economies to be
reaped from increasing a firm's scale of operations is
deeply rooted in British thought (see Chapter 4). During
the decades after the Second World War it seemed plausible
that much of America's productivity was due to the larger
scale of many of its enterprises. The biggest U.S. firms
were and are much larger than the biggest British firms.
The economic growth of the six Common Market countries
after 1957 was taken as further evidence. A strong case
could be and was made.

However, it is not a totally convincing case. Large
scale does require a large market, but it need not be a
domestic or common market: witness Japan's success since
1953. Productivity does not always increase with scale:
studies of U.S. industries indicate that the largest firm
is frequently less efficient than some of its smaller competitors. One should also note that in the postwar years
U.S. productivity, while absolutely higher than British,
increased no faster than did British productivity (see
Chapter 7).

It could turn out to be the French, Germans, Italians,
Belgians, Dutch, and Danes, or even the lagging Irish--
rather than the British--who realize economies of scale and
reap the benefits. The British could end up with less than
they began.

THE EFFECTS OF JOINING THE EEC

A strong case can be made that Britain lost more than
she gained by joining the EEC. The major gains to be made
from joining are those which stem from the discipline of

competition within a large free trade area. A minor gain
is that Britain is a net recipient of the EEC funds devoted
to the development of lagging regions. Only this minor
gain is measurable. The major gains cannot be measured in
advance. Nor can they be measured later on in retrospect,
for the argument that competition will further gains depends
on other things remaining the same, which they never do.
All of which, including the arguments of doubt in the previous sections, does not mean that the gains from comparative advantage, competition, and a large market may not be
great. Rather, the burden of the arguments here is that
they are likely to be much less than has been hoped and
that membership in the Common Market is also likely to involve some unexpected losses and some painfully long and
probably unnecessary adjustments.

Membership in the EEC restricts Britain's independence
in setting her own policies in two important ways: in the
area of foreign trade and exchange and in agricultural and
food price policies.

As a member of the EEC Britain cannot alter her
tariffs against the non-EEC world nor can she levy tariffs
or in any way restrict the importation of goods from EEC
countries. Although she can negotiate ceilings on imports,
as she has done for textiles with Hong Kong and Japan and
is trying to do for automobiles with Japan, Britain is
severely limited in her ability to impose quotas on imports
from non-EEC countries. Insofar as faith in freer trade
is justified, these restrictions on her freedom to interfer
will be beneficial rather than costly, *but* they do mean
that Britain is and will be in a much less powerful position
whenever her balance of payments or the foreign exchange
value of the pound is threatened. No longer can she impose
tariffs or license imports. She is now limited to monetary
and fiscal policies to control domestic demand and to at-
tract foreign funds. When these policies fail Britain has
no choice but to devalue or to do what the IMF demands,
which is almost always to employ more stringent monetary
and fiscal policies and thus limit output and reduce employment.

This is one major reason why the leftwing of British
politics opposed membership in the EEC. It foresaw,
quite correctly, that membership would make it even more
difficult than it has been to introduce and carry out their
programs. That the programs of the British left would be
bad for the British economy, for its balance of payment, or
for the value of the pound in the long run is not at all

clear. (Bacon and Eltis think the left's program makes a
good deal of sense.[1]) It is clear that bankers, businessmen, and foreigners who can sell sterling and bring on a
balance of payments and exchange crisis do regard the left's
programs as bad and they would fulfill their own prophesies
while a leftwing British government could do nothing to
stop them so long as it abided by EEC rules.

THE COMMON AGRICULTURAL POLICY (CAP)

The CAP was designed to create a single price support
policy for the farmers within one common agricultural market in the EEC. The system adopted was very much like the
American system of farm price supports. A minimum support
price is set for each commodity--the list of commodities is
not exhaustive, but it is long. If the price of a commodity falls to the support level, the "intervention agencies"
(several in each country) will buy the commodity and store
it until it can be sold overseas at subsidized prices,
used for aid to Third World countries, or sold within Europe.

As has so often happened in the U.S., large amounts of
agricultural commodities pile up in the silos and warehouses of the intervention agencies of EAGGF (European Agricultural Guidance and Guarantee Fund). Efforts to dispose
of these "surpluses" are often frustrated. In 1977 farmers
did not like EAGGF's attempts to force them to use a minimum
quantity of dried milk in pigfeed. Experience with OPEC
prices may have changed their attitudes, but several years
ago potential buyers were not enthused about using all the
industrial alcohol that could be made from EAGGF stocks of
low quality wines. There is more guarantee than guidance
in the CAP.

CAP guaranteed prices are set annually at a spring review by the ministers of agriculture of the EEC countries.
The minimum prices are stated in u.a. (units of account),
a hypothetical money in which the values of the different
national currencies are expressed. Payments are actually
made by each national government in its national currency.
The governments are reimbursed by EAGGF.

The original scheme for a one-market, one-price CAP
broke down in the face of devaluations and of freely fluc-
tuating exchange rates. If EAGGF had converted units of
account into national currencies at the actual international
market rates of exchange, then a fall in the external value
of a nation's currency would have raised the support price

expressed in that nation's currency. The resulting rise in consumer prices in that nation would have led to demands for compensating increases in wages. Conversely, if the value of a nation's currency had risen on the international market, the prices of agricultural products expressed in that nation's currency would have fallen. While tending to reduce the cost of living, such a fall would have been unpopular with that nation's farmers.

In order to avoid these consequences and to allow member countries to pursue divergent farm and cost of living policies, the EEC developed a system of fixed exchange rates which apply only to EAGGF transactions. These fixed exchange rates between national currencies and units of account are set and changed by negotiation among the member countries' ministers of agriculture and CAP support prices are converted at these rates: hence the phrases "green pound," "green mark," and so on. The result was that the British, whose colorless pound had fallen in value, maintained a "green pound" value more than 20% higher than that of the "real" pound, while the value of Germany's "green mark" has been lower than the market value of the "real" mark. Britain can thus keep food prices in Britain down while Germany can keep prices paid to farmers up. Were this the whole story in a free trade area, agricultural products would flow from low price Britain to high price Germany leaving British shops bare and filling German warehouses. So the EEC has also created a system of compensating taxes and subsidies. A British agricultural export to Germany, for instance, is taxed an amount equal to the difference between its price in British pounds and its higher price in German marks, thus protecting German farmers against cheap imports. Danish exports of bacon to Britain would not reward Danish farmers at the level of reward agreed upon as appropriate at the annual price reviews if Danish farmers received the low British prices. Therefore, the EAGGF pays Danish farmers (through the Danish government) an amount equal to the difference between the receipts from sales in Britain and the u.a. price in Danish kroner. These taxes and subsidies are called Monetary Compensation Amounts (MCAs). The effects of the system are that British farmers receive only as many pounds for exports as for domestic sales, and Danish farmers receive as many kroner for exports to Britain as they do for sales elsewhere.

TABLE 9-1
MCAs Illustrated

Suppose the following situation:

Green £ = 2.4 u.a.
Green Kr = 0.3 u.a.
Green DM = 0.5 u.a.

Then the "prices" of 240 u.a. worth of farm products
would be:

In u.a.	In £s in Britain	In Kr in Denmark	In DM in Germany
240	100	800	480

But suppose also that exchange rates in the international
markets are:

£1 = Kr 6 = DM 3.6

Then:

(1) *British products* sold in Germany would earn DM 480,
which would exchange for DM 480/3.6 = £133.33, a bonus
of £33.33 for the British farmer.
(2) *Danish products* sold in Britain would earn £100 which
would exchange for £100 x 6 = £ Kr 600, a cost of
Kr 200 to the Danish farmer.

The MCA Solution: charge a tax of £33.33 (=DM 120) on the
British export to Germany and pay Denmark an MCA of
£33.33 = Kr 200.

THE COSTS OF CAP TO BRITAIN

Before joining the Common Market the British had a
very different system for maintaining farm incomes: *deficiency payments*. Farmers sold their products on the market,
often through marketing boards, at market prices. These
prices were not free market prices because they were affect-
ed by trade agreements with Britain's major suppliers and
at times by import licensing, but they were fairly free
within Britain. When prices of agricultural produce fell
below levels determined annually by the ministry of agriculture (in close if often disputatious consultation with
farmers' organizations, especially the National Farmers

Union), the government made deficiency payments to the farmers--amounts equal to the differences between the prices set by the government and the actual prices received by the farmers. Furthermore, in contrast with minimum prices set by the CAP, the guaranteed prices set in Britain were relatively low. They were high enough, certainly, to assure efficient farmers a respectable income, but not so high as to allow the inefficient to continue to produce high cost surpluses. British farmers, being relatively few in number, lacked the political power their continental counterparts enjoyed. The major strength of British farmers in the political process was the general realization that the more British farmers produced the less would have to be imported and hence the stronger the pound, the higher its value, and the cheaper the prices of imported goods. The primary objective of British farm policy was to stimulate productive use of Britain's agricultural resources. Achieving this end required that farmers be sufficiently well rewarded to keep them farming and to induce them to look for and adopt more efficient techniques. As a result the incomes of British farmers were maintained without allowing, let alone encouraging, high cost, inefficient farms.

There were two other importantly beneficial consequences of the system. First, agricultural prices were kept low for consumers and other users. Second, no output was wasted by buying it up and storing it in "mountains of meat and wheat" and "lakes of milk and wine."

By joining the EEC, Britain loses all three of these advantages. If or when the CAP succeeds in creating one common price for each commodity throughout the Common Market there will be less pressure on British farmers to be efficient--and so far Britain has had one of the most efficient farm sectors in the world. Second, food prices in Britain have already risen as a result of joining the EEC (they would have risen anyway because world agricultural prices rose after 1973, but British prices would still have been lower than CAP prices). If or when the green pound is eliminated agricultural prices in Britain will rise even more. And third, Britain is now sharing the direct financial costs and wastes of the "mountains and lakes" of produce nobody wants at CAP prices.

The process of joining the EEC has been disruptive both at home and abroad. Rising food prices are resented

in England; there is a feeling that the MCAs are sub-
sidizing continental farmers; and British farmers are
angered at receiving less than farmers on the continent.
The British have therefore been fighting in the Council of
Ministers to maintain a fairly high value for the green
pound (in order to keep food prices and the burden of agricultural subsidies to farmers down) *and* to prevent an increase in CAP prices so that, as other prices rise, the
relative prices of agricultural prices will fall to a level
closer to that received by British farmers. The French
government disagrees with the British on both these counts.

From both the point of view of domestic economic
management and from the point of view of friendly and cooperative foreign relations, the CAP has not served Britain
well.

ENDNOTES

1. Bacon & Eltis, *Britain's Economic Problem*, pp. 64–77.

10

PLANNING

Planning as a major element in British socialist thought goes back to the late 19th century and the Fabian Society. From that time to the Attlee Labour government of 1945-51 little specific content was given to the idea. It was rather assumed that with some careful thought the powers of a socialist government could eliminate the capitalist business cycle and the nation's resources could be reallocated away from less necessary or luxury uses to more important social demands such as hospitals, housing for lower income groups, more education for the working class, and various sorts of payments to assure minimum incomes to the less fortunate. Licensing and prohibitions, publicly financed programs, subsidies, compulsory public insurance programs (health, unemployment, old age, disability), and controls over the types and directions of lending by financial institutions would suffice to do the job of reallocating resources. A not-too-terribly difficult sorting out of problems as they arose, carried out through some appropriate form of government intervention, would integrate the entire system at a level of high employment. As the implications of J. M. Keynes' *General Theory* were absorbed, the left became sure that appropriate Keynesian fiscal policies would suffice to solve the problem of full employment without any need for detailed decisions or administration.

Since major or very-difficult-to-surmount problems were not anticipated and since it was believed that "using the head" was the obvious way to solve specific problems as they arose, the Fabians and Labour did not attempt detailed analyses of how to plan or of how to administer plans. If unkind, it may not be inaccurate to say that the British left thought that Keynes plus controls combined with the powers that would result from the nationalization of basic industries would be sufficient to assure successful planning. Thus when Labour came to power in 1945 it did not have a national plan for the economy--although it certainly did have plans for various sectors of the economy--and no plan for planning the economy.

Since that time Britain has never had a national plan. It has had public policies effecting the entire economy; it has had "strategies." But it has never had a plan on the model of the postwar Monnet plan for the modernization of the French economy or subsequent French plans, nor has it had an organization such as France's Commissariat du Plan, let alone anything in the style of Soviet planning.

The National Economic Development Council, the National Economic Development Office, and the Department of Economic Affairs are discussed below, but none of their activities warrant calling any of them, or all of them together, a national planning body or calling their products a national plan. The Central Policy Review Staff (nicknamed the Think Tank) is a group of senior civil servants released from specific departmental duties to investigate and to think about solutions to all sorts of problems as they arise and as the cabinet thinks they are worth worrying about--from productivity in the automobile industry to the administration of the Foreign Office (the British State Department). The reports of this group do influence national economic policy, but the group does not draw up broad schemes for the management of the economy nor are its recommendations by any means necessarily adopted by the cabinet. When Andrew Shonfield published *Modern Capitalism* in 1965 he had hopes bordering on expectations that the National Economic Development Office would evolve into a Commissariat du Plan, but his description of British planning to 1964 is still a better description of British planning since 1964 than are his anticipations of what it might become.[1]

The closest one comes to a general plan are the "estimates" and the annual budget. During January and February the government publishes "estimates" of expected expenditure by the various departments and under major headings, as well as some changes in the rules governing permissible expenditure. Then, during the first week of April, the Chancellor of the Exchequer delivers his budget speech. This is an occasion for ritual and excitement. The Chancellor begins his speech to the House of Commons at one o'clock in the afternoon. He must spend the first two hours discoursing on general principles and on the outlook and hopes of the government. Were he to announce any of the government's

specific programs before the financial markets closed at
three o'clock, some people would get the information and
others would not. Those who got the information would be
able to take advantage of it on the market; and, in addition, partial information might lead to regrettable mistakes.
Therefore, in the interests of fairness and of the smooth
working of the markets, the Chancellor must dally with wit
and verve until 3 p.m. and thus give the financial community
a night to sleep on the information. Once the markets have
closed, the Chancellor outlines his proposals for changing
the tax laws. The general schema of a Chancellor's budget
speech is a presentation of his forecasts of the total productive capacity of the nation for the next year, of the
demands upon it which will be made by consuming households
and by investing businesses if there is no change in policy,
and of the demands upon it by the government under its
existing policy. There is then a forecast of total government revenue over the next year. If the aggregate demand
upon the country's resources exceeds its anticipated productive capacity the Chancellor will announce increases in
taxes. If the anticipated aggregate demands are less than
the productive capacity of the country, the Chancellor will
announce tax reductions. (It is, of course, the specific
increases or decreases in taxes that are of special interest
to the financial markets). Thus the budget is an aggregate
of gross financial plans for the nation for the next year.
What makes it more of a plan than the U.S. President's budget message or the joint resolutions of the U.S. Congress
is that the Chancellor's "plan" will be enacted as pro-
posed--were Parliament to make major changes, the government would have to resign (see Chapter 3). There is, however, no physical plan, except as provided for in the
government departments' programs which underlie their estimates of expenditure. The budget may affect the nationalized industries, but through provisions affecting their
financial position and not by setting physical programs or
targets for them.

MACROECONOMIC POLICY

Since 1945 British macroeconomic policy has been fairly
successful. Only "fairly," because while policy has largely
solved immediate problems in the short run it has also
exacerbated the difficulties of solving some of Britain's
major longer run problems. Until 1974 the British managed
to keep their level of unemployment low, certainly a good
deal lower than did the United States. [British statistics
will always show lower rates of unemployment than will U.S.

statistics because of the different ways in which the data
are collected. In Britain the estimate is based upon the
number of people seeking work at the employment exchanges.
In the United States the rate of unemployment is computed
from answers to a sample survey asking if people are employed, and if not, if they are seeking work. Perhaps the
American method finds more unemployed than are truly seeking work, although experts assert that the U.S. system
misses many; it is almost certain that the British method
does not find nearly all those who want a job. But after
making due allowance for the differences in method between
countries--and no due allowances are exact--the British
record on unemployment is definitely better than the
American.]

Increasing spending when a shortfall in aggregate demand is expected has not been a problem. The obligations
of the modern welfare state, to say nothing of its aspirations, virtually assure that government demands keep rising.
The expansion of programs designed to increase public welfare directly or through investment can always take up any
slack in the aggregate demand for output. British governments have been less reluctant than others to expand the
services provided to the elderly and to children, to raise
the levels of pension and other benefits; and most of the
time the nationalized industries could usefully absorb additional funds for investment. The problem for a Chancellor
was never "What is there to do?" but "Which of the many
things I might do, will I do?" Not only were there competing demands from different government programs, but
there was always the possibility of lightening the tax burden on some group of people: low income, middle income,
high income people; consumers of automobiles and other
durable goods; homeowners; and so on. That Chancellors always managed to spend enough or to reduce taxes enough to
keep the economy bubbling along with almost everybody employed is to their credit. It is for their failure to use
slack in the economy wisely or as imaginatively as might
have been done to achieve the longer run aims of a more
rapidly increasing productivity and a more appropriate output mix for the economy that Chancellors may be faulted.
But to say that the slack might have been used more wisely
or imaginatively is not to say that there were obvious
things that Chancellors should have done. Any economist
can, in retrospect, think of things that might have been
better done by any particular Chancellor, but doubtless in
retrospect so could each particular Chancellor.

The British have been less successful in avoiding the

inflationary pressures of excessive aggregate demand. During periods of inflation, policy has tended to solve the short run problems at the expense of achieving long run aims. Chancellors have not been afraid to raise taxes, but the already high level of British income taxes has rather limited their ability to raise large sums in that way, and indirect taxes tend to raise prices and thereby the cost of living. Higher costs of living tend to make labor demand higher wages, so Chancellors have not raised indirect taxes much and then largely on tobacco and beer. The solution has therefore often been to cut back on government expenditure. Wages and salaries being otherwise fixed for government employees, and it being poor policy for efficiency and morale to hire and fire civil servants as one might shift from punch bowl to punch bowl at a party, the tendency has been to reduce expenditure on goods. This has largely meant expenditure upon capital goods with the consequence that each restraint upon aggregate demand has meant less capital equipment in subsequent years than would otherwise have been the case.

In part the "blame" lies not upon the choice made by British policy makers but upon Britain's international position. A high level of home demand must always involve for Britain a high level of demand for imports. More imports lead to an increase in the deficit on the balance of trade and this in turn sets off a speculation against the pound sterling in international money markets. To protect the value of the pound the British government must "do something," and those who speculate on international money markets are much given to the view that reducing government expenditures is a "good thing"--and that, for instance, licensing in order to limit imports is a "bad thing"--so that Chancellors are virtually forced to reduce government expenditures. But this is not the whole story: expenditures whose payoff is in the more distant future are dropped rather than less worthy projects whose pay-off will come sooner; cutbacks hit projects with a low rather than a high labor component although the criterion of employment is not clearly related (either way) to desirable changes in the composition of British output or the productivity of British industries. The British may have, in fact, treated speculators with greater circumspection, even fear, than was strictly necessary.

One may summarize the effect of these policies--the British have come to call them "Stop-Go" policies--in the following way: when there has been slack in the economy, Chancellors have encouraged increases in consumption expenditures; when total demand has exceeded productive capacity, it has been investment in capital equipment that has been reduced.

NEDDY, NEDO, AND THE LITTLE NEDDIES[2]

After a decade of Conservative rule during which the British economy grew less than did the other western European economies the Conservative government decided to adapt the French system of "indicative planning." In the French system a Commissariat du Plan, made up of civil servants who consulted closely with private industry, developed a forecast of the growth of the French economy for the coming four or five years. In the process of forecasting, potential bottlenecks were identified. Industries in the private as well as public sector were encouraged to expand greatly if that appeared necessary to achieve the rate of growth which seemed both desirable and possible. Andrew Shonfield has called the system "A Conspiracy to Plan:"

> In some ways, the development of French planning in the 1950s can be viewed as an act of voluntary collusion between senior civil servants and the senior managers of big business. The politicians and the representatives of organized labour were both largely passed by. The conspiracy in the public interest between big business and big officialdom worked, largely because both sides found it convenient. Since the Government had a substantial part of the nation's economic activity under its direct control and exerted an indirect, though powerful, influence on a great deal more, it was not too difficult to convince private business that its decisions would be more intelligently made, over a wider range of industry, if they were made in unison with the public authorities.... The word conspiracy is appropriate because the result depended on a recognition by private business that the government official personally disposed of considerable powers which could be used to influence the success or failure of individual businesses. It all depended, therefore, on a series of bargains between the main centres of public and private economic power....

> The Treasury.... has the authority to underwrite certain favoured borrowing with a state guarantee. Its connexion with the Plan is firmly

established through the Fund for Economic and
Social Development established after the war to
provide public finance for investment projects
deemed to be in the national interest . . .[3]

The system worked through "targets and pressures."[4]
The targets "indicated" what each business or industry
could expect from the other sectors of the economy and from
the growth of the economy as a whole. The targets also
"indicated" what different industries and even specific
business firms were expected to do. The pressures were both
gross and subtle. Easy access to credit was granted to
firms which cooperated, as were special provisions for reducing taxes. More subtly, both the civil servants and the
firms with which they dealt were aware that "scratching of
backs" is a mutual affair. Businesses were aware that much
of the French economy was directly controlled by the government through government ownership and that more was indirectly controlled through government's full and part
ownership of major financial institutions. The result of
these efforts to project the growth of the economy, to discover potential bottlenecks, and to figure out what to do
about them was the "indicative plan"--and to the indicative
plan has been attributed much of the success of France in
changing from one of Europe's slowest growing to one of
Europe's fastest growing economies.

There are several aspects of the system upon which its
success probably depended. First, the plan consisted of
targets jointly arrived at by civil servants and business
leaders: the private business side of the process really
did participate in and approve of the contents of the plans.
Second, the French have long had a tradition of *dirigisme*,
an acceptance that government should and does have an active
role in planning private as well as public business. Third,
in consequence on the one side of the early successes of
the planning process and on the other side of the inability
of coalition governments to formulate and pursue any alternative policies, there developed a silent agreement among
politicians not to interfere with the Commissariat du Plan.
The situation remained effectively the same after de Gaulle
resumed power in 1957 because he always supported the plan-
ners. Fourth, the relationships between the individual
civil servants engaged in planning for each industrial sector were intimate and long lasting. Fifth, perhaps as a by-
product of the tradition of *dirigisme*, the French were quite
willing to be partial, to help these firms most likely to
succeed and to ignore those firms which were unimaginative
or inefficient. Sixth, the civil servants were technologi-

cally (and commercially) quite knowledgeable about the industries and firms with which they dealt.

What the British perceived was a plan for growth which was a product of joint consultation between government and business and which effectively persuaded businesses to pursue activities which would realize the plan: "prophesy contributing to its own fulfillment." So in 1961 Selwyn-Lloyd, the Conservative Chancellor of the Exchequer, proposed a National Economic Development Council--which was immediately nicknamed Neddy--to consist of civil servants, representatives of industry, representatives of the labor unions, and some "outsiders," all supported by a small planning staff in the National Economic Development Office (NEDO). At first the unions were distrustful and refused to join, fearing that they would lack power in the counsels of the Council yet be responsible for the decisions of the Council. They were also opposed to the idea that Council members would not represent specific interests but serve only as wise and competent men. The TUC insisted that union members of the Council should act as representatives of the TUC and its member unions, overtly furthering or defending the interests of the unions and the TUC. Finally the TUC agreed to join and Neddy was set up in 1962. When Labour won the election of 1964 it transferred the planning staff to the government, setting up a Department of Economic Affairs.

In addition to Neddy and NEDO smaller planning groups were set up for a number of specific industries. These groups came to be known as Little Neddies. Through the years the Little Neddies have produced many reports and recommendations. Some have seemed perceptive and potentially helpful. Others have appeared to be no more than standard cliches about productivity, and some fall between these extremes.

A recent proposal, made by Labour after it returned to office in 1974, was that the government enter into "planning agreements" with large firms. These agreements would specify what each firm would do--presumably in the way of investment, technological innovation, reduction of manning levels, or increases in employment offered. Planning agreements are seen as a way of making industrial strategies effective. However, the inducements, obligations, and penalties have not been spelled out for either of the parties to such agreements, so that it is not clear how the system would work, or even that it would work. It is difficult to believe a firm would voluntarily enter into a

contract binding upon itself unless the government offered,
on its side, something a good deal more concrete than a
promise of suitable macro-economic policy, and something
the firm could not get from the banks or financial markets
anyway. Which seems to imply that special privileges would
have to be granted--in other words, a system much more
closely resembling the French system of differential and
therefore, in British eyes, unfair treatment of different
firms.

Neddy and NEDO were to formulate the long-term forecasts for the economy. These forecasts would set the targets which would assure each sector that the profits resulting from pursuing the targets would justify the industries and firms joining in the expansion. Bottlenecks were
to be identified and proposals for widening them made. The
Little Neddies' functions were to find out what specific
sectors could do, what specific sectors needed in order to
fit into the larger scheme, and what the specific sectors
would do to take advantage of the larger scheme.

Neddy and NEDO have produced several national forecasts
and general planning documents.[5] Each has been overtaken
by events before it became a meaningful guide: by the
Labour election victory of 1964; by the foreign exchange
crisis of 1966; by the Conservative election victory of
1970; and by Labour's refusal to cooperate after the intro-
duction of the Conservative's Industrial Relations Bill
(see Chapter 5).

In 1975 Labour proposed what it called "the new industrial strategy."[6] The "new industrial strategy" ex-
plicitly rejected the idea of drawing up a national plan,
but called upon 39 working parties of the Little Neddies to
identify key sectors for future economic growth and to
formulate industry-by-industry strategies to achieve targets
based on assumptions about growth provided annually by the
government. The working parties reported and the government said it was launched upon its new industrial strategy.
A long time reader of the British press should be forgiven
his feeling of *deja vu*. Investment, expansion, innovation,
productivity, redirection of investment and effort away
from the domestic market into exports, greater investment
in industry and less in public and private services--the
analyses of the problems and the recommendations for action
read very much like commentaries from the early 1950s. In
the event the world depression and the struggle to suppress
inflation by limiting demand have meant that targets were
not set and whatever merits the "new industrial strategy"

may have possessed became largely irrelevant.

While frequent changes in government policy might of
themselves have been enough to thwart the operations of
otherwise effective Neddy, NEDO, and Little Neddies, the
British system lacked the traits which in fact made the
French system successful.

British industry never committed itself to carrying
out the plans as thoroughly as did French industry; nor
did British industry participate in the planning process as
completely and continuously as French industry did. There
were several reasons for this. One was the absence of a
tradition of close cooperation between business and government. Business distrusted *dirigisme*, and the civil servants had a tradition of dealing with businesses "at arm's
length," impartially, with a distate for possible intimacy.
Whereas the French firms most closely involved in the planning were selected for their innovativeness, British ideas
of equitable treatment required that all firms be treated
as equally worthy. Then, the British government did not
have as much to give or to withhold as did the French, and
what it had could not be given or withheld discriminatingly.
The unions could be largely ignored in France because they
were always in the opposition, never in the government.
In Britain the active cooperation of the TUC was essential;
and that meant that negotiations were three-sided--government,
business, and labor--instead of two-sided, with consequent-
ly multiplied difficulties in achieving agreement.

Unfortunately for the development of Neddy as an
effective planner by mutual consent, its projections and
proposals never survived as guidelines for policy long
enough to endow Neddy and NEDO with the prestige which the
Commissarriat du Plan enjoyed.

The relationships between civil servants and industrialists, and between civil servants and trade unionists,
were not of the sort to make up for these shortcomings.
People to head the civil service are recruited because they
are broadly educated in the liberal tradition--"able to
administer anything"--and in Britain this usually means with
little or no training in the sciences and almost certainly
with no training in engineering and technology. In contrast,
the top levels of the French civil service are trained in
science, mathematics, and engineering. Thus the government
side in planning discussions often appears to industrial
managements and to the unions alike as knowing less rather
than more about what to do than does the average industrial-

ist or union leader--again, the contrast with France, where
the government's representative in negotiating and planning
may well know more about what to do in a particular case
then many of the managers in the industry.

Despite individual exceptions, and despite good will,
the British civil servant is not attuned to the attitudes
of business. At the upper levels he has likely gone into
government service because he regarded it as superior to
business. The life styles and life experiences of those
who have risen through industry are apt to be foreign to
the successful civil servant. He is unlikely to have had
dealings with an industry and its firms over a long enough
time to have a sense, or "feel," or instinctive understanding of the industry's problems. The lack of mutual understanding can only have been reinforced by the tradition
that the Treasury is the top and best part of the civil
service; for of all branches of the civil service the
Treasury is most devoted to analyzing and evaluating proposals from the point of view of their financial implications only--as opposed to their physical, chemical, or
biological consequences or their consequences for human
relationships.

Strong leadership in planning could not emerge because
British sensitivity to equity, reinforced by the "property
hangup," made it impossible for the government to use the
subtle and not so subtle pressures which are probably necessary to make indicative planning work. Nor could strong
leadership in industrial change emerge when the potential
leaders lacked the technological knowledge--perhaps more
importantly, the instincts and biases of modern industrial
technologists--needed to discover what ought to be done.

ENDNOTES

1. Andrew Shonfield, *Modern Capitalism*. London/Oxford/
    New York: Oxford University Press, 1969, especially
    pp. 71-87, 121-175. The 1969 edition is a "reprint
    with corrections" of the 1965 edition.
2. For a readable if optimistic account of British plan-
    ning since the early 1960s see Michael Shanks, *Planning
    and Politics: The British Experience 1960-1975*.
    London: George Allen & Unwin, for Political and
    Economic Planning, 1977.
3. Shonfield, pp. 128-29.
4. *Ibid.*, p. 134.

168

5. *Growth of the United Kingdom Economy to 1966.* London: HMSO, 1963; *Conditions Favourable to Faster Growth.* London: HMSO, 1963; *The National Plan.* London, 1965; *The Task Ahead: An Economic Assessment to 1972.* London: HMSO, 1969; *Economic Prospects to 1972.* London: HMSO, 1970; *Industrial Review to 1977.* London: HMSO, 1973.
6. *An Approach to Industrial Strategy.* London: HMSO, 1975.

11

THE WELFARE
STATE

A fairly common American view is that "things have
gone badly wrong" with the British welfare state. The British view, by and large, is that some things have gone pretty
well--"the National Health Service is the nicest thing that
ever happened to the British working class"--and that Britain's basic problem is not that she is a welfare state.
Chronically rising prices irritate people. Policies to
limit wage increases do too. One senses a degree of acri-
mony--not of disillusionment, not of cynicism, not of re-
belliousness--but a degree of acrimony not present (some
would say, "merely not so articulated") twenty and thirty
years ago. But despite changes in attitudes there is little
urge to abandon the welfare state.

Britain's problems represent in somewhat exaggerated
form those which arise in the management of all welfare
states. It should not be surprising that there are problems. Managing a welfare state in a changing world inevitably gives rise to new problems, and the experience of living in and managing such a state will inevitably change
people's perceptions of how to achieve their aims. Actually, people and their governments have not had much experience in managing welfare states: thirty years is not so
long a time in historical perspective. The period in British history since 1945 is shorter than the period elapsing
between the rise of the railroads and the establishment of
the Interstate Commerce Commission in the U.S.; certainly
shorter than the period in British history between the
failure of the Grand National Trade Union in the 1830s and
40s and the beginnings of industrial unionism in the late
1880s.

Since the Liberal government's enactment of old age
pension legislation in 1908 and of health and unemployment

insurance in 1911 the British have been developing their
model of the welfare state. For forty years the pace was
slow, consisting largely in extensions of unemployment benefits. Then came rapid changes under Clement Attlee's
government (1945-51), especially during 1946-48. During the
following thirty years there was constant tinkering so that
the model of 1979 was not that of 1969 or 1959, but all the
models fit the architect's conception if not the blueprints
of 1946.

During the Second World War, at the behest of the coalition government (of Conservatives, Labour, and Liberals),
Sir William Beveridge write a Report[1] setting forth a program for comprehensive coverage against any and all those
infirmities and disasters which must or may befall an individual and his family. Beveridge proposed a system of a
minimum payment available to everyone irrespective of previous incomes or contributions. Beyond the minimum each
person, through his own frugality and foresight, was to
make any additional provisions for old age or other unpleasant contingencies as she or he saw fit. (Presumably
frugality and foresight are commonly considered by 19 year
old women when deciding whom to marry.) "There would be
unemployment pay, which would last as long as unemployment
lasted, subject to attendance at a work or training centre
after a certain period; widows', retirement and old-age
pensions; there would be family allowances, payable to all
dependent children after the first, industrial-injury and
disablement pensions, maternity and funeral benefits; there
would be sick pay and medical treatment."[2] The core of
Britain's welfare state is founded in this Report, its
proposals amended as it became legislation, and with numerous changes since. In addition to these programs one should
include the extensions and reforms of the educational system
(see Chapter 2).

Welfare, as conceived by most British, has several
strands. It embraces the ideas of a right to a job, of a
right to a decent living if a job is unavailable, of equality of treatment for all by all in all respects; and, for
Labour at any rate, of increasing equality of income, of
living conditions, and of opportunity.

Very important to the left and of some importance to
the center of British politics has been the theme that welfare is a "right." The contrast--as clear in the British
gut as it is in the British mind--is with "charity." The
idea is that a person should have a decent life and decent
opportunities because he or she is a person, *not* because

some higher authority or higher class or richer person is
willing to be decent to an unfortunate. Hence the recur-
ring slogan, "No means test!" To inquire into the personal
history, character, ethics, life-style, or savings of a
person would deny him or her the full rights of a person by
implying that only "morally deserving unfortunates" should
be allowed to share in the things and the joys which society
provides.

The roots of this view are at least twofold. A "means
test" implies that there are some people who are "superior"
and therefore properly able to sit in judgment on others
(their inferiors). The idea that there are "superiors"
and "inferiors" not only reflects the existence of a class
system: its application in the determination of who is
eligible for assistance tends to reinforce and perpetuate
the class system. Secondly, until recently the people who
inquired into the "means" of applicants for assistance were
of the upper and upper middle classes, and even today many
of the civil servants who inquire come from backgrounds
quite different from the backgrounds of the applicants.
They were (and are) not only unduly prying but also often
callous and rude. "No means test!" expresses resentment at
the class system, at the power of some over others, and at
the humiliations imposed upon those who need help.

The consequence was that the post-1945 welfare legislation tried to provide publicly financed benefits and
specific assistance "as a matter of right." This has meant
that allowances for children, subsidized rents for council
houses (public housing), and access to medical care has
been given without respect to the income or wealth of the
recipient. The "no means test" criterion has not been applied to all programs. Grants to students to study in universities are scaled down as parental income increases.
Recently the law has been changed so that the levels of unemployment benefits and of pensions now depend upon the
level of earned income which the applicant received.

I. INCOME MAINTENANCE

THE ECONOMICS OF INSURANCE AND TRANSFER PAYMENTS

Before describing the way in which everyone is assured
a minimally decent standard of living, a digression on the
economics of pensions and other transfer payments seems in
order.

Confusion often arises from the fact that the language
in which we talk about old age benefits, unemployment benefits, and other forms of social security is very much like
the language spoken by the insurance business. This confusion is compounded by a confusion between the legal and
commercial aspects of insurance and the economic role of insurance in transferring funds. For both insurance companies
and for governments the *economic process* is solely one of
transferring money from members of one group to members of
another group. In the case of insurance companies it is a
transfer from premium payers to beneficiaries (pensioners,
heirs, those whose houses have burned or whose cars have
been stolen). In the case of governments it is a transfer
from taxpayers to the recipients of the pensions or other
benefits; or, what is close to the same thing, from earners
to non-earners.

If a government chooses not to tax it can always create
money by borrowing from the banking system (a process ex-
plained in any elementary economics text). In such cases
there are two possible results: (1) with fairly full employment recipients are given purchasing power with which
to compete with other income recipients in the markets for
currently produced goods and services. There will be some
inflation and a transfer of real income from earners (now
with *relatively* less purchasing power, who must now "do
without") to beneficiaries of the government programs. (2)
Where there is slack in the economy the additional demand
of the recipients of insurance benefits will call forth additional goods and services from the unemployed or under-
employed sectors of the economy: no one will in fact "do
without," and there may be little or no inflation.

There is no way in which society or earners can pay in
advance in *real terms*, and no way in which benefits can be
paid for in *real terms* after the payment of the benefits.
The goods and services available this year to earners and
non-earners alike are those produced during the current
year (plus or minus changes in the stocks of goods in warehouses and on shelves). To allow non-earners to share in
this national product, purchasing power is taken from income recipients and given to the recipients of benefits, who
use this purchasing power to buy their share of the national
product, the taxpaying earners doing without those goods and
services which are bought and enjoyed by the recipients of
the benefits.

The same is true of all forms of insurance. In fire
or theft insurance the policy holders paying premiums are

the equivalent of the taxpayer in a system of national pensions, the poor fellow whose house has burned down is the equivalent of the recipient of a national pension. In the case of life insurance the living premium payers are the taxpayers, the surviving beneficiaries of the insured are the pensioners. In all cases one group, the "undeserving" who earn incomes or live in unrobbed, unburned houses, transfer purchasing power to the "deserving" heirs of someone who died when robbers burned down his house.

"Actuarial soundness" is important in commercial and contractual arrangements. When contracting now with a private company for a pension to be paid many years from now, the purchaser wants to be assured that the company will be able to pay the pension when due; and the company needs to make sure that it will be able to pay the pension even if the incoming premiums at future dates are insufficient to pay the pensions due. The company therefore collects money before the pension is due and lends the money so that it is itself owed money payable at those future dates when it will need money to pay the pension. The same is true of life insurance.

The "actuarial" element enters because no one knows in advance who will die first, who last; who will live a long time and collect a lot of pension money, who will die shortly after starting to receive the pension. The "actuarial" element is a statistical probability prediction about how many people will collect how much in what years. The "average" person pays in just enough to pay his pension and death benefits. Some people are lucky and die young or live on pensions an inordinate time and so benefit at the expense of those who die the day their pensions start.

"Soundness" means that the total inflow of funds to any date (premiums and debt repayments plus the expected earnings on the money lent), less the outflow to that date, is enough to pay the promised benefits. "Soundness" is important because the insurance company has no source of funds at the dates it must pay benefits other than the inflow of premiums in those years plus the debts and interest owed it from its lending of previous premium receipts.

What unites in "actuarial soundness" the earlier payments of premiums with the later payments of benefits is *not the economics* of transfer of real income or wealth from one group, the payers now, to another, the receivers later, *but contract law*. In fact my premium payments now do not

assure me of *actual* pension payments later. What they assure me of is a legal *right* to pension payments later. If
I am actually to collect my pension, there must exist, in
addition to that legal right, an insurance company which is
solvent. If the company has been mismanaged; if the staff
has run off with the funds; if the company has gone bankrupt; in these cases I cannot collect my full pension and
perhaps can collect none of it. I can sue for it, of
course, and if the company cannot pay I can force it into
bankruptcy; but no one else need pay me, for no one else is
obligated to pay me. "Actuarial soundness" is a statement
that the company's cash flows will be sufficient to meet
all obligations for which the company has contracted--a
legal, not an economic matter.

The *economic transfer* is, in these private cases just
as in the public cases, a current transfer of purchasing
power with which to buy currently produced goods and services from those who would otherwise have the purchasing
power to the recipients of money (purchasing power) from
the insurance companies. The differences between the insurance contract and government pensions or other transfer
benefits are that governmental arrangements are not contractual and that the government does not have to depend
upon social security or unemployment taxes to pay the benefits. The government may be morally obligated to pay pensions; the government may feel it is politically obligated
to pay pensions; but it is not legally required to do so
as a matter of contract law. A reading of either British
or American laws on social security benefits will make this
clear, as will even a careful perusal of the information
booklets put out by the governments. Before panicking
about whether participation in such non-contractual systems
is "safe"--participation is inevitable anyway since the law
requires it--consider whether one would rather depend on
the (moral?) sense of a government responsible to an electorate which expects to receive the benefits or upon a contract which depends on the honesty and competence of an insurance company. But most importantly the cash flow to the
government does not depend on a contractual flow of premiums
plus debt repayments from those to whom it has lent, as do
the cash flows of insurance companies, but upon the government's abilities to tax and to borrow. If at any time the
inflow of funds from a social security tax is insufficient
to pay benefits, the government can raise the social security tax *or* borrow *or* use proceeds from other taxes. Thus
the standards by which one judges "actuarial soundness" are
irrelevant when applied to government benefits. The insurance company's word is as good as its bond--but the bonds

it owns are its only word. The government's word is as good
as the police power of the sovereign state--and that is
pretty good.

Thus one can dismiss the fear that the welfare system
is going "to go broke." Recipients of wages, salaries, and
dividends may be unwilling to transfer money to the aged or
disabled, as they may be unwilling to give up money to
social services or to the Glyndebourne Opera (see Chapter
7), but this is a political decision, *not* a matter of
actuarial soundness.

INCOME MAINTENANCE IN BRITAIN

The British systems of guaranteeing a minimum money
income are a bit of a hodge podge--less so than the systems
in the United States, but much more of a hodge podge than
an orderly mind starting from scratch would create. There
are pensions for those over 65 who have been employed and
paying the social security taxes along with their employers.
There are smaller pensions for their widows. There are
pensions in any case for those aged 70 and above even if
they did not contribute to the system earlier. Until recently the pensions were flat rate, the same for each person no matter what his income had been when employed, but
now the pensions are graduated so that those who earned
more while working receive more while retired. For those
who lose their jobs there is unemployment compensation.
There is also a system of workmen's compensation for those
who have been permanently disabled while on the job or have
suffered long term disabilities as a result of industrial
injury.

There are of course those who slip through the gaps in
the safety nets because they are elderly but were not covered during employment, because they are husbandless younger
women with small children, because they have been disabled
but not as a result of their employment. In addition, numbers of people find themselves in a position where their
old age pensions, unemployment compensation, or industrial
injuries benefits are not enough to provide them with what
is regarded as the minimally decent standard of living.
This can occur because specific rates have not been raised
in line with inflation or because of the particular circumstances of the person or family--an unemployed person with
several dependent children, a disabled person with special
needs, a family living in a house on which the rent payments are relatively high. To take care of all of these
who are not properly cared for by the other schemes there

TABLE 11-1
Social Security Payments as Percentages of GNP
(Annual Averages for Selected Periods)

Years	Percent
1949–51	4.8
1953–56	5.0
1961–64	6.1
1967–70	7.4
1971–74	7.6
1975–78	8.9

Source: computed from *Annual Abstract of Statistics*,
various issues, with annual data for GNP
adjusted to fiscal years by weighting.

is a program of "supplementary benefits." All one need do
to qualify for a supplementary benefit is to show that she
or he does not have enough income to buy the minimum re-
quirements of a decent life in Britain and is either looking for a job, disabled, or required to stay home in order
to take care of small children or of disabled parents or
children. The amount of supplementary benefit to which one
is entitled is computed by adding up the amount of money it
is felt that a person or a family needs--about ₤15 a week
for a single adult in 1979, about double that for a couple
with a small child, and a little more for families with
more children--adding to this sum the rent the family pays
and any necessary expenses due to the peculiar circumstances
of the family. From this total is deducted the income which
the family is receiving from pensions, disability payments,
or unemployment insurance. The excess needed is then paid
as a supplementary benefit.

The system does assure that nobody goes homeless or
hungry. For those who are healthy and willing to get their
protein from beans, there is enough for the pint of beer
each evening and an occasional trip to the movies. For
those who have special problems--confined to wheel chairs,
physically unable to wash their own clothes, in need of
someone to go shopping for them, or in need of special
transport to get to the doctor, and so on for all the
peculiar disadvantages to which flesh can be heir--the
minimum income provided by supplementary benefits provides
frugally indeed. The system does, however, provide some
money income to everyone: nobody is left out completely
(as, for instance, are some in the United States, despite
our fairly widespread system of welfare payments).

The number of people receiving supplementary benefits
varies. During times of rapid inflation British governments seem more inclined to increase the minimum level of
supplementary benefit rather than to raise the level of
other benefits so that increasing numbers of people qualify
for the supplementary benefits. Over time, as real incomes
in Britain rise, as they have been doing at about 2% a year
since 1945, what is regarded as the minimum amount upon
which one can ask a person to live rises, and again there
appears to be a tendency to raise the rates at which supplementary benefits are paid faster than the standard rates of
unemployment compensation and old age pensions are raised.

REDUNDANCY PAYMENTS

In the late 1960s the British introduced a system of
compulsory "redundancy payments." A person who is laid-
off--not "for cause" but simply because the work force is
being cut back--is entitled to one week's pay for every
year he has worked for the company (with slight variations
for young people). The system has several virtues, at
least in British eyes. First, it costs a company to make
workers redundant, so the company has some incentive to find
alternative uses for members of its workforce who have
become surplus at one job. Second, it makes it worth the
company's while to keep on older workers, who may be assumed to be more settled, to have a greater "vested interest" in house and neighborhood, and to face more difficulty in finding another job than younger workers. Third,
it allows workers some choice of whether to stay on or to
leave the company. When the company feels it needs to lay-
off workers it asks for volunteers to accept redundancy
payments and to leave. Thus those least desirous of keeping
the job will leave, and only if there are insufficient
volunteers will those who wish to keep the job be made
redundant.

As the system has developed the compulsory redundancy
payments are becoming a minimum payment, with companies
offering higher than the minimum to induce more to volunteer,
as well as to make relations with the workforce a bit happier. While it is true that a company no longer has to
deal with a man after he is dismissed and therefore may feel
there is nothing to gain by being nice to him, it is also
true that the company does have to deal with the workers
who stay on, with workers in that and other unions at other
plants who know whether or not the company has been reasonably generous, as well as with the threat of sit-ins or of
"blacking" (the refusal by those who work for other companies

to handle the company's products or to work on parts supplied by the "selfish" company). So it can be well worth
a company's while to pay a good deal extra in redundancy
payments to gain the willing consent of enough workers.

From the workers' point of view, there is one other
great advantage in the system. For most, a large redundancy
payment is the only time in their lives when they will have
a lot of money all at once--to take their families on long
vacations to the Mediterranean or to buy things they could
never before afford. For those whose skills are easily
transferred to another employment, perhaps even more for
those who do not have special skills, and for those who
have come to dislike their jobs, a large redundancy payment
can be a very cheerful prospect.

II. THE NATIONAL HEALTH SERVICE (NHS)

Every person in the United Kingdom has a right to almost free health care: office calls, hospitalization,
surgery, whatever treatments are necessary, dentistry of all
sorts, eye examinations, and prescriptions. The only
charges are a small charge, about a dollar, on each pre-
scription; a fee of a couple of dollars on the commencement
of each course of dental treatment; and a small charge for
eye-glasses and trusses.

From the patient's point of view, the system works
this way: a person signs onto the "panel" of a doctor who
would be called a GP (general practitioner) in the U.S. and
is usually called a "family" doctor in Britain. When the
patient is sick--even merely "feeling poorly" in the
English idiom--he goes to the doctor on whose panel he is
listed and the doctor treats him; or, if the patient needs
hospitalization or a specialist, the doctor sends him to the
hospital or the specialist, who is called a "consultant" in
Britain and is attached to a hospital. At this point responsibility for the patient passes from his panel doctor
to the consultant and the hospital. The panel doctor will
of course be kept informed, just as would an American doctor who had passed a patient on to another specialist, and
upon release from the consultant's or hospital's care the
patient goes back under the care of his panel doctor. The
patient never sees a bill (minor exceptions as noted above).

The patient has a choice of doctor--as the doctor has
a choice of patient. If the patient comes to dislike the
doctor with whom he has signed up, he can sign up with

TABLE 11-2

Doctors, Dentists, Patients, & Payments
(Great Britain)

	1955	1965	1973
Doctors in family practice		24,260	25,580
Of which, principal doctors*	21,349	22,624	23,965
Patients per principal*	2,246	2,372	2,345
Dentists in general practice	10,511	11,572	12,520
Doctors & dentists in hospital practice	14,498	22,886	31,537
Doctors in hospital practice		22,123	30,594
Of which, consultants		8,042	11,064
Dentists in hospital practice		663	943
Of which, consultants		229	354
Gross earnings per principal (₤s)	2,839	4,398	9,380
Payments per patient (₤s)	1.26	1.85	4.00

Population per doctor, 1973		Population per dentist, 1973	
U. S.	552	U. S.	1,725
Britain	994	Britain	4,115

* Only a "principal" doctor can practice on his own or
  establish a clinic. Payments are made to principals,
  who may employ assistants (only a few do). The figures
  thus slightly overstate the number of patients and the
  earnings per doctor by about 6%.

Source: *Annual Abstract of Statistics*, various issues,
         and *Historical Statistics of the United States,
         Part 1* (U.S. Department of Commerce, Bureau of
         Statistics); *Statistical Abstract of the United
         States*, 1976.

another instead. If the doctor finds the patient too unpleasant, he can ask the patient to sign up with another
doctor. He can refuse to take on a new patient if he feels
that his panel is full enough. As a patient under both
systems, I would hesitate to say that choice is wider in
Britain than in the United States; but I would need a good
deal of persuading to be convinced it was any less wide.
Although a patient in Britain may appear to have less choice
about the consultants who treat him, I doubt that he has any
less choice in fact (do not almost all Americans go to the
specialist recommended by their physician?).

From the point of view of the family doctor--the doctor "in family practice," as the British expression goes--the difference between the American system and the British is largely in the mode of payment. The doctor is paid a capitation fee per patient quarterly, and an annual sum to defray the costs of maintaining an office. He gets paid whether his patients are rich or poor, sick or well. A doctor will generally have over 2,000 on his panel, but rarely over 3,000. He has the same sort of relationship with those on his panel as the American doctor has with his patients (although one suspects that the British doctor can afford to be a bit more brutally honest with hypochondriacs and is inclined to be a bit kinder and more courteous to the "poor but honest" patient).

In recent years the NHS has been encouraging doctors to join together in joint clinical practices and makes grants to help establish clinics for joint practice. While these joint practices are growing rapidly, the majority of doctors still practice alone, or for convenience share an office with another doctor or two. The system of payment remains the same.

Consultants and other hospital staff are salaried. A consultant is in charge of each department in a hospital. The salaries of consultants are higher than those of doctors in family practice. There are grades of pay within the consultant ranks, the consultants themselves awarding the positions with higher pay to those whom the profession regards as most valuable, experienced, and deserving.

Working under consultants are "junior doctors"--but "junior" does not mean "young kids." "Junior doctors" are "juniors" only in the sense that they are subordinate to the consultants. Juniors range in age and experience from beginners in their twenties who have just finished medical training to those well on the way to becoming consultants themselves. Some juniors are career hospital doctors who may never become, may never try to become, consultants. Junior doctors rise through four ranks; from House Officer to Senior House Officer to Registrar to Senior Registrar. Actually most care and treatment and most operations are performed by the junior staff, with the consultant in a supervising and consulting role and performing only some-- presumably the most difficult--operations and actively making final judgments in the more perplexing or dangerous cases (although with a responsibility for all decisions made within his department). Lest an American panic at the idea of being cared for by a "junior" he should understand

that senior registrars and registrars would have passed
their "boards" and be specialists if they practiced in the
U.S.

The salaries of junior staff are low: low in comparison to the incomes of doctors in family practice, and low
even in comparison to people of equivalent experience in
other professions such as teaching. Furthermore, their
hours are long: eighty hours a week including time spent
in hospital available for duty--and I have been told that
when one goes on duty on, say, a Tuesday morning to be available until Wednesday evening, one is unlikely to have enough
time to get one sit-down meal, let alone a nap. The rewards
come later, when one is a consultant: respected, well-to-
do, and, while by no means as rich as his American counterpart, with a power that would be the envy of many American
doctors.

One might well ask why in these circumstances anyone
would choose to make a career of being a hospital junior.
The answer appears to be that Englishmen and Scots do not
choose that course, but become family practitioners or consultants. It is people from the immigrant communities,
especially from India and Pakistan, who undertake careers
as junior doctors. The reasons they do so are that they
may well be better off as registrars or senior registrars
than they would be as doctors in India or Pakistan (especially if one considers the opportunities for their children
which growing up in Britain provides, compared to growing up
in India or Pakistan); and that there is a good deal of
prejudice in Britain, so that an Indian or Pakistani may
wish to avoid the inevitable slights which he would receive
if he set up in family practice--which is not to deny that
a good many Indian and Pakistani doctors have set up successful family practices, but only to say that some may
perceive a salaried career as better in their own particular
circumstances.

An American does not have to read his newspapers or
weekly magazines for long to read that doctors are fleeing
Britain because they are so poorly paid under the NHS.
Plain untrue. Some do leave, but many of those who leave
were not British in the first place but had earlier come to
Britain to study medicine. British medical schools import
students, turn both native born and foreigners into doctors,
export some, but keep most. Britain is *not* running out of
doctors--hardly, when the total number of principal and
hospital doctors and of dentists rose from 46,358 in 1955
to 68,022 in 1973 and to 74,244 in 1977. There has been a

slight rise in the number of patients per doctor in family practice, for which, one suspects, the decline in house calls (just as in the U.S.) compensates. The large increase in hospital practice, including an appreciable increase in the number of consultants, has tended to shift the burden of a larger panel from the family practitioner. (It is, of course, also true that medical advances have increased the work for consultants. I have no idea how one strikes a balance--but clearly it is not all on the side of more work.)

Medical care in Britain is improving: the practice is advancing and there is more of it.

In the case of doctors, as in other cases in British society, it is very misleading to make direct comparisons between British and American incomes, or even between the incomes of British doctors relative to other incomes in Britain with a like comparison for the United States in mind. The earnings of British doctors appear much lower than the earnings of American doctors (and of British dentists even lower, comparatively). The spread of incomes in Britain is narrower than the spread in the United States, while smaller differences in money incomes seem to make a great deal more difference in life styles in Britain than they do in the United States. A typical doctor's income in 1973 of Ł8,000 to Ł9,000 amounted to about $20,000 at the then current exchange rate. While this income would not allow a doctor to buy as many of some things as my spouse and I could buy in America with a combined income over 50% larger, nevertheless our incomes did not seem to provide us with the life style or the "something" which an income of Ł9,000 provided in Britain.

Of course, British doctors complain about their level of earnings. These complaints are probably attributable to several considerations. First, always, and simply, why not complain if the complaints might get one more? Second, while still ranking high among British incomes, the relative position of doctors has declined since the pre-World War II, pre-NHS years of private practice. In this respect, then, old views having a long life, expectations of relative income have been disappointed. In addition, doctors' relative earnings fell at least 12% between 1955 and 1973. Gross earnings per principal doctor rose by 230% (and per dentist by 255%) over these years, while GNP rose 279%. Comparisons with American incomes may also make a number of British doctors feel underpaid. Finally, real incomes in Britain have not risen as fast as have real incomes on the continent (although almost as fast as the United States) so that

British doctors are becoming comparatively poorer. But a
person does not think of his income in terms of his nation's
GNP so much as characteristic of his profession and his
earlier expectations.

The incomes of junior doctors do appear low to an American comparing them with the incomes of businessmen in their
thirties or with the incomes of family practitioners, but
this is probably a British trait rather than a "mistake" in
the management of the NHS. Apprentices in Britain of any
age, class, or occupation have never been particularly well
treated. However, the pay of junior doctors has become a
hot issue and is likely to remain so until the relative pay
of juniors is increased. The proportion of medical treatment provided in hospitals is increasing. In 1965 48% of
doctors worked in hospitals; by 1973 the figure had risen
to 55% (see Table 11-2). They are probably not replacing
family practitioners, but they are providing the new, additional medical services best done in hospitals. The result is that, as hospital doctors take on a larger proportion of the total amount of medical care provided, hospital
practice takes on more the character of a career and becomes less like a period of training. In these circumstances juniors are almost bound to want to be paid a
"doctor's income," not a "trainee's allowance."

Finally, when evaluating doctors' complaints about the
decline in their real incomes since 1973, one should always
remember not only that the whole of the British middle class
has suffered a decline in real income--so have many others,
not least skilled workers (see Chapter 12). Thus an element
in recent complaints is general, not specific to doctors.

By no means entirely consistent with the myth that the
quality of medical care is declining because doctors are
fleeing is the view that medical costs are rising to a most
burdensome level. The increased costs of medical care are
in part mythical, in part due to rising administrative
costs, and in part to rising earnings of non-professional
health workers. One complaint--recurrent since the NHS be-
gan--has been that expenditures on prescriptions and on
glasses have been unnecessarily high. Table 11-3 casts
some doubt on this proposition, especially when one considers the increasing role of modern drugs in health care.
The total cost of health care as a percentage of GNP has
been rising (see Table 11-4), but it is also true that the
total costs of medical care in Britain are a smaller proportion of GNP than they are in the U.S., where they are
estimated to be around 8% and still rising. Some of the

TABLE 11-3
Prescriptions and Glasses

	1955	1965	1973
Prescriptions			
Prescriptions filled, millions	247	270	314
Total cost as percent of GNP	0.29%	0.38%	0.37%
Percent of costs paid by patients	14%	2%	N.A.
Pairs of glasses, thousands	4,628	5,692	5,215
Total cost as percent of GNP	0.07%	0.06%	0.04%
Percent of costs paid by patients	39%	40%	52%

Source: *Annual Abstract of Statistics*, various issues.

TABLE 11-4
Expenditures on the National Health Service
As Percentages of GNP
(Annual Averages for Selected Periods)

Years	Percent
1949–52	3.6
1953–56	2.9
1961–64	3.3
1967–70	3.7
1971–74	4.0
1975–78	4.8

Source: computed from *Annual Abstract of Statistics*, various issues, with annual data adjusted to fiscal years by weighting.

difference is surely due to the smaller ratio of doctors to population in Britain, and hence also to a lower ratio of facilities and equipment to population. It is also likely that health care costs less in Britain because payments to doctors in Britain are subject to hard negotiation between the doctors and the government (as are the prices of drugs, between the manufacturers, pharmacists, and government), whereas in the U.S. the doctors themselves largely set their fees and insurance companies, Medicare, and Medicaid accept the "usual and customary" charges. In any case, the costs of health care in Britain are hardly so high as to threaten her capacity to manage public finance sensibly or to threaten the value of the pound.

Another common criticism of the NHS is that people must wait for long periods before being admitted to hospitals for care and cure. It is certainly true that there are long waits when the operation is postponable (hernias are often cited as a case in point), but whenever a person "needs to be in a hospital *now*," he goes right in and gets fixed as best the profession knows how. One reason there are long waiting lists for postponable treatments is that the existence of the NHS has led to a different system of priorities. Since everyone can now be treated and all know they can be treated as of right, many who formerly were unable to afford the costs of surgery or who feared the strange and unknown doctor, now appear for treatment and when their needs are immediate they go to the front of the line. Formerly, because of costs--and of class, for that matter--many people did not "have doctors" and did not know how to go about seeking proper treatment; now everyone is on some doctor's panel and everyone knows how to go about getting proper treatment. In Britain today medical science, and neither money nor knowledge of how to get treatment, determines priorities in curing patients.

Actually, one does not need to wait for treatment; one can always get cared for privately, outside the NHS, as part of a doctor's private practice and in wards for private patients. That so many wait to be treated under the NHS is not because people cannot get treatment quickly but because they would rather wait to be cured under the NHS than to be treated privately. A doctor on the NHS can have private patients, and anyone can go to a doctor as a private patient. The fact that few people do, that private practice is a miniscule proportion of all health care, is pretty convincing evidence that the system has been working fairly well.

There is, finally, an inconsistency between the criticism that one must wait for treatment under the NHS and the criticism that the costs of the NHS are too great. Waiting lists could be reduced or eliminated if there were more hospital space and if there were more doctors. But building more hospitals and training and paying more doctors would add to the costs of the NHS. There must, of course, be ways to increase the efficiency of health care delivery--there are always ways to be found to increase efficiency in any organization--but there is no evidence that costs could be reduced much, or that facilities are badly under-utilized.

Medical care in Britain is good. With a ratio of doctors to population only a little more than half that in

the U.S., infant mortality is as low in Britain and life
expectancy as long. In fact, after the institution of the
NHS fewer babies died and people lived longer in Britain
than in the U.S. The U.S. only caught up again after the
establishment of Medicare and Medicaid.

III. THE REST OF THE WELFARE STATE

A basic postulate of the welfare state has been that
everyone should enjoy a minimally decent standard of living,
including food, clothing, shelter, health, and help in difficult situations. The first three were to be provided
largely by the guaranteed minimum money income, health by
the NHS, and help in difficulties by what the British call
"personal social services."

However, a minimum money income may not guarantee a
minimally decent standard of living. As average incomes in
a growing economy rise, businesses find it more profitable
to supply more highly processed foods and better quality
clothing and shelter so that those at the lowest end of the
income ladder always find it hard to pay for their basic
necessities. The British have therefore tried various
supplementary measures.

During World War II and the years immediately following
British manufacturers were required to produce some clothing
of servicable if not stylish quality called "utility." A
person could, after the war, always buy better clothing,
but if a family wanted to, it could always get utility
clothing cheaply.

Food had been rationed and subsidized during the war:
consumer choice was not a criterion when half of what was
eaten had to be brought through a U-boat blockade. After
the war--in the face of balance of payments problems, because of the desire to prevent inflation, and to assure the
poorer a supply of basic foodstuffs at cheap prices--sub-
sidies and rationing continued, although the size of the
rations gradually increased while the number of items
rationed gradually declined. Bakeries were required to
supply a "national loaf" of high food value at a low price,
while bottled orange juice for small children was supplied
at a very low price. The system was maintained in part by
bulk purchases of foodstuffs from Commonwealth countries
and in part by the system of deficiency payments to British
farmers (see the section on "The Costs of CAP" in Chapter
9). As in the case of clothing, if one had the inclination

and money, one could buy imported food--processed meats or good cheese, for instance--at the much higher prices prevailing on international markets.

When the Conservatives came to office in the early '50s they abolished rationing, utility clothing, and the national loaf, on liberal principles and in the not ill-founded belief that most people wanted more of better things and more freedom of choice. They also felt that minimum money incomes would still allow people to have enough food and clothing. However, the major program, deficiency payments to farmers, was continued. No one then wanted British food prices to rise to world levels, and after joining the EEC the British have fought in the Council of Ministers to reduce support prices.

What remains--other than deficiency payments to farmers--of the first postwar Labour government's efforts to supply basic clothing and foodstuffs is the provision of school meals and milk and some very small expenditures on welfare foods (see Table 11-5).

HOUSING

Local governments have long been involved in providing low-rent housing. Before the First World War charitable trusts and local governments built housing for low income families. Between the wars more housing was built by local governments (and because built and rented out under the authority of the local governments, it became known as "council housing"). After the Second World War construction of council housing expanded greatly again, providing over half the new housing in some years.

TABLE 11-5
Public Expenditures on
School Meals, Milk and Welfare Food
as Percentages of GNP
(Annual Averages for Selected Periods)

1949-52	1953-56	1961-64	1967-70	1971-74	1975-78
0.5	0.5	0.4	0.4	0.3	0.3

Source: computed from *Annual Abstract of Statistics*, various issues, with annual data for GNP adjusted to fiscal years by weighting.

Three elements have combined to stimulate the growth of council housing. First, the quality of pre-1914 and then of interwar private housing for the working class was perceived as substandard (often, for instance, without baths). Second, rent controls were imposed during the First War and continued after the war. The consequent low returns to investment in housing, combined with the generally depressed condition of the economy during the interwar years, limited the supply of new private housing. The continuation of rent controls after World War II meant that no one would build residential housing as a rental investment. Third, it was felt--and not only by doctrinaire socialists-- that high returns to property were exploitative, especially in conditions of scarcity. Low rents, rising incomes, a backlog in housing construction ever since 1914, and eligibility for council housing for virtually everyone who was not a home owner or actually well-to-do have meant long waiting lists and continued demands that councils construct more houses.

The program of building council housing may have gone somewhat awry. The basic welfare idea was to make sure that there was a supply of decent housing at low rents for people with low incomes, but from the very beginning council housing was also built for the working class so that two ideas--Beveridge's "minimum decent" or "basic welfare" idea and the idea of "housing for the working class"--were confused. As fewer rental properties were built it became more and more difficult to sort out the two separate roots. With the clear need for more housing, the lack of private building for rent--and, one should also note, with the increased willingness of people higher and higher on the income and social scales to live in council housing--the range of those eligible for council houses rose. Councils are now housing a far larger portion of the population than the idea of "basic welfare" would justify.

The confusion of ideas is evident in the sort of housing built. Those in need of the "basic minimum" are apt to be single people or couples: aged and some young people just getting started. The typical council house was built for the "ideal-typical" family, which is not the statistically typical family. The "ideal-typical" family is a nuclear family of parents and two or three children. Since children come in no more than two sexes, two and three bedroom houses fit such families' needs. Although it is true that most people are at some time in their lives parents of two or three children, almost no one fits the "ideal-typical" for more than half an adult lifetime. In

fact, council housing was largely built for people in the
25 to 45 year age group. There has not been a great general
shortage of housing in Britain for ten, perhaps for twenty
years; but there has been a definite shortage of suitable
housing for the single person, the couple, and especially for
the aged, for very young adults, and for the disabled.

The problem is not easy to solve. To build housing
for the groups most in need would only too likely lead to
"young punk," geriatric, and "basket case" neighborhoods--
not at all what a decent society wants. For twenty-five
years now those center and right in British politics have
argued that freeing housing of all controls (other than
zoning) and allowing market rents to solve the problems
would be the proper solution. It would help to move single
sitting tenants out of large houses and large families into
the large houses and would tend to increase the supply of
dwellings for single people and couples. (It is not, however, obvious that large families could afford the rents
for large houses.) There has been some movement in the
direction of decontrolling rents, but each reduction of
legal protection for sitting tenants has been so hedged and
revised that building for sale and selling when moving are
the most sensible options. The recent program of selling
council houses to occupying tenants is based upon the beliefs that owners take better care of houses than tenants,
that sales would reduce the burden of subsidies, and that
more home ownership would make the housing market more effective. There is some truth to each belief, but probably
not so much as believers believe. The belief in the virtues
of owner-occupancy has a color of middle class prejudice;
the real burden of subsidies is less than usually thought
(see the next paragraph); and those who buy council houses
are just the people to stay in them for many more years.

Council housing creates two "burdens." The first,
discussed above, is that it lessens the efficiency of the
market in allocating houses to those in need of different
types of housing. The second is the burden of transfer
payments, in this case from those who do not to those who
do live in council houses. Because people well above any
poverty line live in council houses there is probably very
little Robin Hood effect involved: those who bear the
burden are unlikely to be any better off than those who
live in the houses. However, the 2.5% of GNP devoted to
council housing (recently risen to 3.8%: see Table 11-6)
overstates the burden. The total outlay on council houses
includes the capital costs of building them and the economy
would have to bear this capital cost whether the houses were

TABLE 11-6
Public Expenditures on Housing
(Annual Averages for Selected Periods)

Years	Total expenditures on housing as percent of GNP	Current expenditures on housing as percent of total
1949–52	2.6	19.7
1953–56	2.8	19.2
1961–64	1.9	22.7
1967–70	2.5	22.1
1971–74	2.6	28.4
1975–78	3.8	36.9

Source: computed from *Annual Abstract of Statistics*, various issues, with annual data for GNP adjusted to fiscal years by weighting.

built by councils, by private businesses, or by owner-occupiers. The actual transfer payment, the subsidy to those who live in council houses, is much better measured by the figure for current expenditures on housing. This has amounted to about one half of 1% of the GNP until very recently, and the recent level of about 1.4% of GNP may be best attributed to the post-OPEC depression.

PERSONAL SOCIAL SERVICES

In every society there are those who face specific, often severe difficulties. There are the disabled--by accident or by age--who have trouble moving about or cooking for themselves. There are the lonely: older people without children or who feel they should not park themselves on a son- or daughter-in-law (or who do not like their children, perhaps with good reason). There are one-parent families where the one parent needs to hold a job. There are children, wives, husbands in unpleasant or neurotic family situations. One sort of "solution" to these "problems" is to pack these people off to geriatric homes, hospital wards, and orphanages--but who wants to be put in such institutions? And what sort of person would want to send these people-with-difficulties off to such institutions? (The answer is: "a nasty sort of person.") So the British have been developing programs to provide special services for those with special problems. There are hot-meals-at-home wagons (welfare foods); play groups for small children have been started; local councils employ people to transport the less mobile to places where they have the opportunity to enjoy the company of others, or to visit with the immobile; in some places there are local council employees whose job it is to organize the elderly so that the elderly become effective in demanding their rights. And there are the social workers one finds today in every industrialized country.

In some local government areas the councils provide a good many of these services--although nowhere could one really call the provision generous. Other local governments provide fewer services and are far more penurious in financing them. Camden Town council, in north London, goes so far as to post notices all over the place listing addresses and telephone numbers of offices which take and act on the complaints of people against the council's services. There are councils which do their best to avoid finding out about their deficiencies, and many councils in between.

The costs of running these personal social services has risen, markedly during the 1970s (see Table 11-7). This rise in costs has been a cause of complaint, especially among those who pay "rates" (English for property taxes). Devoting 1.3% of GNP to cheering the aged, teaching children from unpleasant homes to finger-paint, and doing other nice things does not seem an exorbitant price to pay to have a happier society, although it is true that the cost does fall a bit more heavily than it might on ratepayers. The increase in costs does not reflect inefficiency or "office robbery by bureaucrats" but a real improvement in the quantity and quality of services offered. Working women with crippled mothers, and crippled mothers with working daughters, will assure the enquirer they were much better off in 1975 than they were in 1965.

TABLE 11-7
Public Expenditures on Personal Social Services
as Percentages of GNP
(Annual Averages for Selected Periods)

1949–52	1953–56	1961–64	1967–70	1971–74	1975–78
0.2	0.2	0.3	0.4	0.7	0.9

Source: computed from *Annual Abstract of Statistics*, various issues, with annual data for GNP adjusted to fiscal years by weighting.

IV. THE POVERTY TRAP, WASTE, AND EFFICIENCY

By now the reader will be well aware that I find the
objectives of Britain's welfare state admirable, and many
of the means toward those objectives defensible if not
ideal. But some important problems have arisen in the pursuit of what may be called "the decent society."

The efforts to provide minimally decent incomes to all
have created a "poverty trap." A poverty trap exists when
there is an overlap between the minimum level of benefits
provided the unemployed and the incomes which the unemployed might expect to earn if working. The poverty trap
is made worse if people employed at low wages are paying
income tax; and made even worse if benefits are untaxed
while equal wages are taxed. All these conditions exist in
Britain, although the situation is not so bad as some accounts assert. Actually, other things being equal, most
people would rather work at a job for a wage than draw
equal or slightly larger unemployment benefits; because,
actually, most people are pretty decent and want to have a
role in society and contribute their share to keeping
society going. It is usually only when the excess of benefit over wage is large, or the job or the employer most unpleasant, that people choose not to work (at some level of
temptation one always gives in).

There are several aspects to the problem of the poverty
trap. First, it is probably never completely avoidable.
Consider the problem of writing a law which will give the
single mother of two pre-school children a decent income
without making fairly large benefits available to the parents of seven minor children--and if the parents of seven
children are unskilled or semi-skilled, or just lazy, should
their children suffer deprivation?

Secondly, in any society there is a tendency for the
"minimally decent" income to coincide with the incomes of
the lowest paid, for two reasons: (1) the idea of what constitutes a minimally decent income tends to rise as average
incomes rise; and (2) the structure of prices and the quality of goods produced tend to reflect the tastes and abilities to pay of families with average and above average incomes, so that those with well below average incomes have
to buy better and more highly processed things than they
would in a generally poorer society. The larger the portion
of the minimum income which a society is prepared to supply
in kind, the less the pressures arising from the poverty
trap (although supply in kind will never eliminate the

pressures entirely). But it is also true that the larger
the portion in kind, the more the government must enter the
market directly, the more the administrative costs, and the
less the freedom of choice.

To some degree the poverty trap can be blamed on
government policies. The choice could be made to increase
the minimum level at which income tax is charged and raise
the level of indirect taxes (charge value added tax at a
higher rate). The objection is that while the net effect
would leave real incomes pretty much unchanged, it would
raise prices in the shops and be seen as inflationary.
Social security benefits, especially unemployment benefits
and sick pay, could be grossed up with other income and
taxed along with other income. This would involve Inland
Revenue (the department which collects income taxes) in
much more work--or so the Inland Revenue people say. In
Britain income tax withholdings are continually recomputed
by the employer over the course of the tax year and few
people recompute their tax and file at the end of the year,
as Americans do. Another method of assessing taxes might
reduce the burden of work on Inland Revenue. The decision
to provide the minimum income in cash rather than in kind
is also a policy choice, one which has been made by all
successive governments.

How bad a problem the poverty trap is is hard to judge.
The view that it is a great disincentive to work has been
argued mostly on logical grounds or from individual examples; there is little if any general empirical evidence.
However large the problem, it does seem likely that it is
worse during periods of unemployment, and worse during
periods of inflation, than it is during other periods.

Questions are raised about waste and inefficiency in
the welfare services. The questions are not easy to answer:
"waste" is always what one does not want, efficiency that
of which one approves. If there were local government employees who actually did nothing but sit, there would be
general agreement that they were a waste. But when is
visiting an old lady a "waste" and when a fine public service? When is a rarely used extra bed in a hospital "waste"
and when a proper margin for emergencies? "Paperwork" is
much criticized, but paperwork is necessary if one is to
audit actions, reward the virtuous and fire the useless and
sinful. If councillors, MPs, and higher level administrators were willing to take the word of social workers that
the social workers were doing a good job there would be no
need for social workers to make reports and for others to

194

fill out forms. In Britain and the United States one cannot help but feel that the number of people administering
(what an army would call its "tail") is disproportionate to
the number "doing things"; but it is also true that the public and elected officials are reluctant to allow public employees to get on about their businesses without constant
supervision. Perhaps what is badly needed in a welfare
state are new forms of control so that fewer administrators
and records are needed to discover cases of dereliction of
duty.

It is often suggested that the productivity of public
services does not rise, but that it should rise as productivity in manufacturing does. There are fields of endeavor
where one should expect the efforts of public servants to
produce more with fewer inputs: where, for instance, the
use of computers becomes possible, or electric typewriters
are substituted for standard typewriters. But there are
many fields where efficiency in a sense analagous to that
used in industry cannot increase. It takes just as long to
help an old lady across the street today as it did when
Baden-Powell founded the Boy Scouts. Finding the elderly
who need help, organizing clubs for them, cheering disturbed
children by teaching them to finger-paint—these activities
take as much time now as they did twenty years ago, and they
will still take as much time fifty years from now. But the
wages of those who do these things rise more or less in
line with increases in per capita national product so that
services will continue to absorb more and more of the national product—unless, of course, one seriously contem-
plates providing social security clerks and social workers
with the same standard of living (oatmeal and horsehair)
that was provided to medieval monks.

ENDNOTES

1. *Social Insurance and Allied Services*. London: HMSO,
   November 1942. Cmd. 6404.
2. Pauline Gregg, *The Welfare State*. London/Toronto/
   Wellington/Sidney: George G. Harrap & Co., Ltd.,
   1967, p. 21.

12

INCOMES POLICIES

For some years now the British have been trying to develop a workable "incomes policy"--that is, a policy or set of policies which will simultaneously limit aggregate demand to the productive capacity of the economy, prevent costs from rising faster than productivity, and be accepted as fair. So far British governments have not succeeded in developing policies which achieve all these aims; nor, for any appreciable period, any of them. Wage controls which erode differentials between the skilled and the unskilled in an industry seem unfair to the skilled. Wage settlements which create or increase the spread between incomes earned in one industry and incomes in another strike those whose relative incomes fall as unfair. Public sector employees, having achieved "parity" (whatever that may mean) with private sector wages and salaries, object to any policy which will deprive them of the "parity." The increasing burden of taxes and higher prices on middle and upper management call forth protests that the search for greater equality is destroying incentives and making purchases of securities to finance industry a losing proposition. If there is a fairly wide agreement that there should be more for the aged, the infirm, and those distraught through no fault of their own, there is no agreement upon how this burden should be divided up amongst the other groups.

So far incomes policies have been efforts to limit wage and price increases, while limiting increases in dividends to make the policies seem fair to those who own no stock. Incomes policies are neither creations of the 1970s or of either party alone. The Conservatives had a "pay pause" in 1961. Harold Wilson's first Labour government moved from "voluntary cooperation" in 1964-65 to statutory controls on wages and prices in 1966. It was the Conserva-

tive government of Edward Heath that introduced another
system of price and pay controls in 1972 and Wilson's second Labour government which devised the "social contract"
to limit pay and price increases from mid-1975 on. If none
of these efforts proved acceptable for long, neither has
the absence of an incomes policy. In each case--Labour in
the election campaign of 1964, the Conservatives in the campaign of 1970, Labour again in the campaigns of 1974--in
each case the party in opposition promised the electorate
an end to ceilings on incomes, and upon winning the election
abolished the existing system of pay and price controls.
And each time, within a couple of years, each party reim-
posed controls. Each system differed from its predecessor
in detail, and each has been put forward with a new rhetoric
of justification. But despite variations--from "pauses" to
"social contracts," from boards for pay and prices to com-
missions charged with investigating price increases or protecting the consumer--the attempts at an incomes policy and
the problems which arise in its pursuit have had much in
common. The years 1973-79 will serve to illustrate both
the policies and the problems.

PAY AND PRICES: OPEC 1973 TO 1977

In 1972 Prime Minister Edward Heath had introduced pay
and price controls modeled on those imposed in the U.S. by
President Nixon: a freeze, followed by a series of "phases,"
each designed to alleviate "anomalies" created by the previous phase and to move slowly toward a condition of no
controls after the inflation had been brought under control.
Just after the Arab oil embargo of October, 1973, the coal
miners refused to work overtime, demanding much higher
wages. The Arab oil embargo was followed by OPEC's decision to increase the price of oil fourfold. The miners'
refusal to work overtime was followed by their decision to
strike.

Quite aside from its compounding the energy crisis--
and forcing the British economy onto a 3-day workweek during
the winter of 1974--a strike by the coal miners was the
worst possible strike for a government to resist. From the
beginnings of the Industrial Revolution in the late 18th
century until the 1940s the coal miner was the "born loser"
of the British working class. The underground worker was
paid significantly less than workers in other industries
but was doing one of the nastiest and most dangerous jobs
that there is in industrial society. One of the elements
in the decision to nationalize the coal industry had been
the desire to overturn part of the traditional wage struc-

ture and put the miners at or toward the top among wage
earners. No one objected: most people positively favored
doing so. By the end of the 1940s coal miners had become
one of the highest paid groups in British industry. Over
the next twenty years their relative position worsened.
There had been no policy decision to reduce their relative
incomes, nor had there been any change in the feeling that
miners should be very well paid. Rather, it was a result
of slow attrition as other groups managed to raise their
wages more rapidly than did the miners. By the beginning
of the 1970s the coal miners felt that it was time to reverse the gradual decline in their position. In 1972 the
NUM (National Union of Mineworkers) struck and got a large
increase in pay, but the process of attrition set in again.
So they banned overtime, and then struck.

There were two strongly conflicting aspects to the
strike. On the one hand, Phase Three of the pay policy had
just been brought into effect, allowing wages to rise by
Ł2.25 per week per person or by 7% for a group of workers,
no increase to exceed Ł350 for any person in a year. The
miners' demands were completely inconsistent with these
ceilings. The Counter-Inflation Act of 1973, under which
the Pay Board made its decisions about the permissibility
of wage increases, contained no provisions under which the
miners could be exempted as a special case. The miners'
strike was thus a defiance of the government's policy on
pay.

On the other hand, there had come "a point when it
appeared to be widely held that miners ought to have better
wages than those of the Coal Board's current offer, even
though this would mean breaching the current pay limit.
But why? To that question sympathetic members of the public
would answer: because miners' work is hard, dirty and
dangerous and they are less well paid than many other workers whose conditions are much pleasanter: or because miners
have dropped several places in recent years in the table of
earnings: or because with the shortage of oil, coal has
become immensely important to our economy, and miners are
leaving the industry in search of better wages just when
they are most urgently needed in the pits: or because the
pay of some at least of the mineworkers cannot be said to
give them a reasonable standard of living. These were the
real reasons why many people were persuaded of the justice
of the miners' claim. Members of the public interviewed on
radio or television were repeatedly heard to say that they
'wouldn't want to do that sort of work, even for Ł100 a
week'."[1]

Faced with the crisis of short-time work throughout the economy, the Prime Minister called an election. Labour won and gave the miners substantially what they wanted and ended the ceiling on pay. There followed a period of explosive wage increases rising to an annual rate above 30% in early 1975. The Wilson Labour government then reached an agreement with the TUC for voluntary wage restraint.

Voluntary wage restraint was part of what Harold Wilson had dubbed "The Social Compact" or "The Social Contract"-- and which has also been called "The Social Con-Trick." The essence of the 1975 "Contract" was that the labor unions would abide by the voluntary pay limits and the government objectives. During the year from August 1, 1975 to July 31, 1976 (Stage 1), no wages were to increase by more than Ⱡ6 per week. During Stage 2 (1976-77) wages were to rise by at least Ⱡ2.50, or by 6%, but never by more than Ⱡ4.00 per week. It was hoped that enforcement of the Price Code would limit the rate of inflation--a price freeze was out of the question in the face of rising world prices for imported goods and the falling value of the pound.

One cannot say that the price controls did not work at all, but they did work elastically. Before Stage 1 there was a 27% rate of inflation; at the end of Stage 2 the rate had been brought down to 17% and during 1978 it was under 10%. A good deal of the continuing rise in prices should be blamed on the declining exchange value of the pound (see Chapter 8, "Those Foreigners"). In fact, the British reduced their rate of inflation more than any other industrialized democracy. As of early 1979 only France and Germany had lower rates of inflation.

Here a brief digression from the story will serve to illustrate the sort of rules, and the complexities of the rules, which the British have been adopting to control prices. Under the 1975 rules firms could ask to be allowed to raise prices if their costs had risen, but costs would not necessarily justify an increase in price. A reduction in price might be required if profits had also risen appreciably over the rates of profits in a base period (usually the firm's financial year ending in or before 1973)--a requirement imposed only on the telephone division of the Post Office, which was required to give subscribers a rebate in the spring of 1977 because its profits had risen.

Another important limitation on claims that rising costs justified increased prices derived from the idea that the productivity of labor should, by and large, be increas-

ing, and from the idea that at least some of the benefit
from increased labor productivity should be passed on to
customers. To this end "rule of thumb" deductions were
made from actual increases in labor costs. When labor costs
were as small as 8% of total costs, 35% of the increase in
labor costs was "disallowed," but as the percentage which
labor costs bore to total costs rose, the proportion disallowed fell gradually. When labor costs amounted to 94%
or more of total costs the deduction was only 7%.[2]

Price controls could, of course, reduce profits to low
levels, or even cause losses. So another rule of thumb--
that prices should always be allowed to rise until a firm's
net profits before taxes were 10% on capital or 2% of turn-
over--was designed to eliminate this possibility.

Stages 1 and 2 were voluntary: first in the sense that
there was no legislation to enforce the wage ceiling, and
second in the sense that there were virtually no efforts to
evade or avoid or break the limits until February, 1977.
Nevertheless, one must wonder whether wage control legislation would not have been introduced if wages had continued
to rise at anything like a rate of 30% per year. Stages 1
and 2 were, perhaps, more like the social contract of
Hobbes's man in nature in a panic than like Locke's contract between rational, placid adults seeking to make themselves a bit better off.

STRAINS: THE CASE OF THE TOOLMAKERS

One effect of Stages 1 and 2 of pay policy was to reduce wage differentials between skilled workers and the
semi-skilled, absolutely as well as proportionately. Rising
prices and the consequent reduction in purchasing power
made the reduction in differentials more painful. By early
1977 skilled workers were becoming increasingly disgruntled
with the pay policy.

Toolmaking is a highly skilled trade and toolmakers
provide their own equipment, often worth several hundred
pounds. The toolmakers at Leyland (now "BL") had come to
feel that the raises of Ŀ6 in 1975-76 and of Ŀ4 in 1976-77
were mockeries of their skills. They were willing to abide
by the pay limits of the Social Contract until the end of
Stage 2, but they felt that after the end of Stage 2 they
should be treated differently from those members of the
AUEW (the Amalgamated Union of Engineering Workers, Britain's second largest union) whose skills and responsibili-

ties were much less. They therefore demanded the right to bargain separately. Their demand was refused and in February they went on strike.

It was one of those cases in which justice and common sense conflict with justice and common sense, and in which a system of orderly labor relations conflicts with a system of orderly labor relations. By almost all standards for differentiating the pay for one job from another, justice required that the toolmakers be treated differently from many other Leyland workers. But it would also have been unjust to differentiate the toolmakers from other skilled groups in the AUEW and in Britain. Common sense would dictate that workers with the skills and responsibilities of toolmakers be kept happy, that they not be demoralized. But common sense told everyone that acceding to the toolmakers' demands would damage morale elsewhere and start the wrecking of the Social Contract. Orderly labor relations require that groups--who identify themselves as separate and different from other groups and who have their own specific problems, responsibilities, and expectations--that such groups form separate negotiating units so that their representatives can express their worries and desires clearly to management, to other groups of workers and to the public. But orderly labor relations require that the number of groups with which management negotiates be limited; that workers with different problems and different skills sort out among themselves some pattern of wage differentials which all find minimally satisfactory (if not more than minimally), so that a process of constant conflict among groups and leap-frogging of group over group will be avoided.

The toolmakers thus presented the AUEW, Leyland cars, and the nation with a problem for which there was no solution. It was never clear against whom the toolmakers were striking. Since they were not demanding an immediate increase in wages, they were not trying to violate Stage 2 of the pay policy. But the government was opposed to their demands because a separate negotiating body would complicate negotiations between the government and the TUC over Stage 3; because it would lead to a potentially infinite series of demands, with associated labor unrest and strikes; and because it would disrupt the organization of the British trade union movement, a result which the TUC would regard as a most unkind cut by its Labour Party ally (a ground not clearly articulated, for obvious reasons).

The demand of the toolmakers was also a challenge to the authority and the unity of the AUEW and that organization, as an ongoing organization, therefore had to oppose the toolmakers.

In a formal or legal sense, the toolmakers demand was made to Leyland and the strike was against Leyland when it refused to accede to the demand. Leyland was 95% owned by the National Enterprise Board (the NEB: the government's "holding company" for a number of government owned or partly owned businesses). Thus Leyland was, in effect, through the NEB, an arm of the government.

Leyland's management itself was probably not all of one mind. It wanted the toolmakers to return to work; but, as people responsible for running an ongoing enterprise with its own objectives and responsibilities, the management did not want to face further demands or disruptions by others who felt that special treatment for the toolmakers would be unfair. In addition, Leyland's plans to become more competitive in the automobile market required large sums of capital--sums which the government was going to supply *provided* that productivity at Leyland went up *and* that labor relations improved greatly. These sums were in jeopardy because the continuing toolmakers' strike was being interpreted as strong evidence that Leyland was failing to improve labor relations. In the circumstances one is tempted to suspect that many in Leyland's management were secretly hoping to be ordered to do something so that, whatever the results, Leyland's management could not be blamed.

The feelings of the toolmakers represented the feelings of most skilled workers. When asked about the charge that they were demanding special treatment as an "elite," a tool-maker replied, "There's already an elite in the working class--look at the fellows who sweep the floor and at what they get paid." Shortly after the Leyland toolmakers' strike the electricians of the Electricians and Plumbers Union at the new British Steel Corporation plant in south Wales struck for the same reason as had the toolmakers. After a much shorter strike the electricians went back to work with some vague understanding that their grievances would be taken care of after the end of Stage 2.

These strikes were but the disruptive and therefore newsworthy eruptions of a much more widespread feeling among all skilled workers. This strong disgruntlement with the effect of the pay policy on differentials was one major cause of the refusal of the unions in the summer of 1977 to enter into a Stage 3 bargain with the government about ceilings on wages after August 1, 1977. Another reason was the feeling throughout the trade union movement, among low as much as among high paid workers, that continuing inflation at the rate of 17% a year and the rise in unemployment to a post-1945 record were failures on the part of the government to live up to its side of the Social Contract. Then there was the general feeling, quite irrespective of the Social Contract, that real wages were falling entirely too much and that all workers had a right to larger wage increases than would fit within any ceiling to which the government would agree.

PAY LIMITS: STAGES 3 AND 4

Although the unions would not commit themselves to a pay limit in Stage 3 (August 1, 1977 to July 31, 1978), but only to the rule that there would be a twelve month period after any previous increase in pay before the next increase would take effect, the unions did in fact pretty much abide by a 10% limit on increases in pay *rates* (equal to about 14% on take-home pay). For Stage 4 (1978-79) the government originally announced a 5% ceiling but some businesses decided to ignore the limit rather than face industrial disruption. Other businesses claimed that their settlements for over 5% were justified by arrangements for increasing productivity. Then, in January '79, there were widespread strikes, not only in private industry but also in local government services and the NHS. While a few contracts were signed for appreciably higher amounts, increases in wage rates in industry averaged about 10%. The government appeared to be "holding the line" among local government and NHS employees at "9% plus one pound now and more in August." Except for the output lost due to strikes, Stage 4 worked about as well as Stage 3.

THE FUNDAMENTAL PROBLEM

There is a problem more fundamental than any specific inflation or balance of payments crisis, or than the complaints of particular groups of employees. This problem for the modern welfare state is how to distribute the national product--both money incomes after taxes and real incomes after benefits in cash and kind--in a way which will enjoy the consent of so many that the few dissenters will be unable to disrupt the system.

From early in the 19th century until the Second World War there was a general acceptance that the distribution

of income resulting from decisions in the market was *the*
distribution of income. From early days there were protests that such distribution was unjust. The feeling of
injustice was one of the roots of socialist thought from
the early 19th century on; and numbers of people were never
happy with the idea that a person should be rewarded for
owning property, especially inherited property. By the
first decade of this century the majority of the British
had decided that the market's distribution of income to the
aged, sick, and unemployed was wrong and the welfare state
began with the enactment of old age pensions and unemployment and medical insurance. But by-and-large the distribution of income as it resulted from an automatic market
mechanism was accepted. It was accepted joyfully and on
sincere principle by some: the well-to-do, economists,
higher level civil servants, most leaders of political parties. It was accepted regretfully, even resentfully, by
many: large numbers of the working class and socialist reformers who looked forward to a better distribution of income in the distant future. But it was accepted by almost
all as right or as "inevitable in our lifetimes."

This consensus--joyful or resentful--has now been lost.
On the left the distribution of income "resulting from
market forces" is no longer accepted as inevitable. On the
right there are few who believe the distribution is necessarily good: efficient, yes; in many ways a necessary incentive, yes; better than available alternatives in a large
number of situations, yes--but necessarily just or an unavoidable law of nature, no. Faith in the principles of a
free, self-regulating market has been withering away. However, no concensus upon other principles or upon other
mechanisms has emerged.

The class structure makes it even more difficult to
arrive at a consensus about rules or methods for deciding
how to distribute incomes. The well-to-do classes see
their incomes as necessary to the fulfillment of their
roles. At the same time, they appear to have little idea
of what it might be like to be working class. Words flow
across class lines, as do their specific denotations. But
connotations and feelings do not, because they depend upon
experience or upon an empathy which must be developed
vicariously but self-consciously. A class line inhibits
self-conscious efforts to develop a vicarious experience:
it inhibits telling oneself, "Maybe they are saying something different than I think."

The working class believes that the middle and upper
classes have a great deal of wealth that they could give up

to satisfy the needs of the poorer sections of society.
This belief is still supported by the visible differences
in the ways of life of the better-to-do and the worse-to-do.
But it is also a picture of the rich with their "houses on
the hill" enjoying perhaps half the national income and
with much to give up. If perhaps exaggerated, it was not a
grossly false picture two hundred fifty or even one hundred
fifty years ago. Today it is simply false. The middle and
upper classes get a sixth or less of GNP before direct
taxes. After direct taxes and benefits the well-to-do get
a good deal less.

Certainly some of the world's goodies could be transferred from the middle and upper classes, but nowhere near
enough to solve the problems of more investment and of
higher wages and benefits, and more and better government
services. Thus working class views about wealth and in-
come--views which are part of the self-definition of the
working class--tend to phrase both the issue of income redistribution and solutions to the problem in ways which are
largely irrelevant to the existing situation. The same
class line which makes it so hard for the upper classes to
empathize with the hopes, fears, and views of the working
class makes it equally difficult for the working class to
see that the Robin Hood state has now thinned the purses of
the sheriffs and the barons and the church grandees to the
point where their purses will no longer buy ale and meat
for every merry man, poacher, and peasant in need.

The days when the objectives of the welfare state could
be achieved by robbing the rich to give to the poor are
over. Further redistribution of income now requires taxing
the incomes of earners of income to give to non-earners.
Only to a very limited extent can the transfer be across
class lines. Rather, the transfers must be within classes:
from the currently employed to the unemployed; from the
young and middle-aged to the elderly and to the very young;
from the healthy to the sick and disabled; from the child-
less to those with children. The only way for miners to be
paid well above the average is for some other group to be
paid well below the average, or for many other groups to be
paid a little below average. Far from crossing class lines,
transfers must occur even within families. Not only must
taxes on working people go up if Dad and Mum, who are retired, are to receive more, or the years of schooling for
children are to be extended; children's allowances paid to
the mother must increase the burden of taxation upon the
earning father.

Inflationary wage settlements, balance of payments problems, insufficient investment capital, and to a degree poor labor relations all have roots in this more fundamental problem: how to distribute the national product amongst all claimants--earners in different industries or with different skills, mothers, businesses in need of more capital, the aged, social services, and so on--in ways that are acceptable, which seem just and sensible to almost all concerned.[3]

INCOMES POLICIES, 1979 AND BEYOND

As this passage is being revised Prime Minister James Callaghan and other members of the Labour government are saying that Britain must have a permanent incomes policy. They are not specifying what it should be, but suggesting that negotiations between the government, the TUC, and the CBI (Confederation of British Industry) should devise a mutually satisfactory system. Some unions are rejecting the suggestion out of hand and insisting upon a return to "free collective bargaining." Other unions are hinting that they are amenable to further suggestions, and still others have said nothing. The electorate, in opinion polls, is indicating that it rather thinks a continuation of some sort of incomes policy would be a good idea. Margaret Thatcher, hoping to lead the Conservatives to a victory at the polls in 1979, is promising a return to free enterprise in pricing and free collective bargaining in wage settlements. Her party, while supporting her in public, is not, however, entirely behind her. She and her premier advisor, Sir Keith Joseph, believe that strict control of the monetary supply will assure price stability and a low ceiling to wage increases. She is probably in a triple minority: in her opposition to any controls; in her belief that a strict monetarist policy would work; and in her belief that she can carry out such a policy in the face of strong opposition from Labour and the TUC and from businesses badly in need of finance. After the experiences of large and rapid, freely and collectively bargained increases in wages when controls were removed in 1974, it seems likely that any decontrol will be followed by reimposition of controls sooner rather than later.

One cannot predict exactly what these controls will be. They will certainly bear a strong resemblance to the system of the past because the controls that have been and the controls which will be both emerge from the same British social, political, and economic culture. Over a longer period

of time they will evolve. Whether or not the evolution
will solve the problem of how to run an incomes policy
which is acceptable to a large majority is a question about
the future--and if questions about the future could be
answered there would be no gamblers. However, all institutional change is response to new experiences, response
guided by continuous re-evaluation of policies as they are
tried. Just as we would still be living in the old stone
age if we had not tried out new technologies, so we would
also still be killing strangers if we had not been sorting
out better ways to handle interpersonal relationships. So,
although the British may "go down the drain" in an inflationary burst of total social disruption, the odds are that
they will sort out something better to do.

Just what the system will be--just what its techniques,
just what its criteria--are impossible to predict today.
Something along the lines of an annually negotiated standard appears to be the most likely first step. The government, negotiating with the TUC and CBI, might set ceilings,
with increasingly carefully worked out rules for making
desirable or necessary exceptions. There is nothing in
this repugnant to socialist thought, nor to the principles
of the TUC (other than its lingering nostalgia for free
collective bargaining); nor is there anything repugnant in
this to British industrialists who have for years been car-
tellizing, price-fixing, rationalizing their industries,
and calling upon the government for help. The newly established annual convention of the CBI, with its resolutions
on policy, and the increasing frequency with which its
leaders are making public statements on issues of public
policy are strong indications that industry and commerce
will go along with an incomes policy which allows them to
earn some profits, to invest in expansion, and to manage
their firms with some independence and some reward for
being good at managing them.

Other methods may be developed. A legislative body--
Parliament or a cabinet immediately dependent on it--has
so far not worked well in determining which parts of the
electorate should get more and which less. Thus something
of a more "judicial nature" is needed. Early in 1974, in
an effort to find a way out of the impasse created by the
miner's strike, the pay and prices board was turned into a
"Relativities Board" to look into the just relationship between miner's wages and the incomes of other groups. The
election of February, 1974, made the Board's deliberations
moot, but the idea might be adapted. Such a body could
draw upon the traditions of Royal Commissions--investigatory

bodies set up to study a problem in depth and make recommendations, its membership always drawn from a wide variety of political opinions, professions, and backgrounds. It could draw upon opinion polls about who the most deserving groups are, as well as investigate other relevant matters. A Relativities Board might, however, seem to the working class too much like a court of law to be acceptable. On the other hand, experience might make it appear more acceptable than the alternatives.

A somewhat different kind of Relativities Board might be set up by the TUC to sort out which groups of workers should gain more and which less than the national average. Such a TUC Board would not, of course, be a satisfactory way of deciding between wage earners and others, and probably not a satisfactory way of deciding between unionized and non-unionized wage earners.

Systems of tax incentives and penalties could be developed. During 1977-78 the Labour government tried to enforce its wage ceilings by denying government contracts and export credits to some companies which agreed to above-ceiling wages. There was much protest from the Conservatives and from the companies involved, from companies fearing they might become involved, and from the CBI. By December of 1978 the government had to withdraw its sanctions. However, an important element in the protest was that Parliament had never empowered the government to punish companies which violated ceilings which were themselves supposed to be voluntary. The outcome would probably have been different if Stages 3 and 4 had been made compulsory by Parliament.

No one idea alone would be likely to work, but several in combination might well work, especially if combined with systems of guaranteed annual incomes and joint contracts between government, unions, and corporations. All these ideas have been suggested in Britain, in one context or another. Some combination of these methods, and doubtless other methods, does seem much more likely than a long term return to "free collective bargaining" and inflationary leap-frogging of skilled workers over pensioners and unskilled workers, followed by pensioners or school teachers jumping ahead of skilled workers.

The argument in the latter part of this chapter is not that Britain has achieved a viable incomes policy or is on the verge of doing so. Rather it is that the continuing search is likely to discover a workable incomes policy--but slowly, and probably not clearly until 1985 or later.

ENDNOTES

1. Barbara Wootton, *Incomes Policy: An Inquest and a Proposal*. London: Davis-Poynter, 1974, pp. 80–81.
2. Price Commission, *A Guide to the Price Controls in Stage 4*. London: HMSO, 1975.
3. The argument in this section is spelled out more fully in Walter C. Neale, "Income Distribution in the Welfare State: Consequences of a Loss of Consensus in Britain," Chapter 11 in John Adams, ed., *Institutional Economics: Contributions to the Development of Holistic Economics*. Boston: Martinus Nijhoff, 1980.

13

A DECENT SOCIETY IN THE WORKS

British policy may be summarized as attempts to achieve a "decent society"--a society which puts more emphasis on kindliness than on efficiency, more emphasis on considerateness than on productivity--a society which puts more emphasis on the pleasant enjoyment of the even tenor of one's way than rapidly increasing material wealth. But to say that this is what the British are after is not to say that they have figured out just how to achieve their aim, nor to say that they have figured out just what such a society will look like or just what it will cost whom.

To say that the British put more emphasis upon an even tenor of life than upon material wealth does not mean that like some ideal Hindu they have no interest in material comforts and enjoyments, but rather that compared to Americans or Germans of Japanese they are relatively less interested in more things and relatively more interested in pleasantness, security, and their ideas of economic justice than are Americans, Germans, and Japanese. The evidence for this assertion is in the day-by-day, year-by-year behavior of the British, in the history of the choices they have made when they had to make choices, and not in the public utterances of their leaders or in the urgings of their press. Whether it is Margaret Thatcher addressing a group of businessmen or James Callaghan addressing a convention of the TUC, a constant theme is the need to increase productivity. *The Economist* is not alone among British journals and newspapers in pressing for "dashes to growth." And like everyone else on this planet, any Englishman, Welshman, or Scot would like to have more rather than less. If there just happens to be a "free lunch" somewhere around, who wouldn't want it? It is "the actions, not the words" which are the evidence for the argument here. When faced with the threatened closure of British Chrysler, the government steps in with financial aid to keep it open, as the government did to keep Upper Clyde Shipbuilders in business, as it did when British Leyland was going bankrupt, and as it did when it nationalized shipbuilding because that industry too was going bankrupt. A more efficient economic allocation of resources would have been achieved with higher coal prices in the early 1950s, or with higher natural gas prices in the 1970s. More goods, but fewer public services, could have been had during the 1960s and 1970s if funds had been channeled to manufacturing investment and away from increased social services. The British Steel Corporation would be more productive today if it had invested more heavily in modern plant ten years ago and closed down its older plant more quickly. But in every case, whenever there was a choice between keeping open a high cost plant or causing many redundancies, between more social workers or more machine operators, between more houses or more machines, between more consumption now or more long term investment, the choice actually made has always been for the former. This has been true no matter what Prime Ministers, Chancellors of the Exchequer, and leaders of the opposition have said, and true no matter which party has been in power. It stretches credulity beyond the breaking point to ask that one believe all these decisions have been foolish errors of judgement. Rather, they reflect a national bias.

British attempts to achieve the decent society are complicated by the class structure. A national bias does not constitute general agreement on the specifics of what should be done. In any society there are going to be different points of view just because people are differently situated in that society--in different regions, with different jobs and family composition, to say nothing of different vested interests and different experiences of life. In addition, British perceptions are divided by outlooks or folkviews given by the history of British class structure. Thus the upper classes and the ruling elites see themselves as especially suited to the roles of deciding how a decent society should be created and of administering the changes needed to achieve it. The middle classes see themselves as the bearers of the solid (they would not call them stolid) virtues which the decent society should reflect. Both groups see themselves as requiring certain statuses or perquisites if they are to fulfill their roles. But what the working class sees is unwarranted privilege, not necessary perquisites, and the abuse of power and of propertied position to assure more material welfare, more economic

security, and greater access to justice than is right--and
much more than is available to the working class. An inability of the higher classes to understand the feelings of
the working class is matched by a working class distrust
of every action or proposal of the higher classes.

I do not wish my readers to infer, when I write that
the British are striving for a decent society, that other
peoples want indecent societies, or care not a whit for
decency. Again, I am not contrasting opposites but trying
to bring out variations in emphasis and to point out that
British values, while not all that different from the values
of other peoples, are ordered differently (and, admittedly,
that I rather like their ordering). The contrasts (the
variations, not the opposites) are with, for instance, the
Japanese, who put a strong emphasis upon a high level of
investment, and induce a corresponding high level of saving
and low level of consumption by making niggardly provisions
for public pensions in old age; with the Germans, whose
Social Democratic (labor, socialist) Party is inclined to
trust the big banks and the big industrialists to manage
the economy, and who prefer efficiency to quiet comfort;
with the French, who also prefer efficiency and rapid growth
to quiet enjoyment, and whose public officials happily play
private favorites rather than insist that public justice be
seen to be done; and with the Americans, who would--on one
reading of their recent record--rather enjoy the quiet
tenor of the British economy, but who fear (or say they
fear) the bureaucrat and political "interference" with
lives and livelihood and who are given to measuring pleasure
in things. The peoples of all these other countries would
like the things the British are striving for, but they do
not want them as much. The British would like to have the
things these other countries have or are getting, but not
so much that they will accept the rough edges which can
cause so much discomfort.

There are many traits which differentiate the British
economy from the economies of the other developed democracies, and the preceding chapters have dealt with the most
important. But what contributes most to the differences--
what perhaps best explains the economic structure and the
policies followed--is the ongoing struggle of a society
imbued with a history of class to create institutions which
will assure everyone a civilized equality, a comfortable
life (which is not the same as an easy life), and freedom
from all those fears which can be allayed by courteous and
considerate public policies. Where the British economy is
very much like the economies of the other industrialized
democracies is in its imperfect ability to achieve its aims.